Reliable and Intelligent Optimization in Multi-Layered Cloud Computing Architectures

One of the major developments in the computing field has been cloud computing, which enables users to do complicated computations that local devices are unable to handle. The computing power and flexibility that have made the cloud so popular do not come without challenges. It is particularly challenging to decide which resources to use, even when they have the same configuration but different levels of performance because of the variable structure of the available resources. Cloud data centers can host millions of virtual machines, and where to locate these machines in the cloud is a difficult problem. Additionally, fulfilling optimization needs is a complex problem.

Reliable and Intelligent Optimization in Multi-Layered Cloud Computing Architectures examines ways to meet these challenges. It discusses virtual machine placement techniques and task scheduling techniques that optimize resource utilization and minimize energy consumption of cloud data centers. Placement techniques presented can provide an optimal solution to the optimization problem using multiple objectives. The book focuses on basic design principles and analysis of virtual machine placement techniques and task allocation techniques. It also looks at virtual machine placement techniques that can improve quality-of-service (QoS) in service-oriented architecture (SOA) computing. The aims of virtual machine placement include minimizing energy usage, network traffic, economical cost, maximizing performance, and maximizing resource utilization. Other highlights of the book include:

- Improving QoS and resource efficiency
- Fault-tolerant and reliable resource optimization models
- A reactive fault tolerance method using checkpointing restart
- Cost and network-aware metaheuristics
- Virtual machine scheduling and placement
- Electricity consumption in cloud data centers

Written by leading experts and researchers, this book provides insights and techniques to those dedicated to improving cloud computing and its services.

Madhusudhan H. S. is an Associate Professor in the Department of Computer Science and Engineering at Vidyavardhaka College of Engineering, Mysuru, Karnataka, India.

Satish Kumar T. is an Associate Professor in the Department of Computer Science and Engineering at BMS Institute of Technology and Management, Bengaluru, Karnataka, India.

Punit Gupta is an PostDoc Fellow, School of Computer Science, University College Dublin, Dublin, Ireland.

Dinesh Kumar Saini is a Full Professor at the School of Computing and Information Technology, Manipal University Jaipur, Jaipur, Rajasthan, India.

Kashif Zia is a Research Associate at the MRC/CSO Social and Public Health Sciences Unit, University of Glasgow, United Kingdom.

Reliable and Intelligent Optimization in Multi-Layered Cloud Computing Architectures

Edited by
Madhusudhan H. S., Satish Kumar T.,
Punit Gupta, Dinesh Kumar Saini, and Kashif Zia

CRC Press
Taylor & Francis Group
Boca Raton London New York

CRC Press is an imprint of the
Taylor & Francis Group, an **informa** business

AN AUERBACH BOOK

First edition published 2024
2385 NW Executive Center Drive, Suite 320, Boca Raton FL 33431

and by CRC Press
4 Park Square, Milton Park, Abingdon, Oxon, OX14 4RN

CRC Press is an imprint of Taylor & Francis Group, LLC

© 2024 Taylor & Francis Group, LLC

ISBN: 978-1-032-55380-1 (hbk)
ISBN: 978-1-032-55996-4 (pbk)
ISBN: 978-1-003-43329-3 (ebk)

DOI: 10.1201/9781003433293

Typeset in Adobe Garamond Pro
by Apex CoVantage, LLC

Contents

Contributors

Sanjit Bhagat
Manipal University
Jaipur, India

Lavanya M. C.
Department of Computer Science
  and Engineering
Vidyavardhaka College of
  Engineering
Mysuru, India

Vaishali Chourey
Adani Institute of Infrastructure
  Engineering
Ahmedabad, India

P. K. Gupta
Jaypee University of Information
  Technology
Solan, H. P., India

Punit Gupta
School Of Computer Science
University College Dublin
Dublin, Ireland

Shivani Jaswal
National College of Ireland
Dublin, Ireland

Akshatha M.
Department of Computer Science
  and Engineering
Vidyavardhaka College of Engineering
Mysuru, India

Manisha Malhotra
Chandigarh University
Punjab, India

A. V. Krishna Mohan
Department of Computer Science
  and Engineering
Siddaganga Institute of
  Technology, Tumkur

Ashwini N.
Department of Computer Science and
  Engineering
BMS Institute of Technology
  and Management
Bengaluru, India

Seema H. R.
Department of Artificial Intelligence
  and Machine Learning
Vidyavardhaka College of
  Engineering
Mysuru, India

Dheeraj Rane
Indian Institute of Technology
 Indore (IITI) Drishti CPS
 Foundation
Indian Institute of Technology (IIT)
 Indore
Indore, India

Madhusudhan H. S.
Department of Computer Science
 and Engineering
Vidyavardhaka College of Engineering
Mysuru, Karnataka, India

Shashank S.
Research Scholar
Indian Institute of Science (IISc)
Bengaluru, India

Dinesh Kumar Saini
Department of Computer and
 Communication Engineering
School of Computing and
 Information Technology
Manipal University
Jaipur, India

Satish Kumar T.
Department of Computer
 Science & Engineering
BMS Institute of Technology and
 Management, Bengaluru
Karnataka, India

Righa Tandon
Chitkara University Institute of
 Engineering and Technology
Chitkara University
Punjab, India

Ajay Verma
Jaypee University of Information
 Technology
Solan, H. P., India

Rohit Verma
National College of Ireland
Dublin, Ireland

Preface

One of the major developments in the computing field is cloud computing, which enables users to do complicated computations that local devices are unable to handle. The finest feature of cloud computing is the pay-per-use model, which requires customers to pay only for the resources they use for a specified amount of time rather than receiving payment for the entire year or month. A collaborative environment is provided by multi-layered cloud computing, where diverse resources in the form of data centers support various services. Data centers are a diverse group of resources that are deployed across multiple geographic locations in multi-layered cloud computing and have varied computational capacity, architecture, and performance.

It is particularly challenging to decide which resources to use, even when they have the same configuration but different performance, because of the variable structure of the available resources. As a result, it is necessary for a broker's intermediate layer to have a knowledge bank about the historical performance of the resources, which in this example may be a data center, host, or virtual machine. The broker will be in charge of assessing each resource's performance and assigning it a score that may be used to make decisions at different levels, such as choosing the best resource for scheduling, load balancing, or migration. There are several explanations for why such a mechanism exists. Millions of virtual machines are hosted in cloud datacenters in the real world on computer nodes, and where to locate them in the cloud is a difficult problem. Additionally, it is a crucial step in fulfilling optimization needs.

The aim of the virtual machine placement includes minimizing energy usage, network traffic, economical cost, maximizing performance, and maximizing resource utilization. This book is all about several techniques where virtual machine scheduling and placement may be a big deal in cloud service models. Electricity consumption in cloud datacenters is substantial and inversely correlated to the volume of user requests. Due to this, there are high operational expenses and carbon dioxide emissions.

The chapters proposed for the book chapter include virtual machine placement techniques and task scheduling techniques that optimize resource utilization and minimize energy consumption of the cloud datacenter. The placement techniques provide an optimal solution to the optimization problem using multiple objectives.

The book chapter focuses on basic design principles and analysis of virtual machine placement techniques and tasks allocation techniques. The virtual machine placement techniques are also used for quality of service improvement of the service-oriented architecture-supported computing paradigm.

Chapter 1 covers the general introduction to cloud computing and optimization in cloud. Cloud computing has become a popular model for providing a variety of services to users on a pay-per-use basis. The rapid development in the number of cloud users and the types of services offered to cloud has led to the creation of massive datacenters with thousands of processing nodes all over the world. In the real world, cloud datacenters host millions of virtual machines on computing nodes, and virtual machine placement is a challenging issue in the cloud. It is also a critical process for meeting optimization requirements. The aim of the virtual machine placement is to achieve energy optimization, network traffic optimization, economical costs optimization, performance optimization and resource utilization optimization.

Chapter 2 focuses on improving QoS and resource efficiency. In this chapter, artificial neural network, a supervised machine learning approach, is proposed with the goal of reducing makespan and increasing resource utilization. The experiment has been carried out using real-time workload from the San Diego Supercomputer Center's (SDSC) blue horizon log.

Chapter 3 presents a machine learning-based optimization approach. Here, the suggested approach aims to increase case reviews using text accuracy. Text reviews are typically neglected since they are difficult to categorize into any of the classes and are thus ignored. With the help of this study, we will be able to categorize these reviews into any of the classes and so enhance the analysis.

Chapter 4 addresses energy-aware optimization using a hybrid approach based on GA and ANN is proposed. The objective of the proposed work is to reduce energy consumption while enhancing resource utilization and performance through load balancing among available resources. The experiment uses real-time workload traces from over a thousand Planet Lab virtual machines.

Chapter 5 explores the fault tolerant and reliable resource optimization model. A fault-tolerant and trustworthy resource optimization paradigm for cloud computing settings is covered in this book chapter. The approach seeks to increase cloud resource allocation effectiveness while preserving the system's high availability and fault tolerance. Based on demand characteristics, service-level agreements (SLAs), and system availability, the model dynamically allocates resources using a combination of predictive analytics, optimization algorithms, and fault-tolerant mechanisms. In order to guarantee that the system continues to function even in the case of hardware or software failures, the model also includes fault-tolerant methods such as redundancy and failover. Simulation studies used to test the usefulness of the proposed model show that it can increase resource utilization, decrease downtime, and guarantee the dependability of cloud-based services. For cloud service providers, IT administrators, and researchers working in the field of cloud computing, the model is anticipated to be helpful.

Chapter 6 covers a reactive fault tolerance method using checkpointing restart mechanism. The proposed approach is divided into three parts: (1) Firstly, algorithms are developed to detect virtual machine failure owing to many faults (2) A checkpoint interval time optimization technique is proposed. (3) Finally, unsuccessful tasks are restarted using an asynchronous checkpoint/restart using a log-based recovery method. When compared to the non-optimization technique, the valuation findings produced via a real-time data set reveal that the model proposed in this work minimizes power consumption and increases performance by a superior fault tolerance result.

Chapter 7 highlights the existing fault tolerance approaches as well as the challenges yet to be overcome. Also, a framework has been proposed for predicting faults in cloud environments with performance evaluation and validation. The evaluation results also reveal that the proposed framework model has high availability, better throughput, and lesser checkpoint overheads. The result analysis reveals the effectiveness of the proposed approach.

Chapter 8 examines how blockchain and Pravega may work together, showing both the advantages and disadvantages of the pairing. Data input, transaction processing and consensus methods, and data synchronization are some of the important elements and architectural issues we examine while integrating Pravega with blockchain. The overall goal of this research is to present a thorough review of the integration of Pravega with blockchain, including its possible advantages, difficulties, and ramifications.

Chapter 9 covers the scaling and cost prediction model. Scaling is a progressive process where resource can only be scaled up to the server (vertical) or out of the server (horizontal) or both but increasing order only. In elasticity, resources can be scaled up or scaled down according to the user requirement fulfilling pay as you go concept. It is more suitable for public cloud services. Scalability and elasticity are prime components to make a cost-efficient cloud system with proper resource utilization.

Chapter 10 addresses the cost and network aware metaheuristic approach. Networking is one of the major components of cloud environments. Private networks can be built on premises while public networks are available at the provider's end. Security was major concern about a public cloud network, so a hybrid model was proposed. In this model confidential data and configuration was stored at the user end while rest of the data and configuration was taken from the public cloud network. There has been an increase in data and migration of enterprises over the cloud in recent years. It is a challenging task to handle all the data over cloud networks while maintaining SLA, minimum downtime, and better resource utilization while minimizing the cost and power consumption.

Chapter 11 explores scheduling, estimation, and scalability in cloud computing to subsidize costs and represent it in the SLAs fairly. Also, it provides a concise overview of cloud economics and the function of SLAs within the context of imposed limitations. A comprehensive enumeration and justification of cost optimization techniques is presented. Practice and research will surely benefit from the findings on cost optimization methods and attributes in a cloud. An efficient decision-making strategy is finally proposed for cost optimization and ways to formulate this strategy in SLAs are discussed.

We hope that the works published in this book will be able to serve the concerned communities of cloud computing and its services.

Acknowledgements

The editors are thankful to the authors and reviewers of the chapters of this book who contributed their scientific work and useful comments, respectively.

Chapter 1

Introduction to Optimization in Cloud Computing

Madhusudhan H. S. and Punit Gupta

1.1 Introduction

Cloud computing is a model for providing on-demand network access to a collective pool of computational resources. Users and businesses may load and process data in third-party data centers with the aid of cloud computing and storage solutions. Cloud computing applications, like distributed computing, are operated on a network of computers. Cloud computing services include Software as a Service (SaaS), Platform as a Service (PaaS), and Infrastructure as a Service (IaaS).

Through SaaS, users may access application software and databases. A supplier licenses an application to users as a service on demand or as a subscription via SaaS. PaaS is a collection of tools and services that enable developing and deploying software easier. PaaS models often contain a database, operating system, web server and programming-language execution environment which are all provided by cloud providers. Application designers may develop and run software solutions on a cloud platform without the cost and complexity of procurement and handling the underlying software and hardware layers.

IaaS is a method of offering Cloud Computing infrastructure, such as storage, servers, operating systems and network, as a pay-as-you-go service. Virtualization is one of the most essential technologies in IaaS. Virtualization is a potential method for dividing hardware resources on one or more computers into several execution contexts, each of which may serve as a complete system, using complete or partial

DOI: 10.1201/9781003433293-1

device simulation, time-sharing, software and hardware partitioning. Virtualization allows several programs to operate on various performance-isolated platforms called virtual machines (VMs) on a single physical machine, allowing for dynamic allotment of physical resources in cloud computing settings. As a result, each physical machine in the datacenter network houses a large number of virtual machines. This setting is depicted in Figure 1.1. On-demand or utility computing is a just-in-time resource provisioning approach in which computing resources like memory, CPU and bandwidth are made accessible to requests only when they are required rather than being assigned statically based on peak task demand [1].

The IaaS provides clients with virtual machines on which they may build their own services [1]. Virtual machine placement (VMP) is one of the most difficult challenges in cloud infrastructure management, as datacenters house millions of virtual machines. VMP is the task of deciding which virtual machines should run on every individual physical machine (PM) in a datacenter. In cloud infrastructures, VM placement is a key strategy for increasing resource usage and power efficiency [2].

The goal of the virtual machine placement is divided into five functions:

 i. Energy Consumption Minimization
 ii. Performance Maximization
 iii. Minimization of Network Traffic
 iv. Maximization of Resource Utilization
 v. Optimization of Economical Costs

Because of the widespread use of cloud computing, large-scale data centers with thousands of compute nodes have been deployed all over the world. Cloud data centers, on the other hand, require a lot of electricity, resulting in high operating cost and in terms of energy usage, keeping servers underused is extremely inefficient. This thesis focuses on the challenge of energy-efficient resource management in cloud data centers, that is, assuring that computing resources are suitably utilized to service application workloads to reduce energy utilization while maintaining apt performance.

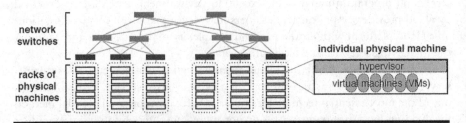

Figure 1.1   A typical datacenter network.

1.2 Multi-layered Cloud Architecture

Users in a variety of professions utilize cloud computing technology to store data in the cloud and access it over the internet from anywhere, at any time. Many different types of cloud service layers are stacked on top of one another to produce a reliable, scalable and pay-per-use model with outstanding service quality.

Buyya et al. described a layered cloud design in [3], as depicted in Figure 1.2. Cloud resources in addition to significant capabilities of middleware provide the foundation for providing IaaS. The purpose of user-level middleware is to provide PaaS features. The top layer can focus on application amenities by exploiting services delivered by the bottom layer services (SaaS).

User-Level Middleware: Web 2.0 interfaces (IBM Workplace, Ajax) are examples of software frameworks that let developers create cost-effective, rich user interfaces for browser-dependent applications at this layer. Composition tools and programming environments are also included in the layer, making it easy to design, deploy, and execute cloud applications.

Core Middleware: Platform-level services implemented at this layer enable cloud computing by providing a runtime environment for request services constructed using user-level middleware. In this layer, essential services comprise accounting, billing, dynamic SLA (service level agreement) management, pricing,

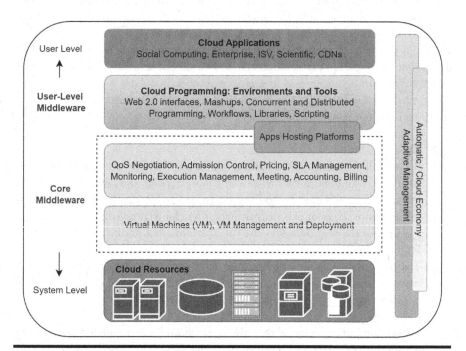

Figure 1.2   Layered cloud computing architecture.

execution monitoring and management. At this layer, companies providing cloud services are Google App Engine, Amazon EC2 and Aneka [4].

System Level: Cloud computing infrastructures are supported by a network of data centers, each of which has hundreds to tens of thousands of servers. Enormous physical resources (application servers and storage servers) drive data centers at the system level layer. Higher-level virtualization services and toolkits operate these servers invisibly, allowing capacity sharing between virtual instances of servers. Since these virtual machines are isolated from one another, they provide fault tolerance and a secure environment.

1.3 Cloud Characteristics

The majority of individuals and IT firms are now discussing cloud computing. Cloud architecture might be viewed as a model for providing simple, direct and on-demand ingress to a common group of computing resources (e.g., networks, servers, applications, storage etc.) that can be provided and decommissioned with nominal management effort. The United States' National Institute of Standards and Technology (NIST) provides a set of operational ideas that divide cloud infrastructure into operation and implementation models [5]. Figure 1.3 depicts these models, as well as their linkages to important cloud system operations.

Cloud computing is a TCP/IP-based computer platform that incorporates large amounts of memory, powerful microprocessors, trustworthy device architecture, and rapid networks. If there were no standard connecting protocols and established data canter principles in place, cloud systems would not be possible. Clouds and/or cloud storage can be interpreted in a variety of ways.

Some of the qualities of cloud computing that make it superior to other systems are listed here [6, 7]:

■ Pay-per-use model
  Because cloud computing is affordable in an industry with so much infrastructure, a small business owner may simply manage and devise their specific infrastructure and high computing system at a small cost. Instead of purchasing an entire server or private infrastructure, cloud computing allows users to pay just for the resources they use for a certain amount of time.
■ High availability
  The continual availability of resources like storage, processing power, and high network bandwidth are the most important properties of the cloud. According to this attribute, the resources are also available in overloaded situations.
■ Reliability
  Cloud computing ensures that the user obtains exceptionally trustworthy computing resources and services, implying that the user will receive services that are uninterrupted and of the same high quality as assured to the user.

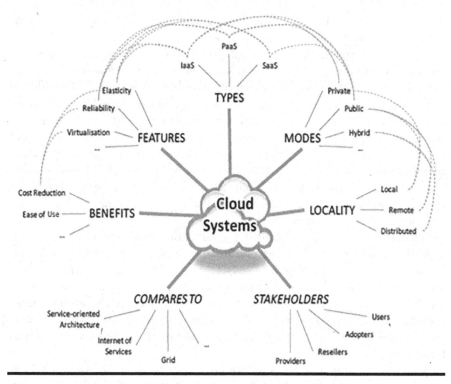

Figure 1.3 Perspective on the key aspects of cloud computing.

■ Elasticity
  Cloud computing is thought to be scalable and versatile. This capability permits the cloud to scale its resources up or down depending on the user or corporate demands for a limited time. This lets the cloud to retain high availability even when it is overwhelmed, guaranteeing that customers get consistent, and high-quality service.
  Most of the elements that make up a cloud system are seen in Figure 1.3.

1.4 Optimization in Cloud Computing

Traditionally, computing system development has been driven by the need for applications from the consumer, scientific, and corporate sectors, which has resulted in rising productivity. Virtual machine placement has a significant influence on the power efficiency and optimizing resource utilization of a cloud datacenter in cloud computing. Optimization focuses on power optimization, load balancing, resource optimization, cost optimization, network optimization, etc.

to fulfil the needs of users and also optimization is critical from the cloud provider perspective.

Cloud computing has revolutionized information technology by allowing virtual machines to do operations such as scheduling, consolidation, migration, and other support functions. Cloud computing has altered the system's network and architectural creation. Cloud computing is a type of computing that allows for large-scale computations, storage virtualization, and cloud customers frequently choose the pay-per-use model to access cloud services. Scheduling is the process of assigning appropriate tasks to hosts for execution. This process is critical in a cloud environment for efficient resource utilization. A virtual machine is the software employment of a computing environment to install or run a program. Important aspects include allocating resources to the virtual machine and transferring applications across virtual machines.

Virtual machines are scheduled for numerous data centers in the cloud architecture, which may be geographically spread. The optimization of scheduling process in a cloud computing context defines resource and infrastructure utilization. Scheduling aids in improving service quality and maximizing profit for cloud service providers. Companies may save money by conserving energy and using cloud computing services. The optimization process results in lower energy consumption, quicker task execution, and more efficient resource allocation parameters.

Cloud computing offers various levels of service to users. To assess cloud services (PaaS, SaaS, and IaaS), we must first understand the metrics. Performance, economics, and general characteristics are the measures associated with various elements of cloud services. The following optimization metrics are used in cloud computing.

1.4.1 Performance Metrics

These metrics are a variety of possibilities provided by cloud providers to meet the needs of companies. Performance is judged on a greater scale. It is related to throughput, response time, and timeliness in general. Table 1.1 summarizes some of the key performance indicators. [8–10].

Table 1.1 Performance Metrics

Features	Description	Metrics
Computation	In Cloud systems, this term refers to the processing of data or tasks (jobs).	Instance Efficiency (% CPU peak)
		CPU Load (%)
		Benchmark OP (FLOP) Rate

Features	Description	Metrics
Communication	Data movement between internal service instances or between an external consumer and the cloud	MPI Transfer Bit/Byte Speed
		Connection Error Rate
		Packet Loss Frequency
Time	For projects to be successful, they must be completed on schedule while retaining high quality.	Communication Time
		Computation Time
Memory	Designed to quickly retrieve and temporarily store information from a slow-access hard disc device.	Mean Hit Time (s)
		Response Time (ms)
		Random Memory Update Rate
		Memory Byte/Bit Speed

1.4.2 Economic Features

Economic factors have been cited as a driving force behind cloud computing adoption. Cost and elasticity are two economic factors that may be roughly characterized. [11]. Since it provides so many alternatives, cloud services come at a variety of options. Table 1.2 outlines the key economic features [12–14].

1.4.3 General Features

The cloud's services are often dispersed across a number of cloud providers. Delivering services to users while maintaining a high level of QoS is a difficult task. It is critical to assess QoS in a simple manner. Table 1.3 lists some of the most general features and metrics. [12, 15–19].

1.5 Classification of Schedulers

There are several approaches used in achieving optimization in cloud computing. Here, scheduling of tasks and VMs in cloud computing is addressed to optimize few parameters. Figure 1.4 depicts the hierarchical structure that classifies different schedulers at various layers of cloud infrastructure. In this work, the schedulers are designed in application layer and virtualization layer to address some of the metrics discussed

Table 1.2   Economic Features

Features	Description	Metrics
Elasticity	Describes system ability to swiftly add and remove cloud resources in a very fine-grained manner. Particularly, an elastic cloud service handles both workload increase and decrease, and places a premium on the speed with which it responds to changing workloads.	Speed of scaling
		Precision
		Deployment or Provision Time (measured in seconds)
		Time Spent on Acquisition (measured in seconds)
Cost	Important and straightforward indicator to highlight, but also cost-effective when using Cloud Computing. Moving computing to the cloud might theoretically cover a wide range of costs.	Total Cost ($)
		Cost over a Fixed Time ($/year)
		Price/Performance Ratio
		Users Supported on a specified Budget
		Cost of Component Resources ($)

Table 1.3   General Features

Features	Description	Metrics
Scalability	Represents the possibility of improving the service provider's applications calculating power and the product's capacity to handle a large number of clients' requirements in a short period of time.	Assigned Resources
		Response Time
Availability	Users of traditional devices access services over the internet using a web browser, however access to those services is not guaranteed here.	Flexibility
		Response time
		Accuracy

Features	Description	Metrics
Efficiency	The resources used for services while offering the desired operation, and hence the level of efficiency, in a predetermined condition, that is to say it evaluates how well the web services make use of the resources.	Resource Utilization
		Time Behavior
		Ratio of Waiting Time
Reliability	It is a service's ability to remain operational over time without malfunction. The service's capacity to continue functioning at a high level of efficiency in a timely manner.	Service Constancy
		Fault Tolerance
		Recoverability
		Accuracy of Service
Composability	It has something to do with the interoperability properties.	Service Interoperability
		Service Modularity
Reusability	The degree to which an application component or other work system may be employed in several programs or applications.	Coverage of variability
		Readability
		Publicity
Usability	The extent to which a service may be utilized by specific customers to achieve specific goals while maintaining effectiveness, usefulness, and approval in a given context.	Operability
		Learn Ability
		Attractiveness
Adaptability	The efficiency with which solutions are adjusted for the use of each service-based software.	Coverage of Variability
		Completeness
Sustainability	For the purpose of defining the environmental impact of the cloud service used, it could be measured as the standard carbon imprint or even the amount of energy that cloud services consumed.	Data Centre Performance per Energy (DPPE), PUE (Power Usage Efficiency)

(*Continued*)

Table 1.3 *(Continued)*   **General Features**

Features	Description	Metrics
Modifiability	When service interfaces are published and used by programs, the capability to make changes to a product rapidly and cost-effectively may be required. However, customization may cause problems as a result of when service interfaces are delivered and utilized by programs.	Mean Time to Change (MTTC)

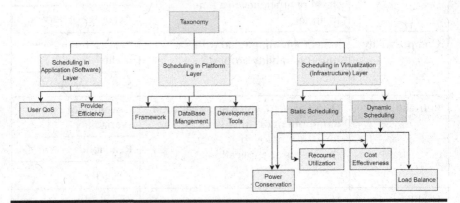

Figure 1.4   Classification of schedulers.

in the previous section. In the application layer, task schedulers are designed to focus on QoS and cloud provider efficiency. Scheduling in the platform layer intended for DB management, handling tools etc. Scheduling in virtualization is broadly classified as static scheduling or dynamic scheduling. When the system is in offline mode or at startup, static VMP is performed. In a cloud computing environment, this is the first VMP. The states of VM, states of PM, and pace of virtual machine requests are not taken into account in this VMP. Further, values such as the tasks it will serve, the resources available to serve the requests, and other information are not available. In dynamic scheduling, information on incoming requests, resources that are present, physical machines state and virtual machines state are available.

1.5.1 Scheduling in Application Layer

Scheduling is used in the application layer to allocate virtual or physical resources to provision user applications or tasks. User QoS includes factors such as response time, makespan, and cost. Parameters like resource utilization [20], fault tolerance, and energy consumption are crucial from the provider's standpoint.

1.5.2 Scheduling in Virtualization (Infrastructure) Layer

VMP is a significant approach in cloud infrastructure's IaaS. Virtualization enables for the most efficient use of the underlying resources. While selecting a viable solution for the VMP problem in a cloud datacenter with a set of available PMs and VMs, there are numerous criteria that may be picked based on optimization objectives and policies. The objective functions may be categorized into five types based on their common goals [21]. It is divided into the following sections:

1. Energy Consumption Minimization: Most of the researchers have considered this as the main objective in their research work. Some of the objective functions comes under this group are a) energy/power consumption minimization b) minimization of power consumption in IP layer c) minimization of number of PMs d) minimization of network power consumption e) energy efficiency maximization.

2. Economical Cost Optimization: Objective functions under this group are a) electricity cost minimization b) economical revenue maximization c) operational cost minimization d) server cost minimization e) thermal dissipation costs minimization f) SLA violations minimization g) total infrastructure cost minimization

3. Network Traffic Minimization: Some of the researchers have considered Network Traffic Minimization along with energy consumption minimization in their work. Objective functions classified under this group are a) minimization of average traffic latency b) minimization of cloud service response time c) minimization of time required for data transfer d) minimization of end-to-end delay e) migration number minimization f) link congestion minimization g) migration overhead minimization h) network cost minimization i) migration time minimization j) network traffic minimization k) network performance maximization l) node cost minimization m) worst case cut load ratio minimization n) overall communication cost minimization.

4. Resource Utilization Maximization: Cloud data center provides set of virtual and physical resources like RAM, CPU, network bandwidth, storage and graphical process units. A balanced and efficient utilization of these resources is a significant issue to address. A few objectives functions in this optimization group are a) maximum average utilization minimization b) elasticity maximization c) resource wastage minimization d) resource utilization maximization.

5. Performance Maximization: Objective functions include a) QoS maximization b) security metrics maximization c) total job completion time

minimization d) availability maximization e) resource interference minimization f) performance maximization g) CPU demand satisfaction maximization falls under this category.

1.6 Summary

The notion of computer resources as a utility has taken another step closer to reality through cloud computing. The paradigm of distributing computing power remotely via the Internet will grow as technology progresses and network connectivity gets quicker and with reduced latency. As a result, cloud data centers are likely to expand and amass a bigger share of the global computing resources. In this context, optimizing several aspects of cloud infrastructure is a critical issue. This chapter presented scheduling mechanisms and the parameters that can be used in optimization in cloud computing.

References

[1] Gao Y., Guan H., Qi Z., Hou Y., & Liu L. "A multi-objective ant colony system algorithm for virtual machine placement in cloud computing". Journal of Computer and System Sciences, 79(8), pp. 1230–1242, 2013.

[2] Lopez-Pires, F., & Baran, B. "Virtual machine placement literature review". arXiv preprint arXiv:1506.01509, 2015.

[3] Buyya, R., Ranjan, R., & Calheiros, R. N. "Modeling and simulation of scalable Cloud computing environments and the CloudSim toolkit: Challenges and opportunities". In High Performance Computing & Simulation. International Conference, vol. 21, pp. 1–11, 2009.

[4] Chu, X. et al. "Aneka: Next-generation enterprise grid platform for e-science and e-business applications". Proceedings of the 3rd IEEE International Conference on e-Science and Grid Computing, 2007.

[5] Badger, L., Grance, T., Patt-Corner, R., & Voas, J. "Draft cloud computing synopsis and recommendations". National Institute of Standards and Technology (NIST) Special Publication 800–146. US Department of Commerce. May 2011.

[6] Schubert, L., Jeffery, K., & Neidecker-Lutz, B. "The future of cloud computing, opportunities for European Cloud computing beyond 2010". Expert Group Report, public version 1, 2010.

[7] Zhang, Q., Cheng, L., & Boutaba, R. "Cloud computing: State-of-the-art and research challenges". Journal of Internet Services and Applications, 1(1), pp. 7–18, 2010.

[8] Li, Zh., O'Brien, L., Zhang, H., & Cai, R. "On a catalogue of metrics for evaluating commercial cloud services". 13th International Conference on Grid Computing, ACM/IEEE, pp. 164–173, 2012.

[9] Li, Z., O'Brien, L., Cai, R., & Zhang, H. "Towards a taxonomy of performance evaluation of commercial cloud services". Proceeding 5th Int. Conf. Cloud Computing (IEEE CLOUD 2012), IEEE Computer Society, 2012.

[10] Hazelhurst, S. "Scientific computing using virtual high-performance computing: A case study using the amazon elastic computing cloud". Proceeding 2008 Annual Research Conference of South African Institute of Computer Scientists and Information Technologists (SAICSIT 2008), ACM Press, pp. 94–103, 2008.

[11] Armbrust, M., Fox, A., Griffith, R., Joseph, A. D., Katz, R., Konwinski, A., Lee, G., Patterson, D., Rabkin, A., Stoica, I., & Zaharia, M. "A view of cloud computing, communications". ACM, 53(4), pp. 50–58, 2010.

[12] Li, Zh., O'Brien, L., Zhang, H., & Cai, R. "On a catalogue of metrics for evaluating commercial cloud services". 13th International Conference on Grid Computing, ACM/IEEE, pp. 164–173, 2012.

[13] Kondo, D., Javadi, B., Malecot, P., Cappello, F., & Anderson, D. P. "Cloud computing service composition: A systematic literature review". Expert Systems with Applications, 41(8), pp. 3809–3824, 2014.

[14] Bientinesi, P., Iakymchuk, R., & Napper, J. "HPC on competitive cloud resources". In Handbook of Cloud Computing, pp. 493–516. Springer, Boston, MA, 2010.

[15] Duan, Q. "Cloud service performance evaluation: status, challenges, and opportunities–a survey from the system modeling perspective". Digital Communications and Networks, 3(2), pp. 101–111, 2017.

[16] Reixa, M., Costa, c., & Aparicio, M. "Cloud services evaluation framework". Proceedings of the Workshop on Open Source and Design of Communication, ACM, pp. 61–69, 2012.

[17] Kumar Garg, S., Versteeg, S., & Buyya, R. "A framework for ranking of cloud computing services". Future Generation Computer Systems Journal, 29, pp. 1012–1023, 2013.

[18] Nadanam, P., & Rajmohan, R. "QoS evaluation for web services in cloud computing". Third International Conference on computing Communication & Networking Technologies (ICCCNT), pp. 1–8, 2012.

[19] Al-Qutaish, R. E. "Measuring the software product quality during the software development life-cycle: An international organization for standardization standards perspective". Journal of Computer Science, 5(5), pp. 392–397, 2009.

[20] Madhusudhan, H. S., Punit, G., Dinesh Kumar, S., & Zhenhai, T. "Dynamic virtual machine allocation in cloud computing using elephant herd optimization scheme". Journal of Circuits, Systems and Computers, 32(11), p. 2350188, 2023.

[21] Lopez-Pires, F., & Baran, B. "Virtual machine placement literature review". arXiv preprint arXiv:1506.01509, 2015.

Chapter 2

Improving QoS and Resource Efficiency in the Cloud Using Neural Networks

Madhusudhan H. S., Satish Kumar T., and Punit Gupta

2.1 Introduction

A front end and a back end are common components of cloud computing architecture. Clients and mobile devices make up the front end. CPU, storage, RAM, Graphical Process Units (GPU), and network bandwidth are all examples of physical and virtual resources used at the back end. Resource management, maximum performance, reliability, and security are few of the challenging issues encountered with cloud computing [1].

The goal of resource management is to make the best use of the available computer resources. Task scheduling is critical in the optimization process. Task scheduling plays a vital role in the cloud since it impacts overall system performance and load balancing. Developing an effective task scheduling algorithm would not only increase the system's performance, but will also allow the users to meet their requirements. Platform as a Service (PaaS), Infrastructure as a Service (IaaS), and Software as a Service (SaaS) are examples of cloud services. While providing these services, a variety of issues have arisen. One of the most significant issues among them is task scheduling [2]. Task scheduling allows for more efficient resource utilization. NP-complete problems include

DOI: 10.1201/9781003433293-2

task scheduling [3]. Several parameters must be considered while building an effective task scheduling algorithm. Task completion time, response time, cost, SLA (Service Level Agreement), and makespan are considered as essential factors from the perspective of cloud users, to mention a few. Parameters including resource utilization, fault tolerance, and energy/power consumption will be considered by the cloud provider as goals to be accomplished [4]. An artificial neural network, which is a supervised machine learning technique, is employed in this chapter to design a task scheduling algorithm that aims to decrease resource utilization and makespan.

2.2 Literature Review

Here, some of the research work that has been done in the field of task scheduling is presented.

The authors of [5] proposed a technique for resolving the problem, in which a queue is maintained, forcing incoming tasks to wait. All of these tasks will be recomputed and sorted throughout the scheduling process. Following that, during scheduling, the first task is taken from the queue, and resource allocation is done using a genetic algorithm based on best fit. The focus of this research is to maximize resource utilization while reducing execution time.

S. Singh provides an overview of genetic algorithms in [6]. Several types of job scheduling have been established in the cloud environment. The Max-Min technique is utilized to produce the initial population in this research. As a scheduling algorithm, a modified genetic algorithm is utilized. The goal is to achieve good outcomes by focusing on makespan.

A method for resource scheduling is introduced by the authors in [7]. They took into account each task's execution time, as well as the type of workload, which influences performance, which is the most essential factor in this situation. That means different QoS needs and QoS requirements that are comparable. [8] Hybrid bacteria foraging algorithm has been proposed by Sobhanayak Srichandan and Turuk Ashok Kumar to reduce energy consumption and limit makespan. [9] To decrease makespan, Tripathy Binodini and Smita Dash developed scheduling algorithm using a neural network trained with DSO.

2.3 Proposed Work

The system model and the proposed technique are described in this section. When the number of user tasks increases, the complexity of task scheduling often increases linearly. In this circumstance, cloud providers will need an effective algorithm to schedule the user's task in order to offer Quality of Service (QoS), decrease makespan, and ensure efficient resource usage of cloud resources [10]. As a result, task scheduling may be thought of as a problem of optimization.

2.3.1 Task Scheduling using an Artificial Neural Network

The system model is depicted in Figure 2.1. The user task is received by the cloud request manager and forwarded to the scheduler. The tasks that users issue should be assigned or allocated to a virtual machine for execution. We employ an artificial neural network (ANN) to create a scheduler that allocates income tasks to appropriate virtual machines. The use of numerous hidden layers in the construction of a neural network allows for better training. The round robin algorithm is used to place virtual machines on the physical machines.

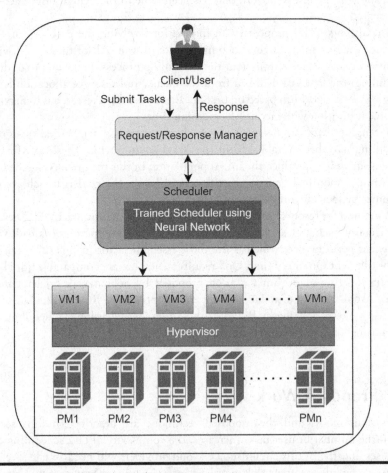

Figure 2.1 System model of task scheduling.

Figure 2.2 depicts a multilayer artificial neural network, having an input layer, several hidden layers, and an output layer.

Each layer of an artificial neural network is made up of one or more artificial neurons. Figure 2.3 depicts an artificial neuron. The dot product of the input features and the weights is the net input to the activation function. At each layer, different activation functions might be used. Two hidden layers were employed in this work.

Firstly, consider the input layer. Here, the input for the activation function along with bias can be mathematically expressed as shown in equation 2.1.

$$\text{inputsum}_1 = \sum w_i \cdot x_i + b \qquad (2.1)$$

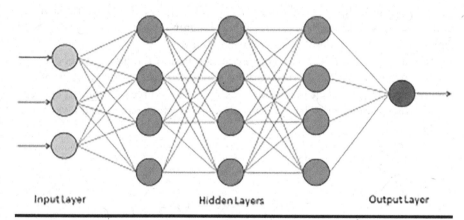

Figure 2.2　ANN with hidden layers.

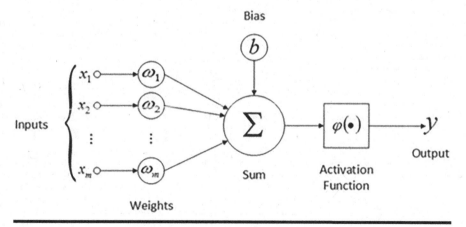

Figure 2.3　A neuron representation.

The output of the neuron can be derived by wrapping the net input with activation function Φ, as shown in equation 2.2

$$Ai = \varphi(\text{inputsum}_i),$$
$$\text{i.e } A_i = \varphi\left(\sum w_i * A_i + b\right) \tag{2.2}$$

This activation value of a neuron is considered to be the value which will be forwarded to the succeeding layer. Next, in the hidden layers, net input is mathematically expressed as in equation 2.3. Net input here is activation from neurons of the previous layers.

$$\text{inputsum}_i = \sum w_i \cdot A_i + b \tag{2.3}$$

Several activation function like tanh, sigmoid, softplus, ReLU (rectified linear unit), and leaky ReLU can be adapted while designing ANN. In our work sigmoid and leaky ReLU activation functions have been used.

Sigmoid activation function is expressed as equation 2.4. Sigmoid can decrease extreme values or outliers in data without eliminating them. A sigmoid function converts near infinite range independent variables into simple probabilities between 0 and 1with majority of its being extremely close to 0 or 1 represented by y axis in the Figure 2.4.

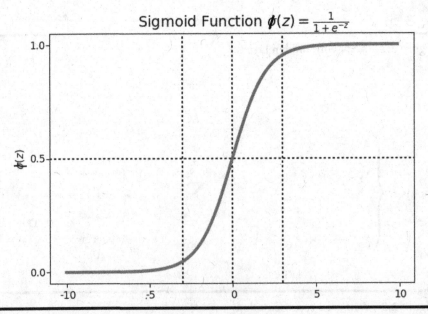

Figure 2.4 Sigmoid activation function.

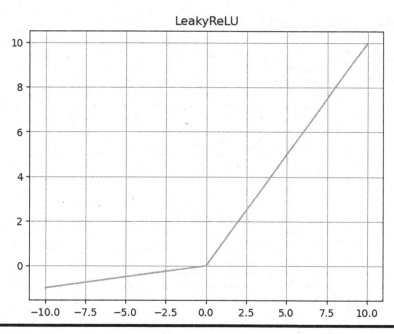

Figure 2.5   Leaky ReLU activation function.

$$\varphi(z) = 1/1 + e^{-z} \tag{2.4}$$

Leaky ReLUs are an approach to diminish the "ReLU" issue. Figure 2.5 shows Leaky ReLU activation function. When x is less than zero, the leaky ReLU's function will have a slight negative slope instead of being zero (e.g., "around 0.01"). The equation is given by

$$\varphi(z) = \begin{cases} z, \text{ if } z > 0 \\ \alpha z, \text{ if } z \le 0 \end{cases} \tag{2.5}$$

When creating a multilayer artificial neural network, the back propagation learning process is used, and weights can be altered incrementally as the algorithm discovers the solution. Weights are treated as a vector in this case, and they must be optimized to reduce errors. To minimize errors, the back propagation process is used. The difference between the actual output and the value obtained by the ANN must be kept to a minimum. The notations used in ANN are listed in Table 2.1.

In backpropagation algorithm, following steps are adapted to update weights:

1. Begin the algorithm, set artificial neural network and loop through.
2. Calculate the neural network output for the given input. Compare actual output with network output and find the error.
3. Update weights using equation 2.6.

Table 2.1   Notations used in an Artificial Neural Network

Notation	Meaning
i	A neuron's index
j	Neuron's index values of preceding layer linking to neuron i
a_i	Neuron naïve Activation value, i.e neuron i output value
A_i	Activation values as an input for neuron i
φ	Activation function
φ'	Derivate of activation function
err_i	Error: difference between actual output of training data and network output
W_i	Weights Vector to neuron i
W_{ji}	Weight on input connection from preceding layer neuron j to neuron i
$inputsum_i$	Added Weights of inputs to neuron i
$inputsum_j$	Added Weights of inputs of neuron j of preceding layer
α'	Learning rate
Δ_i	Error term for neuron i; $\Delta_i = err_i \times \varphi'\ (inputsum_i)$
Δ_j	Error value for connected neuron j in preceding layer

$$W_{ji} \leftarrow W_{ji} + \alpha' \times a_j \times err_i \times \varphi'(inputsum_i) \qquad (2.6)$$

4. For each successive layers in the network:

Compute the error at each node/neuron as given in equation 2.7.

$$\Delta_j \leftarrow \varphi'(inputsum_j) \times \sum W_{ji}\Delta_i \qquad (2.7)$$

Update the weights leading into the layer.

$$W_{kj} \leftarrow W_{kj} + \alpha' \times a_k \times \Delta_j \qquad (2.8)$$

5. Reiterate loop till maximum epoch is reached.

In this chapter, the training algorithms simulated annealing (SA) and genetic algorithm (GA) are proposed. In this case, an ANN is being trained to assign tasks to virtual machines.

2.3.2 Simulated Annealing Algorithm

Simulated annealing is on the meta heuristic technique. Simulated annealing will overcome local optima and provide an approximate global optimization solution when tackling an optimization issue with a vast search space. Annealing is a metallurgical process in which metals are gently cooled to allow them to reach a low-energy state, which makes them extremely strong.

1. The algorithm's stages are as follows: Initial configuration:
   In initial configuration, assignment of tasks Ti (i=1, 2 . . . m) to Virtual Machines (VMs) VMj, (j=1,2 . . . m) is prepared in random fashion. We have used array list to denote the assignment as T={t1, t2, t3 . . . . tm}. The task/cloudlet number is used as an array index in the array list, and the value of that index is the virtual number to which the task is assigned. Initial configuration is expected to be the best configuration and it is considered as the current configuration.

2. Generation of new configuration:
   Simulated annealing will look for neighbor states in order to improve outcomes. A neighbor configuration is a randomly generated and it also indicates the task allocation to a virtual machine. The neighbor's two index values are picked, and their virtual machines are exchanged. The new resulting configuration is compared to the original configuration. Goal of SA is to find a good configuration in terms of objective function.

3. Objective function for the optimization problem:
   An acceptance probability is the definition of an objective function. The acceptance probability specifies how long each task will take to complete on the virtual machine that has been assigned to it. Acceptance probability is used to compare the present configuration with the resultant neighbor configuration. If the neighbor configuration can do all tasks faster than the current configuration, it becomes the best configuration; otherwise, the current setup remains the best configuration. By lowering the temperature as specified in the following, phase 2 was repeated.

4. Temperature scheduling: Cooling down the temperature is an important feature of simulated annealing, because quick cooling might result in a result that isn't close to ideal. There is no universal method for adjusting temperature. We experimented with several parameters before settling on a starting temperature of 100 degree and a cooling rate of 0.003.

Algorithm 1: SA algorithm for Placing Task on Virtual Machine

Input: Task list, virtual machine list
Output: Assignment of tasks to VM
1. temp← 100
2. c_rate←0.003 (cooling rate)
3. Generate initialize assignment randomly, assume initial assignment is the best_solution
4. current_solution=initial solution
5. **while** temp>1 do
6.   create a new neighbor by generating assignment randomly
7. select 2 points(tasks) randomly from neighbor
8.   swap the placement of virtual machines of the selected tasks
9.   calculate the objective function value of both current_solution and neighbor
10. **if** (acceptance_probability of neighbor) then
8.   current_solution=neighbor
9.   best_solution= current_solution
10. **else**
11.   set placement as old placement
12. temp*= 1-c_rate (decrease temp)
12. **end while**
13. **end**

Finally, a best configuration will be obtained, and this mapping data set (best configuration) will be utilized to train the artificial neural network as depicted in Figure 2.6.

2.3.3 Genetic Algorithm

GA is a type of evolutionary algorithm. It is a meta heuristic technique influenced by natural selection. GA may be used to address issues that are both constrained and unconstrained. It is frequently utilized to find near-optimal or ideal solutions to complex issues. It works on the entire population, increasing the chances of achieving global optimal while avoiding local optimum [11].

In our approach, the subsequent steps are applied:

1. Initialize Population: The population is initialized by randomly mapping all tasks T_m (m=1 to x) to virtual machines VM_n (n= 1 to y).
   An example for initial population is shown in Figure 2.7. Here 7 tasks are allocated to 5 virtual machines.
2. Fitness function: The ability to determine fitness function is critical since it determines the best option when selecting the proper individuals from a large

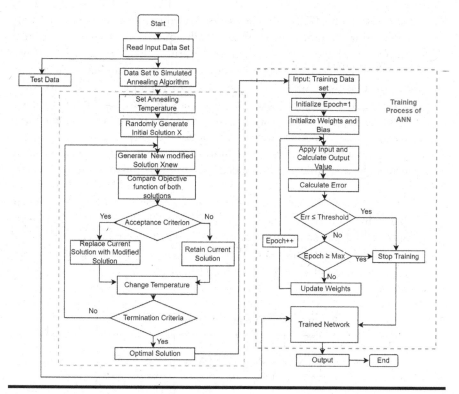

Figure 2.6   SA-ANN workflow.

T₁₁	T₁₂	T₁₃	T₁₄	T₁₅	T₁₆	T₁₇
VM3	VM5	VM2	VM4	VM1	VM3	VM2

Figure 2.7   Initial population with VM mapping.

group. The execution time is used to derive the fitness function here. Task T_m execution time on virtual machine VM_n is written as

Execution time=ET[m, n], where m ∈ T, x=1, 2 . . . x and n ∈ VM, y=1, 2 . . . y

Individuals with the best execution times are regarded the fittest and are chosen for reproduction.

3. Selection: Many strategies come to notice while selecting individuals for crossing. We employed the tournament selection strategy in this case. The tournament size is denoted by the letter K, and K individuals are chosen at random from the population. The individual with the highest fitness value is declared the tournament winner and will be used for crossover operation.

4. Crossover: To begin, two of the fittest individuals from the population are chosen using the tournament selection technique. The crossover procedure is then used to create new individuals or offspring. There are various crossover strategies available, including single point crossover, multipoint crossover, and uniform crossover. We have employed a two-point crossover in this work. Following crossover, newly created individuals are reintroduced into the population to improve its diversity. Figure 2.8 depicts two parents, parent 1 and parent 2, and two points are chosen to perform crossover.

Figure 2.9 represents new child/individual after crossover operation. Here we keep the first child and it is added back to the population.

5. Mutation:

There are several mutation operations available, including move, swap, rebalancing, and move and swap. To alter individuals, we picked swap. Figure 2.10 depicts a mutation procedure in which two points from the child are randomly picked and values of two points are exchanged to generate a new child, i.e. virtual machines assigned to tasks are switched.

Parent 1:		2-point crossover				
T_{11}	T_{12}	T_{13}	T_{14}	T_{15}	T_{16}	T_{17}
VM3	VM5	VM2	VM4	VM1	VM3	VM2

Parent 2:						
T_{11}	T_{12}	T_{13}	T_{14}	T_{15}	T_{16}	T_{17}
VM2	VM3	VM1	VM5	VM4	VM2	VM3

Figure 2.8   Two-point crossover (before cross over).

Child 1						
T_{11}	T_{12}	T_{13}	T_{14}	T_{15}	T_{16}	T_{17}
VM3	VM5	VM1	VM5	VM4	VM3	VM2

Child 2						
T_{11}	T_{12}	T_{13}	T_{14}	T_{15}	T_{16}	T_{17}
VM2	VM3	VM2	VM4	VM1	VM2	VM3

Figure 2.9   New child after crossover.

Before Mutation:

T$_{11}$	T$_{12}$	T$_{13}$	T$_{14}$	T$_{15}$	T$_{16}$	T$_{17}$
VM3	VM5	VM1	VM5	VM4	VM3	VM2

After Mutation:

T$_{11}$	T$_{12}$	T$_{13}$	T$_{14}$	T$_{15}$	T$_{16}$	T$_{17}$
VM3	VM3	VM1	VM5	VM4	VM5	VM2

Figure 2.10   Mutation operation.

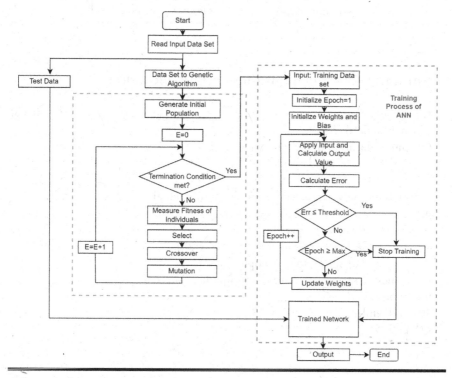

Figure 2.11   GA-ANN workflow.

The steps from 2 to 5 are repeated until the termination condition is satisfied. We used a 100 evolution of genetic algorithm to come up with a better solution based on the fitness value. At the end, the data set is derived containing mapping of tasks to VMs and further it is used to train the ANN as shown in Figure 2.11. The values of GA parameters used in this work are presented in Table 2.2.

Table 2.2   Parameters of Genetic Algorithm

Parameter	Value
Population Size	100
Initial Population	Randomly Generated
Number of Generations	100
Mutation Probability	0.15
Crossover Probability	0.9
Selection Scheme	Tournament Selection
Crossover Type	2 Point Crossover

Algorithm 2: Genetic Algorithm for task allocation

Input: population_size, generation_size, mutation_rate, task list, virtual machine(VM) list
Output: Allocation of tasks to apt VMs
1. start
2. While(g≤generation_size) do
3.   derive new_population from fittest individuals
4.   for j = 1 to new_population_size
5.   select parent1, parent2
6.   offspring = crossover(parent1, parent2)
7.   add offspring to new population
8.   newoffpsring = mutate(offspring, mutation_rate)
9.   end for
10. end while
11. end

2.4 Experimental Results and Discussion

In two scenarios, we conducted the experiment. In the first case, three physical machines (PMs) and eight virtual machines (VMs) were employed, whereas in the second scenario, five PMs and 20 VMs were used. The experiment uses data from the blue horizon log at the San Diego Supercomputer Center (SDSC), which is a real-time workload. This log contains information on tasks that have been in production for more than two years. This was done on an IBM SP system with 8 processors per node. In each of the aforementioned scenarios, 500 to 10,000 tasks were rendered ten times and the outcomes were recorded. The results are averaged over ten trials and rounded to the closest integer.

2.4.1 Makespan

From the user's perspective, makespan is one of the most important parameters. Makespan represents total time taken to execute all the tasks. As a result, it is utilized to assess the performance of a scheduling technique.

The makespan of several methods are shown in Tables 2.3 and 2.4.

Scenario 1:

Table 2.3   Makespan (msec) of GA, NNGA, and NNSA

No. of Tasks	GA	NN-GA	NN-SA
500	1099	809	913
1000	2627	1680	1736
3000	12366	8992	8691
5000	24005	19720	20413
10000	70066	64075	64225

As depicted in Figure 2.12, in comparison to default genetic algorithm and ANN trained with simulated annealing, the results show that ANN trained with genetic algorithm reduces makespan by 23% and 3%, respectively.

Scenario 2:

Table 2.4   Makespan (msec) of GA, NNGA, and NNSA

No. of Tasks	GA	NN-GA	NN-SA
500	1042	698	838
1000	2531	1602	1639
3000	12810	8485	8509
5000	25748	19375	20019
10000	71377	62451	62890

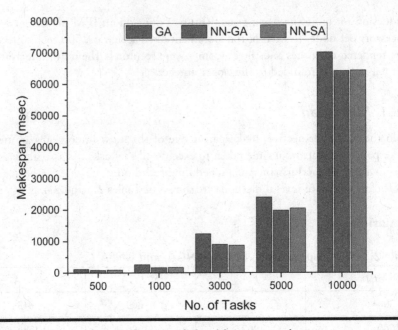

Figure 2.12 Comparison makespan of algorithms (scenario 1).

In scenario 2, as shown in Figure 2.13, the makespan of ANN trained with GA is reduced by 28% and 3% when compared to default genetic algorithm and ANN trained using simulated annealing.

2.4.2 Resource Utilization

The sum of all the virtual machine's busy time divided by the overall duration for the application's execution represents resource usage. It is expressed as equation 2.9.

$$\text{Utilization} = \frac{\sum \text{Virtual Machine busy time}}{\text{Total execution time}} * 100 \qquad (2.9)$$

Resource utilization in the datacenter through different algorithms are shown in Table 2.5 and Table 2.6.

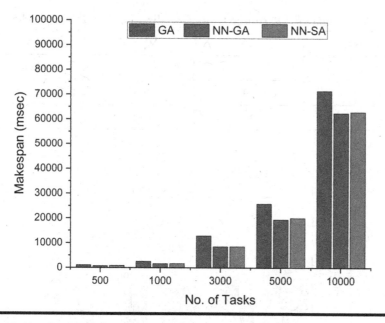

Figure 2.13   Comparison makespan of algorithms (scenario 2).

Scenario 1:

Table 2.5   Resource Utilization through GA, NN-GA, and NN-SA

No. of Tasks	GA	NN-GA	NN-SA
500	26	33	40
1000	21	37	34
3000	26	51	48
5000	28	38	34
100000	17	25	25

Scenario 2:

Table 2.6   Resource Utilization through GA, NN-GA, and NN-SA

No. of Tasks	GA	NN-GA	NN-SA
500	9	21	14
1000	9	28	26

(Continued)

Table 2.6 *(Continued)*　**Resource Utilization through GA, NN-GA, and NN-SA**

No. of Tasks	GA	NN-GA	NN-SA
3000	9	30	29
5000	9	15	13
10000	10	10	10

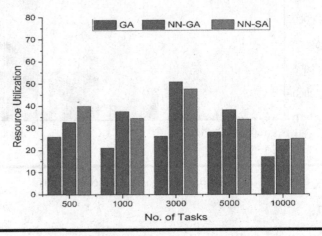

Figure 2.14　Resource utilization via different algorithms (scenario 1).

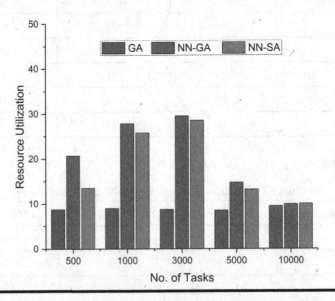

Figure 2.15　Resource utilization via different algorithms (scenario 2).

As shown in the Figure 2.14, when compared to default GA and ANN trained with SA, resource utilization using ANN trained with GA is improved by 35% and 2%, respectively. In scenario 2, as depicted in Figure 2.15, the overall resource utilization using ANN trained with GA is greater by 48% and 11% when compared to default genetic algorithm and ANN trained with SA respectively.

2.5 Summary

In this chapter, artificial neural network, a supervised machine learning approach for task scheduling is proposed. The objectives are to reduce the makespan and maximize resource utilization. Data sets obtained from two meta heuristics techniques, gAs and SA algorithms, are used to train an ANN. The results show that ANN trained with genetic algorithm outperforms both the default genetic algorithm and ANN trained with SA. When compared to the default genetic algorithm, an ANN with GA outperforms by an average execution efficiency of 25.56% and average resource utilization by 41.5%. It has been proven that machine learning produces better outcomes than conventional techniques.

References

[1] Furht, B. Armando Escalante Handbook of Cloud Computing. ISBN 978-1-4419-6523-3, Springer, New York, 2010.
[2] Hadi, G., & Pedram, M. "Energy-efficient virtual machine replication and placement in a cloud computing system". In Cloud Computing (CLOUD), 2012 IEEE 5th International Conference on, pp. 750–757. IEEE, 2012.
[3] Ullman, J. D. "NP-complete scheduling problems". Journal of Computer and System Sciences, 10(3), p. 384e93, 1975.
[4] Ge, J. W., & Yuan, Y. S. "Research of cloud computing task scheduling algorithm based on improved genetic algorithm". Applied Mechanics and Materials, pp. 2426–2429, 2013.
[5] Ravichandran, S., & Naganathan, D. E. "Dynamic scheduling of data using genetic algorithm in cloud computing". International Journal of Computing Algorithm, 2, pp. 127–133, 2013.
[6] Singh, S., & Kalra, M. "Scheduling of independent tasks in cloud computing using modified genetic algorithm". In Computational Intelligence and Communication Networks (CICN), 2014 International Conference on, pp. 565–569, 2014.
[7] Singh, S., & Chana, I. "Cloud resource provisioning: survey, status and future research directions". Knowledge and Information Systems, 49(3), pp. 1005–1069, 2016.
[8] Srichandan, S., Kumar, T. A., & Bibhudatta, S. "Task scheduling for cloud computing using multi-objective hybrid bacteria foraging algorithm". Future Computing and Informatics Journal, 3(2), pp. 210–230, 2018.
[9] Tripathy, B., Dash, S., & Padhy, S. K. "Dynamic task scheduling using a directed neural network". Journal of Parallel and Distributed Computing, 75, pp. 101–106, 2015.

[10] Kaur, R., & Kinger, S. "Enhanced genetic algorithm based task scheduling in cloud computing". International Journal of Computer Applications, 101, 2014.

[11] Kumar, T. S., Sakthivel, S., & Kumar, S. "Optimizing code by selecting compiler flags using parallel genetic algorithm on multicore CPUs". International Journal of Engineering and Technology (IJET), 6(2), pp. 544–555, 2014.

Chapter 3

A Machine Learning-Based Optimization Approach to Analyze the Text-Based Reviews for Improving Graduation Rates for Cloud-Based Architectures

Akshatha M., Lavanya M. C., Seema H. R., and Shashank S.

3.1 Introduction

Analyzing the views of individuals, sentiments, and emotions is the focus of the natural language processing (NLP) subfield known as sentiment analysis (SA). Data retrieval, extraction, preprocessing, and feature extraction are all steps in the multi-step SA process. There is a critical need to monitor this enormous volume of internet data and automatically extract relevant information given the quick uptake of social media comments in a variety of businesses. Models for sentiment analysis are crucial

DOI: 10.1201/9781003433293-3

in this activity. Emotion detection is used in many industries, including marketing, public policy, disaster management, and public health. There is extensive usage of facial expression and image-based emotion recognition software. Hand motions have been recognized using human action recognition technology. investigation of emotion detection models may also be done through interaction. Emotionally rich text data from social networks may be handled for a variety of real-world uses.

Recently, there has been a sharp rise in the use of text on the Internet. Ideograms and smileys made it easier for people to convey their feelings in electronic messages and on websites. Texts like "Face with Tears of Joy" have transformed how we converse on social media and microblogging platforms. People frequently employ them when it is more challenging to convey their expressions using words alone. A single Text symbol can improve a text message's expressiveness. When a city's name is displayed by itself, it has no sentimental meaning. But if the user also included a Text with this name, the content may have sentimental meaning. Emoticons are a more basic form of text, and research published in the Social Neuroscience magazine shows that the brain perceives them as actual faces. Dr. Owen Churches from the psychology department at Flinders University has discovered that emoticons are now more significant than previously thought. They now seem to elicit the same responses from us as a real human face would. For the first time, the "Face with Tears of Joy" or "Text was picked as the Oxford Dictionaries Word of the Year in November 2015. This followed the widespread use of this Text character online, particularly on social networks.

3.2 Background and Related Work

A substantial amount of research focused on sentiment analysis models. The methods and models differ between fields. However, only a few studies looked at how Text characters were used on social media. The first machine-learning-based sentiment analysis research was conducted by Pang et al. [1]. They tested supervised classifiers likenaïvee Bayes, Maximum Entropy, and Support Vector Machine (SVM) on a dataset of movie reviews. When compared to traditional text classification, the classifiers are ineffective in classifying sentiment. The main justification could be that they are frequently used with conventional text classification approaches, which establish words in a document as belonging to a "bag of words" (BOW) concept. Grammatical structures, word order, and semantic relationships between words are essential components of SA [2] but are not stored in BOW. As a result, this approach required a stockpile of labeled data, which may be expensive or even prohibitively expensive, the poor scalability of fresh data was a disadvantage.

The benefits of DL have led several researchers to utilize various forms of SA for artificial neural networks. These benefits include [3]: automated feature generation

(AFG), which generates new features from a small collection of features in the training data to help them generalize more effectively; and scalability (DL), which examines massive amounts of data and performs various calculations quickly and efficiently.

Models for sentiment analysis have been developed for a variety of purposes, including projecting financial and economic variables, measuring customer happiness, and even predicting political events like election results before voting. For instance, using a sample of 3516 tweets as a model of consumer brand sentiment, the study in [4] analyzed consumers' attitudes toward prominent companies. A pre-set lexicon of 6800 seed adjectives with predetermined orientations was used for the model analysis. By combining qualitative and quantitative methods to analyze the data, the algorithm was able to forecast how customers will feel about well-known brands.

In [5], MJ Rust, M. Bates, and X. Zhuang employed a multi-knowledge strategy that used WordNet, statistical analysis, and movie expertise to create a powerful model for mining and summarizing movie reviews. A real-time sentiment analysis method for the 2012 US presidential elections expressed on Twitter was proposed by Wang et al. [6]. Utilizing the Nave Bayes model, the system had a four-category classification accuracy of 59%.

Bollen et al. used Google Profile of Mood States (GPOMS), which measures mood in terms of six dimensions (Calm, Alert, Sure, Vital, Kind, and Happy), and Opinion Finder, which measures positive and negative moods, to analyze the text content of daily Twitter to predict changes in DJIA closing values in 2011 [7]. According to the methodology, adding certain public mood components can increase the precision of DJIA projections. They were 86.7% accurate in anticipating the daily up and downshifts in the DJIA stock market index closing values.

A sentiment model was put up by Cheong, Marc, and Vincent C. S. Lee [8] to gauge public opinion and reaction in the event of terrorism. The model produced helpful graphical visualizations of data that revealed viable responses to terrorist threats when used in conjunction with data mining, visualization, and filtering techniques.

The expressivity of the characters must be examined to gauge how employing texts will affect Sentiment Analysis models. Researchers often exclude all punctuation and special characters from the text unless they are the primary focus of the study. Information for sentiment analysis and text mining. Text characters are eliminated throughout the text mining process just like any other group of special characters. Our aim in this work was to investigate how Text characters affect Sentiment Analysis models. While creating a sentiment analysis model, we investigated whether people use text more frequently in good or bad life events and assessed the effects of ignoring such characters.

The objectives of this study are summarized as follows:

- We intend a model for the emotion category applied to the college dataset (Vidyavardhaka College of Engineering) datasets. which could extract contextual information from the text in the review.
- Word cloud models are used to extract context information from text for the fine-tuning process.
- We employed training models on text datasets and then tested the hypothesis of texts' advantage as a cue in classification by training the same model but eliminating texts in the preprocessing stage and observing the impact.

The order of the chapter is as follows. The method recommended for determining the emotional components of reviews is explained in the methodology section. The most significant findings are highlighted and discussed in the experiment and results section. The Conclusion and Future Work Section concludes by summarizing the findings and outlining potential future study avenues.

3.3 Methodology

Tracking the reviews given by the stakeholders is considered a rigorous task by the patron. In this work, a simplified, robust approach is presented to trace and analyze the text-based reviews on college websites using the word cloud sentiment analysis tool for a cloud-based architecture. Conversely, the reviews given by the students may provide some insights that could not be plausible to get from institutionally conducted student surveys. Additionally, we can consider a large set of data, and can apply the fact-finding, and the intended future work.

3.4 Dataset

With the help of the open-source (R) packages RSelenium and rvest, clients may create software that can be launched virtually, access any website for communication with a specified website, for extracting HTML code from the various sources of the pages. We create (R) scripts using various methods that will browse the college websites, examine the reviews of institutions based on program conditions [9], scrape all comments, and then store and export them to reviews.csv file. We gather a total of 360 multi-dimensional observations by directing these scripts to look for the college that this study is focusing on 250 of them, or the great bulk of them, are from the public cloud—officially named collegedunia.com.

3.5 Data Analysis

As part of the initial phase of our analysis, we clean each comment by web scraping, eliminating extraneous whitespace, punctuation, and stop words (as specified in the (R) package tm [10]), as well as changing all characters to lowercase and stemming all words. Web scraping software is now a variety of web scraping technologies available or being developed specifically for users to extract desired information from millions of websites. Web scraping tools were created expressly to obtain data from the internet. These tools, which are often referred to as web harvesting tools or data extraction tools, are helpful for anybody attempting to gather certain data from websites since they give the user structured data after gathering data from a variety of websites. The following are some of the most used web scraping tools: Import.io, Webhose.io, Dexi.io, Scrapinghub, and Parsehub. Legalizing web scraping is a touchy subject since, depending on how it is applied, it may either be a blessing or a curse. On the one hand, effective online scraping allows search engines to index web material and price comparison services to help customers save money. Web scraping, however, can be used to serve more nefarious and harmful purposes. Web scraping is sometimes associated with other hostile automation techniques known as "bad bots," which facilitate destructive actions including denial of service assaults, competitive data mining, account takeover, data theft, etc. The legality of web scraping is a murky issue that inevitably grows with time. Web scraping is the main cause of the rise in copyright violations, terms of service violations, and other activities that are seriously detrimental to a company's operations, even while it technically speeds up data surfing, loading, copying, and pasting. Problems with web scraping have challenges from several different issues in addition to the question of its legality.

Future of Data Scraping: Since data scraping has both potential and difficulties, it can be properly said that unintentional data scrapers are more likely to target businesses and steal their data, which might lead to moral hazard. Data-scraping in combination with big data, however, may give the organization market information, assist them to uncover important trends and patterns, and find the greatest prospects and solutions since we are on the cusp of a data transformation. Therefore, it would be accurate to suggest that data scraping will soon be improved.

We start separating the information from the reviews by estimating the word frequencies; after that, we perform Natural language processing and sentiment analysis because the data that is in the form of reviews is better suited for computational analysis. We use the National Research Council of Canada (NRC) [11] and Finn Arup Nielsen (AFINN) [12] lexicons in a lexicon-based approach to sentiment analysis. By doing so, we may go over the restrictive and binary character of many other lexicons that solely use the concepts of "positive," "neutral," and "negative" [13]. The lexicon then serves as an essential complement by enabling us to gauge the strength of sentiment by rating words on a discrete scaling as 0, 1 and

2, where "0" denotes extreme negativity, "1" complete neutrality, and "2" denotes extreme positivity [14].

3.6 Word Cloud Creation

We use the clustering technique for grouping similar items, hence both the K-means clustering technique and fuzzy C-means clustering is been adopted to find the similarities and differences using all the characteristics, including the fraction of phrases expressing anger [15] In contrast to supervised learning, this clustering does not use labeled data. K-Means divides objects into clusters that have things in common and are different from those in another cluster.

Figure 3.1 shows the word cloud creation technology that uses many sources of textual data to construct word clouds. A user-entered text document is the most basic source. Additionally, users have the option of entering a website's URL or a PDF link. In this instance, a word cloud is created using the text that was retrieved. Another choice is to include the URL to a Reddit or YouTube conversation. The technology analyses every remark on the video for the scenario and creates a "comment cloud" as a result.

The input text is preprocessed using the following processes before creating a word cloud:

Term Extraction: Using Apache OpenNLP, sentences from the input text are first divided into groups of words called tokens. Stop-words like "a," "the," and "is" are eliminated from the collection. The Porter Stemming Algorithm is used to group the remaining words by their stems, reducing terms like "dance," "dancer," and "dancing" to their root, "dance." The final word cloud uses the term's most prevalent variant.

Ranking: The terms are ranked in order of relative significance in the next step. Depending on the word used in the supplied text, we utilize one of three possible ranking functions. Words are arranged in each ranking function according to their weight (rank). The most fundamental ranking criteria, Term Frequency, is

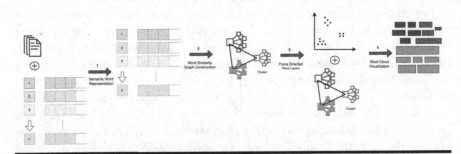

Figure 3.1   Word cloud architecture.

employed in many conventional word cloud visualizations. Even after eliminating frequent stop-words, many semantically worthless terms still have high-term frequency rankings. By normalizing a word's frequency by its frequency in a broader text collection, Term Frequency-Inverse Document Frequency addressed this issue. The Lex Rank algorithm serves as the foundation for the third-ranking method. The approach uses eigenvector centrality to calculate the relative significance of textual units. The ranked list of words is used to create a matrix of pairwise similarities, to give related terms high similarity scores. Depending on the input text, we employ three similarity functions: cosine similarity, Jaccard similarity, and lexical similarity. The similarity function always yields a number between 0, which denotes that a pair of words are unrelated, and 1, which denotes that the words are extremely similar.

After extracting terms, ranks, and similarities, we build an edge-weighted network with vertices representing the phrases and weights representing the calculated similarities. An axis-aligned rectangle with a height proportionate to the rank of each word is produced [16].

3.7 Star Forest Word Cloud Creation Algorithm

A star is a tree with a maximum depth of 1, and a star forest is a forest in which all of the linked trees are stars. Our method consists of three parts. The given graph, which we obtained from the dissimilarity matrix, is first divided into individual stars. The next step is to create a word cloud for each star (realizing star) [17]. The final word cloud is produced by combining the various responses.

We greedily remove stars from the provided graph. We identify the vertex v that has the highest neighboring weight, or the one for which P uV sim(v, u) is greatest. The vertices V v are then treated as the star's leaves and the vertex as its center. The words that will be close to star center v are predicted and are then eliminated from the graph. Until the graph is empty, this procedure is repeated with the smaller graph.

The Knapsack issue, which is described as follows, is comparable to the challenge of determining the optimal group of words to be close to a star center: Pack a maximum-valued subset of objects into a rucksack with the specified capacity given a collection of items, each with a size and value. Let B0 represent the star's center-corresponding box. There are four boxes B1, B2, B3, and B4 in every optimum solution, each of which sides contains a corner of the center box B0.

Given B1, B2, B3, and B4, the issue is reduced to allocating each of the four remaining boxes Bit to the side of B0 which fully includes the contact between Bi and B0 for each of the other four boxes. The assignment of boxes to B0's side is automatically transformed into a Knapsack instance: the dimensions of a box are its height and breadth for its vertical and horizontal sides, respectively, and its edge weight between Bi and B0. The Knapsack problem algorithm is now performed for the top side of B0, the realized boxes are removed, and we continue to the bottom, left, and right sides of the center box. We apply the polynomial-time approximation strategy presented to solve Knapsack.

This paper investigates the reactions of students to a word frequency-based method for condensing electronically accessible material. Using this method, students produced word clouds that they then utilized to supplement their individual and small-group learning. This investigation is qualitative. Student opinions were gathered using small focus groups. According to feedback, students modified how they used word clouds to suit their preferred learning styles. It was done using Kolb's learning styles inventory. Word clouds may be used in the workplace, according to student responses.

A pictorial representation of the number of occurrences of the terms in any chosen written material, such as notes, a book chapter, or any website, is a word cloud, also known as a tag cloud or a weighted list. Font size serves as a proxy for frequency; hence, the bigger the font, the more frequently a term is used. Figure 3.1 depicts an instance of a word cloud taken from the text of this article. This abstract was made using a free online program called Wordle, which may be found at www.wordle.net. Wordle gave us the option to control aspects like word count, typeface, layout, and color. Common terms like conjunctions and prepositions may be removed, but we were unable to add or remove nouns, verbs, adjectives, or adverbs. Within the constraints we were able to specify, the word cloud abstract depicts the terms that appear the most frequently in this article. The pupils mentioned in this article utilized Wordle as their program. Word clouds have the benefit of producing a clear visual representation.

They highlight the words that are used the most, make them available for students to concentrate on the reviews, and consider if the same terms are being highlighted. Word clouds may be a helpful tool for students who are studying for semester end Exams since they can serve as a memory aid for previously read content or a summary of written material. Word clouds have a few drawbacks: terms that consist of one or more clusters of words, like "word clouds," are treated as two separate words; the word cloud generated by Word cloud can only be changed within a pre-defined set of parameters; the important concepts may be omitted as the words used to label a concept appear rarely. The main goal of this study is to showcase the real working of the word cloud.

The secondary goal [18] is to describe how accounting students proactively changed their word cloud usage. This demonstrates how adaptable the method is. The fact that students only tended word clouds in ways that matched their preferred learning styles, however, may have limited the value of word clouds as an efficient methodology for individual learning because it proposes that students were only receptive to learning strategies that were easy for them rather than those that were difficult for them. Due to the moderately small group of students (69 students) and the brief duration of the study (two semesters with 13 teaching weeks per semester), it is possible that the strong tendency of the accounting students to only use word clouds in ways that are consistent with their learning styles was an anomaly or coincidence.

Word clouds were created by the students utilizing information from websites and PowerPoint presentations used in the lectures. We are also cautioned about the drawbacks of word clouds and are told to use them in conjunction with other learning strategies rather than as a replacement for them. The students were actively modifying their learning processes to meet their unique requirements in line with a responsible attitude to learning by actively investigating new uses for word clouds beyond those presented in class (White, 1988). If students can own the process of learning rather than just the subject matter being covered, learning will be more successful (Enghag & Niedderer, 2008). The literature supporting [19] This research is reviewed after explaining word clouds, and then student reactions to utilizing word clouds are investigated. This article looks at the substance of focus group replies about word clouds, how students customized word clouds to fit their preferred learning styles, and the benefits students perceived from utilizing word clouds at work. It sheds light on how students applied a teaching strategy they believed to be both current and ongoingly relevant.

Students were properly informed of word clouds' restrictions. All students eagerly accepted word clouds, which were first offered as an optional learning tool to be used sparingly with other learning strategies, to summarize lecture notes and PowerPoint for review. However, the majority used word clouds in considerably more extensive ways. In voluntary focus groups, students' responses revealed a clear pattern of employing word clouds in ways that matched their preferences for learning techniques. Students have already self-assessed their preferred learning styles in another setting. We were concerned that kids might interpret their usage of word clouds as being in line with what they already understood about their preferred learning styles. The academic staff saw the association; the students were utilizing word clouds in ways that were congruent with their preferences, but they were unaware of it. The use of word clouds by students did not appear to be related to their preferred learning styles. According to them, "it just seemed the obvious thing for me to do," to use the words of one student.

The passionate student response to word clouds was first noted in their casual comments made in class. All students voluntarily participated in focus groups that were independently moderated as a result. We employed focus groups, each with 12 students, to gather input. The groups were led by academic personnel [20]. Given the paucity of existing research on the use of word clouds to improve student learning, it was deemed crucial to collect the richer data of an unstructured focus group discussion with the facilitator remaining as uninvolved as possible. Responses were verbatim recorded, then transcribed. Although students had been utilizing the terminology of learning styles for over three years, they were only reporting on their experiences with word clouds across two semester-long periods. Only four students were of legal drinking age, and there were 56 men and 13 women among the student body, with only two being of Australian descent. The international students came from Singapore and New Zealand. All of the students were enrolled in a bachelor's program in business.

The constructivist student-led learning approach, in which students worked in small, self-selected groups to promote peer learning, was a key component of the teaching technique. Peer learning offers advantages, according to research (Evans & Cuffe, 2009; Miley, 2004), and working collaboratively is essential in many corporate situations Focus groups offered the benefit of allowing students to hear about the experiences of their peers and compare those experiences to their own. This was seen to be in line with the constructivist mindset, allowing students the chance to reflect on word cloud usage as part of their learning while also offering the academic teaching staff and researchers information. Additionally, it was believed that focus groups would yield more detailed information on the student experience than other methods of data gathering would have, which appeared crucial given the paucity of published studies on the usage of word clouds. Focus groups established an environment in which students may predominately direct the discourse, in line with a student-led approach to instruction.

In focus groups, undergraduates brought up the topic of graduate qualities and noted that their knowledge of education styles informed them about themselves, while their knowledge of word clouds informed them about the outside world. The intellectuals noted that while information managing skills which they categorized word

Figure 3.2 Word cloud created for college reviews.

clouds into were crucial in the profession, universities that prioritized the knowledge itself at the time overlooked them. In response to focus group remarks, the literature on graduate characteristics was consulted, and the additional material listed in Figure 3.2 served as a thinking framework for the use of word clouds in teaching and learning.

3.8 Discussion

3.8.1 Learning Preferences

Unexpectedly, a significant link existed between preferred learning styles and word cloud usage. Had the students' knowledge of their preferred learning styles accustomed them to utilize word clouds in ways that complemented those tasks? Although they disagreed, the students found it difficult to comprehend that the alignment could be that precise, especially when many of them were on the cusp of having preferences for one learning method vs another. If this assumption is confirmed, it shows that students may have rejected word cloud applications that they judged to be incompatible with their preferred learning styles. However, given the enthusiastic response from the students, perhaps what counts is that word clouds were a successful teaching tool. If this assumption is confirmed, it shows that students may have rejected word cloud applications that they judged to be incompatible with their preferred learning styles. The fact that word clouds were an effective teaching tool may be more important, given the enthusiastic student reaction. According to student feedback, word clouds helped accounting students become more motivated by providing them a sense of control over the discipline's content since they could change how it was presented.

3.9 Educating Strategy

To improve peer learning, all students took part in small learning groups. Students were urged to create their organizations. Although most students had formed groups of peers who preferred similar learning styles, viewing this as an arbitrary assignment as it was not explicitly addressed learning style preferences with other peers before choosing their group. Because students were encouraged to establish groups with people who shared their views towards and expectations for learning and their study habits, it is impossible to perceive it as total. There was a lot of disagreement concerning the usage of word clouds, according to groups whose members had mixed preferences for learning styles; in one group, this issue was still unresolved. With one exception, groups with members who preferred comparable learning styles proved to be more amicable. That disagreement was unrelated to the usage of word clouds since it included a team member who frequently avoided engaging with his teammates. The students created their own group and they met periodically to form their word clouds because it was expected that group members would bring their finished word clouds to meetings. They could see how the introduction of word clouds as a teaching tool and constructivist teaching methodology were complementary.

3.10 Ownership of Learning Strategies by the Student

There will always be some students who are not adequately motivated to participate completely in it, as there will be other elements of student learning. This study and the accounting teaching strategy presupposed that most students wanted to participate in deep learning but sometimes lacked the knowledge to do so. Students were given a tool—word clouds—to help them connect with accounting more deeply. They offered a system for education. Three points sparked a lot of student fervor. First, mastering a method, like creating word clouds, might interest people in a topic almost as much as interesting material. Second, regardless of the intended learning goals or expectations of the teacher, students lacked the motivation to participate in deep learning until they could identify the workplace applicability of either the specific content or a proper learning tool offered to them. Third, two main factors influenced student adoption of word clouds: the ability to customize it, either by changing the appearance of the word clouds or by utilizing the goals that are fit for the selected, and the small-group teaching approach, where they either had the chance to showcase their word cloud artwork for others to admire or where they could put their knowledge to use. These findings bring up some crucial teaching-related issues, such as whether teaching processes are more relevant for learning than teaching content, how much workplace relevance should influence how we teach rather than what we teach, how to help students feel unique while trying to teach a class of students, and the role of teaching processes in encouraging students to take accountability for their learning. The student population will determine how these concerns are handled.

The ability to choose how word clouds are used to further learning has been cited by students as increasing their desire to comprehend accounting and enhancing their feeling of self since they can take charge of the learning process. Employers seem to place a high emphasis on having a strong sense of self. That a computer-mediated procedure seems to improve something so private as a person's sense of self is counterintuitive. It is unknown if this reflects the age bounds of the students who, for the most part, grew up using computers, but it would be interesting to find out how much technology may have an impact on how they feel about themselves.

3.11 Developing Professional Skills

The students may have been more inclined to consider word clouds as a talent transferrable to the industry since they were close to graduating and were particularly anxious to develop transferable abilities to the profession. The students said word clouds were best suited to provide them with some method of organizing this evidence and the copiousness of evidence offered to them online since they defined the knowledge base obligatory for business management as uneven, heterogenous, and always varying. Word-clouds therefore, served the intended function for which they had been presented to the pupils. It is never easy to strike a balance between preparing accounting students for the present while also preparing them for the future. The research implies that this trade-off in accounting should be expanded to encompass learning methods instead of just the academic material delivered.

3.12 Conclusion and Future Work

This study outlines an effort to address students' worries about controlling the amount of information they will be exposed to at work. We investigate the word cloud tool to help students in the workplace summarize information that is readily available electronically. Additionally, word clouds are investigated as a technique to aid in student learning. We investigated the ways text symbols are used on social networks and how they affect sentiment analysis and text mining. To determine whether there was a difference in text usage between good and negative events, we examined some significant worldwide positive and negative occurrences. We found that including text when conducting sentiment analysis helps to raise overall sentiment ratings. Text characters may be used to communicate both positive and negative thoughts, however, in our investigation, the employment of text characters seemed to increase the expressivity and overall sentiment ratings of the positive opinions relative to the negative ones.

According to this research, word clouds serve as a helpful complement to other learning techniques. Using bits requires prudence since they summarize word frequency, which could not correspond to word importance. Generalizing from a single, limited case study is always risky. This study included a limited number of participants and was conducted during a brief period. However, the flexibility of word clouds and the students' overwhelmingly positive response to them imply that this approach is worthwhile as a teaching aid and that additional investigation into students' use of word clouds is necessary.

References

[1] Thapa B. Sentiment analysis of cybersecurity content on Twitter and Reddit. arXiv preprint arXiv:2204.12267, 2022.

[2] apple_twitter_sentiment_texts. www.kaggle.com/seriousran/appletwittersentiment-texts. Accessed Jan 2022.

[3] Preslav N, Ritter A, Rosenthal S, Sebastiani F, Stoyanov V. SemEval2016 task 4: sentiment analysis in Twitter. In Proceedings of the 10th International Workshop on Semantic Evaluation. San Diego, California, USA, SemEval'16, pages 1–18, Apple Twitter

Sentiment (CrowdFlower), 2016. www.kaggle.com/slythe/apple-twitter-sentiment-crowd fower. Accessed Jan 2022.

[4] Jaiswala PJN, Umac M. Opinion mining of Twitter data for recommending airlines services. International Journal of Control Theory and Applications, 2016, Twitter US Airline Sentiment. www.kaggle. com/crowdfower/twitter-airline-sentiment. Accessed Jan 2022.

[5] AlBadani B, Shi R, Dong J. A novel machine learning approach for sentiment analysis on Twitter incorporating the universal language model fine-tuning and SVM. Applied System Innovation. 2022;5(1):13.

[6] Tan KL, et al. RoBERTa-LSTM: a hybrid model for sentiment analysis with transformer and recurrent neural network. IEEE Access. 2022;10:21517–25.

[7] Jain PK, et al. Employing BERT-DCNN with a semantic knowledge base for social media sentiment analysis. Journal of Ambient Intelligence and Humanized Computing. 2023;14(8):10417–29. https://doi.org/10.1007/s12652-022-03698-z

[8] Prottasha NJ, Sami AA, Kowsher M, Murad SA, Bairagi AK, Masud M, Baz M. Transfer learning for sentiment analysis using BERT-based supervised fine-tuning. Sensors. 2022;22:4157.

[9] Nimmi K, et al. Pre-trained ensemble model for identification of emotion during COVID-19 based on emergency response support system dataset. Applied Soft Computing. 2022;122:108842.

[10] Filippini C, et al. Facilitating the child–robot interaction by endowing the robot with the capability of understanding child engagement: the case of the mioamico robot. International Journal of Social Robotics. 2021;13(4):677–89.

[11] Jain PK, Saravanan V, Pamula R. A hybrid CNN-LSTM: a deep learning approach for consumer sentiment analysis using qualitative user-generated content. Transactions on Asian and Low-Resource Language Information Processing. 2021;20(5):84.

[12] Kumawat, S., et al. Sentiment analysis using language models: a study. In 2021 11th International Conference on Cloud Computing, Data Science & Engineering (Confluence). IEEE; 2021.

[13] Dang NC, Moreno-García MN, De la Prieta F. Sentiment analysis based on deep learning: a comparative study. Electronics. 2020;9(3):483.

[14] Liberatore, S. A new study finds Face with Tears of Joy is the world's most popular text. Daily Mail, 2017. Retrieved Jan 30, 2017, from www.dailymail.co.uk/sciencetech/article-4089052/Crying-waychart-Face-tears-joy-revealed-world-s-popular-text.html

[15] Janjua SH, et al. Multi-level aspect-based sentiment classification of Twitter data: using the hybrid approach in deep learning. PeerJ Computer Science. 2021;7:e433.

[16] Demotte P, et al. Enhanced sentiment extraction architecture for social media content analysis using capsule networks. Multimedia Tools and Applications. 2021;20:1–26.

[17] Indrayuni E, Nurhadi A. Optimizing genetic algorithms for sentiment analysis of Apple product reviews using SVM. SinkrOn. 2020;4(2):172–8.

[18] Bansal B, Srivastava S. Hybrid attribute-based sentiment classification of online reviews for consumer intelligence. Applied Intelligence. 2019;49(1):137–49.

[19] Ma Y, et al. Sentic LSTM: a hybrid network for targeted aspect-based sentiment analysis. Cognitive Computing. 2018;10(4):639–50.

[20] Zainuddin N, Selamat A, Ibrahim R. Hybrid sentiment classification on Twitter aspect-based sentiment analysis. Applied Intelligence. 2018;48(5):1218–32.

Chapter 4

An Energy-Aware Optimization Model Using a Hybrid Approach

Madhusudhan H. S., Satish Kumar T., and Punit Gupta

4.1 Introduction

Cloud computing provides a wide range of services, prompting many applications to migrate to the cloud. It is a sort of distributed computing which uses utility ideas to provide quantitative and expandable (scalable) resources through the internet. Cloud computing embodies grid computing, parallel computing and distributed computing [1]. Customers can access a collective group of resources on an "on-demand" basis in the cloud as a service [2]. Because of the cloud's tremendous processing capabilities and huge storage capacity, users may use cloud services at any time and from any location. A cloud data center contains servers, communication devices, databases, networks, and software systems.

As client requests for resources of cloud grows, providers of cloud services must expand the quantity of servers and other equipment. Consequently, adding additional physical nodes will increase the energy consumption of the data center. Currently data centers devour 2% of the world's electricity. By 2030, it is predicted that it will have risen to 8%. The three biggest power users in a data center are networks, servers, and cooling systems. The network consumes 10–25% of total energy, cooling systems 15–30%, and servers 40–55% [3].

Virtualization is a popular technique in Infrastructure as a Service (IaaS). It enables resource sharing by allowing virtual machines to run on real computers

DOI: 10.1201/9781003433293-4

to handle various applications. Clients can create their own services using virtual machines. IaaS makes computer resources such as Network, CPU, RAM and Storage available as a service, with service level agreements (SLAs) governing how they are used. The amount of energy we utilize is influenced by how we utilize resources. Minimum resource usage is one of the factors for the data center's energy inadequacy [4]. Lesser the workload, power consumption is larger than 50% of the highest power if the CPU use is less than 10%. Virtualization technologies are important in IaaS for optimizing resource or cloud utilization [5]. Virtualization allows virtual machines (VMs) to fulfil user requests on physical machines (PMs), allowing for resource sharing. Virtualization may be utilized to do three separate tasks: virtual machine isolation, virtual machine migration, and virtual machine consolidation. Virtual machines are moved from one physical machine to another using virtual machine migration technology. In the virtual machine consolidation procedure, VMs executing on various hosts would migrate from that host, then reside on lesser hosts to conserve energy via turning off or shifting the original running or executing host to hibernation mode [6]. A technique known as virtual machine placement (VMP) is adapted for operating virtual machines over real-world hosts. To increase resource utilization and power efficiency, an effective VMP strategy is essential.

By combining all VMs into a small number of PMs, an efficient virtual machine placement reduces energy usage. In a cloud data center, load balancing can be achieved through a variety of methods: a) performing task scheduling, b) implementing efficient virtual machine placement (VMP) techniques, and c) by migrating present VMs from overloaded PMs to underloaded PMs and vice versa. This work implements load balancing technique comprising virtual machine placement and also migrating VMs from one host to another.

A scheduler, which schedules VMs on to PMs, processes user requests to the cloud data center. Data centers have a stable capacity of resources to service user queries, resulting in failure of request or minor processing interruptions. A method for selecting an energy-efficient and minimum-fault-rate PM to accomplish user requests is proposed in this chapter. This will increase the cloud datacenter's power efficiency, throughput and reduce the execution time.

The proposed approach splits the problems into four sub-problems:

1. Performing virtual machine placement over a suitable physical machine.
2. Determining if the host is regarded to be overloaded, to facilitate some virtual machines to be migrated from one host to another host.
3. Selecting VMs to migrate from an overloaded host.
4. Placing selected VMs on other physical machines.

The hybrid model based on a GA-RF model and HHO model for VMP are proposed in this chapter. Objectives of this work to reduce consumption of energy, makespan and maximize resource utilization of the cloud datacenter. One of the

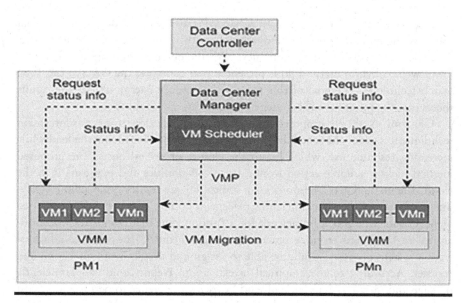

Figure 4.1 System architecture for VMPs in cloud computing.

meta-heuristic approaches applied to discover a global feasible solution is the genetic algorithm (GA). To begin, the GA emphasizes on creating an ideal resource allocation schedule that acts as a training data set which includes virtual machine to physical machine mapping. The hybrid model utilizes the best optimum solution derived from GA to train the random forest model, and then use the trained model to anticipate the optimal solution in a stable time in the next iteration, avoiding the time wasted by evolutions looking for the global best solution.

Figure 4.1 illustrates the system architecture. A data center is made up of a large number of physical machines. On a single physical machine, several virtual machines can operate. A virtual machine monitor (VMM), often identified by means of a hypervisor, is software that makes creating, monitoring and managing VMs easier. Moreover, it maintains a virtualized environment over set of physical hosts. After the VM execution request is received, the data center administration congregate status data from every accessible physical machine and provides it to the virtual machine scheduler. Here, the virtual machine scheduler was built via the GA-RF approach and HHO model. The VM scheduler then evaluates the status data and assigns VMs to physical hosts that are appropriate.

4.2 Literature Review

Some of the research work that has been carried out in the field of VM placement is described in this section.

In [7], the author has provided an enhanced transformation-dependent GA that uses less energy and minimize resource usage. This work is compared to various heuristic and meta-heuristic techniques, with the outcome indicating that it performs well. A hybrid method [8] is presented that combines the GA and the Tabu search technique. The goal of this project is to reduce energy usage. The results shows that the recommended strategy produces superior results.

Ghasemi et al. [9] proposed a learning-based solution using reinforcement technique to tackle VM scheduling. The work focuses on balancing the load while increasing resource use, which led to the closure of several hosts. The proposed method picks a suitable action from a list of possibilities and performs it in the cloud. The method gets a reinforcement indication as a result of that action, verifying the aptness of the virtual machine placement option. Khan et al. [10] proposed HeporCloud, which is a framework for a fusion cloud that comprises workload-aware, an integrated resource orchestrator and scheduler. The resource administration system proposed would be able to assign and predict work allocation and transfer. According to the empirical investigation, HeporCloud can proficiently manage and merge various sorts of workloads with reference to performance, cost and energy. [11] Presented a simulator with enhanced version to increase the simulator's precision and accuracy. In terms of power usage, resource allocation performance, and even consolidation in heterogeneous datacenters, the enlarged version outperformed the conventional version.

[12] Proposed a consolidation strategy that favors the most effective migration that might be a virtual machine, or a specific application executing inside a container. The authors of this research viewed how the coalition of diverse containers, apps and VMs influence heterogeneous datacenter energy efficiency and performance. [13] Developed resource management using game-theoretic concept for Multi-access edge computing. To evaluate the proposed work, Google's workload traces were used. The objective is to develop an energy-efficient, high-performance and cost-effective resource management strategy.

[14] Ilias Mavridis and Helen Karatza presented a way for improving cloud isolation and usefulness by combining virtual machines with containers. The authors concentrated on the advantage of running containers on VMs, along with an examination of how diverse virtualization methods and its organization impact the method's enactment. Docker container was designed to execute on Linux container running on Windows Server, as well as KVM and XEN virtual machines. By performing many benchmarks in addition to mounting real-world programs as use cases, the authors could establish the performance impact of Windows' additional virtualization layer. Finally, the authors investigated how virtual machines and containers are isolated using various operating systems developed to host containers, in addition to approaches for storing permanent data. Authors in [15] proposed energy and resource efficient VMP method using a metaheuristic approach.

4.3 System Model

An environment like IaaS is exemplified by a massive data center with N (numerous) heterogeneous physical machines or nodes as the target system. The CPU performance, measured in millions of instructions per second (MIPS), as well as the quantity of RAM and network bandwidth, are all factors that influence the performance of each node. To support VM live migration, the servers do not have direct-attached storage, instead relying on a Network Attached Storage (NAS) or Storage Area Network (SAN). Because of the environment's nature, no information about application workloads or the duration for which VMs are deployed is available. To put it another way, the resource management system must be independent of the applications it manages.

Numerous individual users make requests for housing of M heterogeneous virtual machines, each with specific processor power, RAM, and network bandwidth needs.

As stated earlier, the method to VM placement technique proposed in this chapter follows a distributed model, where the problem is divided into two sub-problems:

1. VM Placement
2. Load Balance
   2.1 Host Overload and Host Underload Detection
   2.2 VM Selection
   2.3 VM Migration

A user desires to execute a group of k services or applications on the cloud; they may be known all at once or in sequence. Each Ai application makes use of Ji virtual machines (VMs), which must be installed on the datacenter's M physical machines. More than one VM can run on each machine as long as the CPU constraints are met. Each VM has a CPU demand, which represents the amount of CPU required to complete its computations.

The system is frequently overwhelmed as a result of a small number of servers handling a large number of requests and other servers being idle. This causes overloaded servers' performance to deteriorate and requests to fail. The average response time of the server increases for these overloaded servers. As a result, a load-balancing algorithm must be developed to optimize reaction time, resource utilization and minimize overload on any single resource. Since the host overload detection runs locally on each computing host, splitting the challenges enhances the system's scalability. As a result, the system's software layer is split into two parts: local and data center administrators. Figure 4.2 depicts the system model, in which the data center manager gets physical node status information from the local manager after receiving requests from the user. The virtual machine scheduler examines the status information before placing virtual machines on physical machines. The virtual machine scheduler is created using a GA-RF. Machine learning models are trained using the data set derived from genetic algorithm.

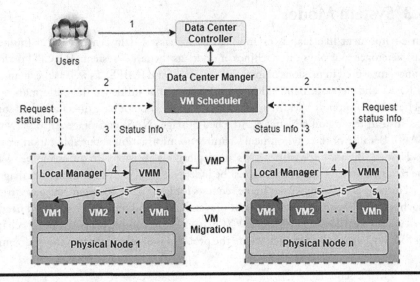

Figure 4.2 Proposed system model.

As a VMM module, the local managers are installed on each node. Their goal is to keep a close watch on the node's CPU use and detect any instances of host overload (4). In the case of an overloaded host, the overloaded host's local manager starts the specified VM selection procedure to choose which VMs to offload. The datacenter manager is based on the master node and gathers data from the local managers in order to keep an overview picture of the system's resource use (2). The global manager provides VM migration instructions to optimize VM placement depending on the decisions made by the local managers (3). Actual VM migration as well as changes in node power modes are handled by VMMs (5).

4.3.1 Host Overload Detection

To reduce performance degradation and violations of SLA, each computing host executes a host overload detection algorithm periodically to de-consolidate virtual machines as required. The proposed heuristics for the host overload recognition problem are described in this section.

4.3.1.1 Interquartile Range

This subdivision provides a robust statistic-based technique for ascertaining an adaptive CPU usage limit. The interquartile range (IQR), often known as the mid-spread or middle 50 in descriptive statistics, is a measure of statistical dispersion. The variation between the third and first quartiles is equal to IQR: Q3–Q1. The interquartile range, contrasting the (total) range, is a strong statistic with a breakdown threshold of 25%, and is therefore repeatedly chosen over the complete range. Using IQR, the CPU utilization threshold is defined in (4.1)

$$T_u = 1 - s * IQR \qquad (4.1)$$

where s is a method parameter that specifies the method's safety.

4.3.1.2 Local Regression

Local regression is a heuristic method proposed by Cleveland. The local regression method's fundamental idea is to fit simple models to restricted sections of data in order to create a curve that approximates the original data. The tricube weight function (equation 4.2) is used to assign neighborhood weights to the observations (xi, yi).

$$T(u) = \begin{cases} (1 - |u|^3)^3 & if \ |u| < 1, \\ 0 & otherwise \end{cases} \qquad (4.2)$$

4.3.2 VM Selection

Virtual machines running on overloaded physical machines must be relocated to an underloaded host to achieve load balancing. We chose virtual machines to migrate from overloaded physical computers using the minimum utilization (MU) approach. All virtual machines that can be migrated are identified by MU and added to the list. The CPU usage of each virtual machine on each actual system is then determined. After that, the virtual machine with the lowest CPU utilization rate is chosen for migration.

4.3.3 Host Underload Detection

First, all encumbered hosts are identified via the overload detection technique and the VMs that will be migrated are assigned to the destination hosts. The system then attempts to deploy all of the VMs from this host on other hosts with minimal utilization relative to the other hosts, while ensuring that they are not overloaded. The VMs are configured for migration to the identified destination hosts if such a placement is possible. To save energy, the source host is put to sleep mode once the migrations are done. The source host is maintained operational if all the VMs from the source host cannot be moved to other hosts. For all non-overloaded hosts, this step is done repeatedly.

4.4 Genetic Algorithm

A hybrid model based on a genetic algorithm and machine learning approaches for VMP is proposed in this chapter. In this work, a genetic algorithm will generate the data set that will be used to train the machine learning algorithms. The training data set includes the mapping of VMs to PMs.

One of metaheuristic method for finding a global optimum solution is Genetic algorithm (GA). We employ the evolutionary algorithm to produce a mapping of virtual machines to actual machines that are available.

In our work, GA comprises the subsequent steps:

1. Population initialization:
   Initial population is created at random, with all virtual machines VM_k (k=1 to n) being allocated to PMs PM_r (r=1 to m). An example of the initial population is depicted in Figure 4.3.
2. Fitness function: Fitness values of the PM is expressed as

$$Fitness(i) = \beta * Power\ Efficiency \qquad (4.3)$$

   where β represent the random constant. For the reproduction process, individuals with better fitness values are chosen.
3. Selection:
   The Tournament Selection technique is used to pick the fittest entities from the population. N (individuals) is the tournament size, and they are picked at random from the population. Tournament winner is chosen for a crossover process.
4. Crossover:
   A two-point crossover was applied in this work to create new individual/offspring from the top individuals. There are also multipoint, single-point and uniform crossovers to choose from. A newly produced individual is introduced back into the population to enhance diversity. Figure 4.4 shows an example of a two-point crossover.
5. Mutation: Swap, move, move & swap, and rebalancing are all methods for mutating individuals. We have used swap to mutate individuals. To generate a new individual, two points are found, and their values are exchanged. As illustrated in Figure 4.5, the swap procedure will switch the physical machine allotted to the virtual machine.

VM_2	VM_1	VM_3	VM_5	VM_7	VM_4	VM_6
PM_3	PM_7	PM_1	PM_2	PM_4	PM_6	PM_5

Figure 4.3   Random population formation at the initial stage.

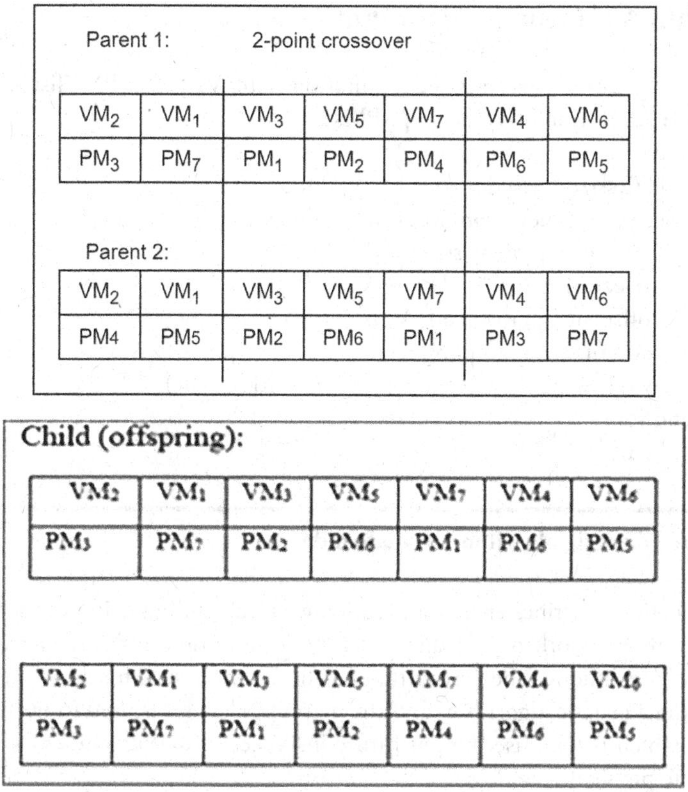

Parent 1:		2-point crossover				
VM_2	VM_1	VM_3	VM_5	VM_7	VM_4	VM_6
PM_3	PM_7	PM_1	PM_2	PM_4	PM_6	PM_5

Parent 2:						
VM_2	VM_1	VM_3	VM_5	VM_7	VM_4	VM_6
PM4	PM5	PM2	PM6	PM1	PM3	PM7

Child (offspring):

VM_2	VM_1	VM_3	VM_5	VM_7	VM_4	VM_6
PM_3	PM_7	PM_2	PM_6	PM_1	PM_6	PM_5

VM_2	VM_1	VM_3	VM_5	VM_7	VM_4	VM_6
PM_3	PM_7	PM_1	PM_2	PM_4	PM_6	PM_5

Figure 4.4 GA crossover process.

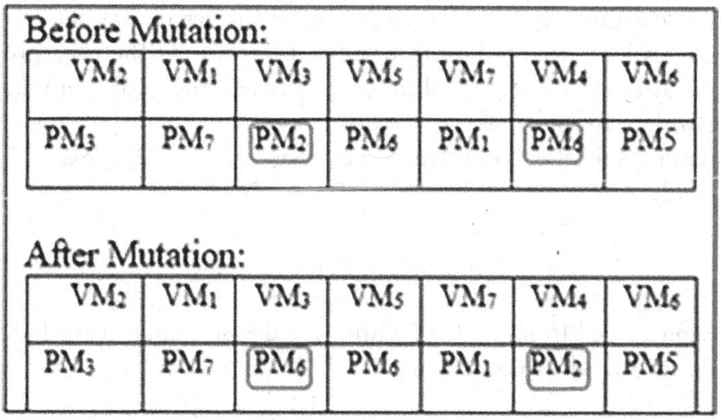

Before Mutation:

VM_2	VM_1	VM_3	VM_5	VM_7	VM_4	VM_6
PM_3	PM_7	PM_2	PM_6	PM_1	PM_4	PM5

After Mutation:

VM_2	VM_1	VM_3	VM_5	VM_7	VM_4	VM_6
PM_3	PM_7	PM_6	PM_6	PM_1	PM_2	PM5

Figure 4.5 Mutation operation in GA.

Algorithm 4.1: Genetic Algorithm

Input: population_size, size_gen, mutation_rate, VMs list, PMs list
Output: Allocation of VMs to apt PMs
1. start
2. while (g≤size_gen) do
3.   derive pop_new from finest individuals
4.   for j=1 to pop_new_size
5.   select p1, p2
6.   offspring = crossover(p1, p2)
7.   add offspring to pop_new
8.   newoffpsring = mutate(offspring, mutation_rate)
9.   end for
10. end while
11. end

Figure 4.6 Genetic algorithm's Pseudocode.

This section describes energy and fault aware scheduling using GA and ANN. Objective of this work is to reduce energy consumption and also derive a fault aware VMP technique. The best virtual machines to physical machines mapping is found using a genetic algorithm, and the mapping data set is used to train a neural network, which is then used to put future instances/virtual machines on the most appropriate physical machine.

In this work, a multilayer neural network was employed, which consists of multiple layers, each of which contains one or more artificial neurons. Tanh, sigmoid, ReLU, leaky ReLU, and softplus are activation functions that may be applied to neurons in a neural network. They can also be used in diverse layers of a ANN. The ReLU leaky activation function was employed here. The back propagation learning algorithm is used in a multilayer neural network to alter weights progressively as the algorithm seeks the solution. The back propagation algorithm is used to reduce the difference between the actual output and the neural network's output value.

In equation 4.4, the input layer's net input along with bias is illustrated mathematically

$$input\_sum_1 = \sum w_p \cdot x_p + b \qquad (4.4)$$

The activation gained from previous neurons is the net input in the hidden layer. Equation 4.5 is used to express it.

$$input\_sum_p = \sum w_p \cdot O_p + b \qquad (4.5)$$

To bind net input and produce the neuron's output, we use the activation function. This process is depicted in Equation 4.6.

$$O_p = f\left(input\_sum_p\right), i.e\ O_p = f\left(\Sigma w_p \cdot O_p + b\right) \tag{4.6}$$

This is the output value, which is a neuron's activation value that is transferred to the next layer.

Tanh, sigmoid, ReLU, leaky ReLU, and softplus are examples of activation functions that may be employed to neurons in a ANN. Leaky ReLU is employed as an activation function here.

Leaky ReLU is expressed as

$$f(y) = \begin{cases} y, if\ y > 0 \\ \alpha y, if\ y \leq 0 \end{cases} \tag{4.7}$$

Here, α is a small -ve slope

In the backpropagation algorithm, there are several steps to updating the weights.

1. Start the algorithm, set up the neural network, and put it into a loop.
2. Calculate the network output for the given input. Calculate the error by comparing the network output to the actual output.
3. Update the output layer weights

$$W_{qp} \leftarrow W_{qp} + \alpha' \times o_q \times err_p \times f'\left(input\_sum_p\right) \tag{4.8}$$

4. for each of the neural network's subsequent layers do
   Calculate each neuron or node error

$$\Delta_q \leftarrow f'\left(input\_sum_p\right) \times \Sigma W_{qp} \Delta_p \tag{4.9}$$

Update the weights that lead into layer k.

$$W_{kq} \leftarrow W_{kq} + \alpha' \times o_k \times \Delta_q \tag{4.10}$$

5. re-run the loop until the maximum epoch has been attained.

Work flow of the GA and ANN procedure is shown in Figure 4.7. There are two phases in this hybrid model, in the first phase, genetic algorithm is used to generate the training data set. In phase 2 ANN is trained using the data set derived from GA. ANN training is halted when either maximum epoch is reached or when threshold crosses the pre specified value. Finally ANN is tested with the test data.

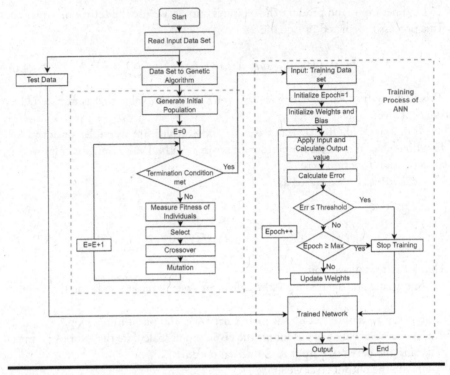

Figure 4.7   Workflow of the hybrid model.

The proposed method is compared with Power Aware Best Fit Decreasing (PABFD) algorithm.

Algorithm 4.2: PABFD

Input: List of VMs (VL), List of Hosts (HL)
Output: Virtual machine placement
a.   sort VL in declining order of CPU consumption:
b.   for every VM in VL do
c.   minPow = MAX
d.   assigned_Host = NULL
e.   for every host in HL do
f.   if sufficient resource is in host
g.   pow= calculate_Power(H,VM)
h.   if minPower > pow then

i.   assigned_Host = host
j.   min_Pow=pow
k.   end if
l.   end if
m.   end
n.   end
n.   if assigned_Host ≠ NULL then
o.   add(assigned_Host,VM) to vm_Placement
p.   end

4.4.1 Fitness Value using Fault and Power Model

The proposed method will place virtual machines on real machines with strong processing capabilities and low failure rates. The data center's energy efficiency is determined using a linear power model. Because of storage/network failure or resource unavailability, certain user requests may fail at random in the data center. When placing virtual machines, all available hosts are first evaluated, and they are sorted according to their fitness value. The fitness value is determined using the physical machine's power efficiency and failure probability. After that, we'll assign virtual machines to hosts with superior power efficiency and lower failure rates.

Fitness function of an individual host i is expressed as

$$\text{Fitness}(i) = \alpha * \text{power efficiency} + \beta * \text{failure probability} \qquad (4.11)$$

Where α and β denote the random constants.

Following are the parameter used to derive fitness function:

D_C: Data center C.
PE_k: Power efficiency of host k in C.
U_k: Current Power Utilization of host k in C.
FLP_k: Failure probability of host k.
F_k: Fitness value of host k.

Power efficiency of host k is computed via linear power utilization as articulated in equation 4.12

$$PE_k = LinearPower\left(\frac{(PowMax - PowMin) * Uk}{100}\right) \qquad (4.12)$$

Here, PowMax denotes extreme power and PowMin is the lowest power consumption of the data center.

The data center Utilization (U_k) is given in equation 4.13

$$U_k = \left(\frac{(TotalMIPS - AllocatedMIPS)}{TotalMIPS} \right) \tag{4.13}$$

In a data center, faults arise randomly and it is based on Poisson distribution over period of time t and time t+ΔT is expressed in equation 4.14

$$FLP_k(t \leq T \leq t + \Delta T \,|\, T > t) = \left(\frac{exp(-\lambda t) - exp(\lambda(t + \Delta T))}{exp(-\lambda t)} \right)$$

$$FLP_k(t) = (1 - exp(-\lambda \Delta t)) \tag{4.14}$$

Utilization U_k of the host is calculated using allocated total MIPS in the data center. Equation 4.12 represents the calculation of power consumption which is based on linear power efficiency [16]. Failure probability is computed using equation 4.14. Finally, fitness value is derived using equation 4.11, is a combination of power efficiency and the failure probability. Fitness value lies in the range 0 to 1.

4.5 Experimental Results and Discussions

In this section, we provide the simulation results and examine the performance of various methods.

4.5.1 Experimental Setup

As a simulation platform, the CloudSim toolkit is employed. It's a simulation framework for cloud-based environments. Many features are included in CloudSim, such as on-demand resource provisioning, energy consumption modelling, and the capability to simulate applications with dynamic workloads.

Our simulation data center had 800 heterogeneous hosts (physical machines), half of which were HP ProLiant ML110 G4 servers and the other half were HP ProLiant ML110 G5 servers. The server setup is shown in Table 4.1. Failure probability of the hosts is between 0.15 and 0.20.

The simulation uses real-time workload data from PlanetLab's CoMon project, which is a monitoring infrastructure. It contains CPU utilization traces from over

Table 4.1   Server Configuration

Machine Type	Description
HP G4	4GB RAM,1860 MIPS, 1.5 GB storage and 2 GB network bandwidth
HP G5	4GB RAM, 2660 MIPS, 1.5 GB storage and 2 GB network bandwidth

Table 4.2   Workload Traces

Workload	No. of VM's
20110303	1052
20110306	898
20110309	1061
20110322	1516
20110325	1078
20110403	1463
20110409	1358
20110411	1233
20110412	1054
20110420	1033

1000 virtual machines running on hosts in over 500 different locations across the world. The workload traces are shown in Table 4.2.

We have defined four types of virtual machines, each of different configurations: Micro instance (500 MIPS), Small Instance (1000 MIPS), Medium Instance (2000 MIPS) and Extra-large instance (2500 MIPS).

4.5.2 Results

Two situations are used in the experiment. In the first case, we employed IQR and MU for host overload detection and virtual machine selection, respectively, as explained in the previous section. Second, for the identical process, we employed local regression and MU.

4.5.2.1 Performance Metrics

Two measures are utilized to evaluate and compare the performance of the algorithms. The overall power usage of the data center's physical servers is one metric. The model specified in 4.4.1 was used to determine power usage. The execution time is another parameter to consider.

1. Energy Consumption:

Figures 4.8 and 4.9 illustrate the average power consumption of the proposed technique, PABFD and the Genetic Algorithm in scenarios 1 and 2. The minimum energy consumption of an ANN trained using GA is 85.19 kWh, while the highest energy consumption is 156.45 kWh. The average amount of energy used is 110.6 kWh. The results show that ANN trained with GA decreases energy consumption by 59% and 5% in comparison to PABFD and GA in scenario 1 and 25% and 8% in comparison to PABFD and GA in scenario 2.

2. Execution Time:

One of the most important parameters in the cloud is execution speed, and cloud users expect their requests to be completed in less time. As a result, it is used

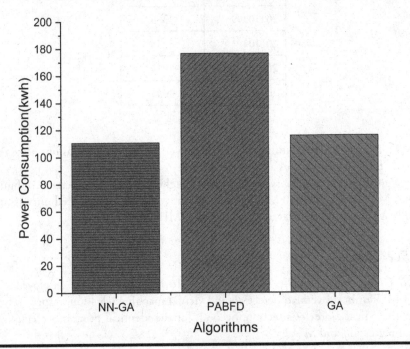

Figure 4.8 Average power consumption: scenario 1.

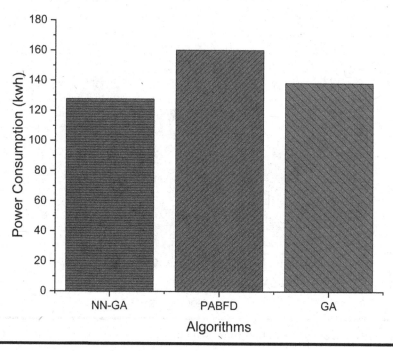

Figure 4.9 Average power consumption: scenario 2.

Table 4.3 Average energy consumption.

Algorithms Scenario	ANN trained with GA	PAFBD	GA
IRQ-MU (Scenario 1)	110.6 kWh	176.46 kWh	115.7 kWh
LR-MU (Scenario 2)	127.78 kWh	160.29 kWh	138.42 kWh

to compare the performance of various algorithms. Before a virtual machine is placed on a host, the fault aware virtual machine allocation proposed in this paper will analyze the host's failure probability. If the host's failure rate is high, the virtual machine's execution time may increase since the host might be unable to process the VM owing to resource constraints, and the VM will need to be rescheduled to another host that can handle it. This rescheduling will take more time, hence the overall VM execution time will increase. If the host's failure rate is low, the virtual machine will be executed on that host, resulting in a shorter execution time. Execution time of NN with GA outperforms PAFBD and GA by 19% and 43%, respectively, as depicted in Figures 4.10 and 4.11, shows that NN with GA is 18% and 35% quicker than PABFD and GA, respectively, in terms of execution time.

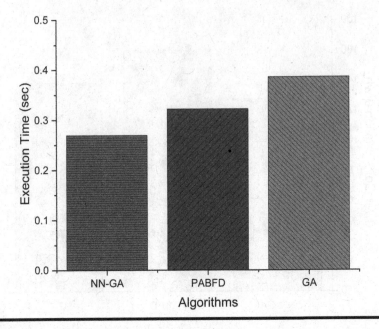

Figure 4.10 Average execution time: scenario 1.

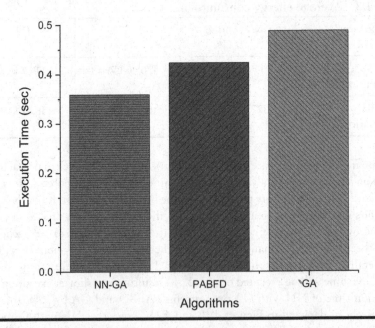

Figure 4.11 Average execution time: scenario 2.

Table 4.4 Average Execution Time

Algorithms Scenario	NN trained with GA	PAFBD	GA
IRQ-MU (Scenario 1)	0.26 sec	0.322 sec	0.38 sec
LR-MU (Scenario 2)	0.35 sec	0.42 sec	0.48 sec

4.6 Summary

We used an artificial neural network and genetic algorithm to develop energy and fault aware virtual machine placement. Our aim is to lower the data center's power usage and to complete execution of requests in minimal time. The result shows that the artificial neural network trained using a genetic algorithm approach outperforms PABFD and the default genetic algorithm.

References

[1] I. Foster, Y. Zhao, I. Raicu, and S. Lu, "Cloud computing and grid computing 360-degree compared," in Proceedings of the Grid Computing Environment Workshop, pp. 1–10, Austin, TX, USA, November 2008.

[2] R. Buyya, A. Beloglazov, and J. Abawajy, "Energy-efficient management of data center resources for cloud computing: a vision, architectural elements, and open challenges," Eprint Arxiv, vol. 12, no. 4, pp. 6–17, 2010.

[3] K. Zheng, X. Wang, L. Li, and X. Wang, "Joint power optimization of data center network and servers with correlation analysis," in Proceedings of the IEEE INFOCOM 2014—IEEE Conference on Computer Communications, pp. 2598–2606, Toronto, ON, Canada, May 2014.

[4] A. Beloglazov, R. Buyya, Y. C. Lee, and A. Zomaya, "A taxonomy and survey of energy-efficient data centers and cloud computing systems," Advances in Computers, vol. 82, pp. 47–111, 2011.

[5] V. Petrucci, O. Loques, and D. Moss'e, "March. A framework for dynamic adaptation of power-aware server clusters," in Proceedings of the 2009 ACM symposium on Applied Computing, pp. 1034–1039, Honolulu, Hawaii, USA, March 2009.

[6] M. Masdari, S. S. Nabavi, and V. Ahmadi, "An overview of virtual machine placement schemes in cloud computing," Journal of Network and Computer Applications, vol. 66, pp. 106–127, 2016.

[7] A. S. Abohamama and E. Hamouda, "A hybrid energy–Aware virtual machine placement algorithm for cloud environments," Expert Systems with Applications, vol. 150, pp. 113306, 2020.

[8] D.-M. Zhao, J.-T. Zhou, and K. Li. "An energy-aware algorithm for virtual machine placement in cloud computing," IEEE Access, vol. 7, pp. 55659–55668, 2019.

[9] A. Ghasemi and A. Toroghi Haghighat, "A multi-objective load balancing algorithm for virtual machine placement in cloud data centers based on machine learning," Computing, vol. 102, pp. 2049–2072, 2020.

[10] A. A. Khan, M. Zakarya, I. U. Rahman, R. Khan, and R. Buyya, "HeporCloud: an energy and performance efficient resource orchestrator for hybrid heterogeneous cloud computing environments," Journal of Network and Computer Applications, vol. 173, pp. 102869, 2021.

[11] M. Zakarya and L. Gillam, "Modelling resource heterogeneities in cloud simulations and quantifying their accuracy," Simulation Modelling Practice and Theory, vol. 94, pp. 43–65, 2019.

[12] A. A. Khan, M. Zakarya, R. Khan, I. u. Rahman, M. Khan, and A. u. R. Khan, "An energy, performance efficient resource consolidation scheme for heterogeneous cloud datacenters," Journal of Network and Computer Applications, vol. 150, p. 102497, 2019.

[13] M. Zakarya, L. Gillam, H. Ali, I. Rahman, K. Salah, R. Khan, O. Rana, and R. Buyya, "Epcaware: a game-based, energy, performance and cost efficient resource management technique for multi-access edge computing," IEEE Transactions on Services Computing, vol. 15, no. 3, pp.1634–1648, 2020.

[14] I. Mavridis and H. Karatza, "Combining containers and virtual machines to enhance isolation and extend functionality on cloud computing," Future Generation Computer Systems, vol. 94, pp. 674–696, 2019.

[15] H. S. Madhusudhan, P. Gupta, and G. McArdle, "A Harris Hawk optimisation system for energy and resource efficient virtual machine placement in cloud data centers," Plos one, vol. 18, no. 8, p. e0289156, 2023.

[16] Z. Zhou, Z. Hu, and K. Li, "Virtual machine placement algorithm for both energy-awareness and SLA violation reduction in cloud data centers," Hindawi Publishing Corporation Scientific Programming Volume 2016.

Chapter 5

Fault Tolerant and Reliable Resource Optimization Model for Cloud

Righa Tandon, Ajay Verma, and P. K. Gupta

5.1 Introduction

A common method for delivering and administering different apps and services in recent years is cloud computing. However, the distributed and dynamic nature of the cloud makes it susceptible to various faults and failures, including software errors, network failures, and hardware failures. A concept for providing on-demand computer services, such as processing speed, storage space, and software programmes, through the internet is called cloud computing. Organizations must take into account fault tolerance and dependability while implementing cloud computing models. The ability of a system to function even in the case of a failure or outage is referred to as fault tolerance. Redundancy and distributed computing are two ways to create fault tolerance in cloud computing. For example In order to ensure that the workload can be easily shifted to another data centre without interruption in the event that one data centre fails, a cloud provider, for instance, may employ many data centres in various geographical locations. The ability of a system to offer the desired level of performance consistently and without interruption or downtime is referred to as reliability. By structuring their systems to manage heavy traffic and usage surges, implementing load balancing and auto-scaling

DOI: 10.1201/9781003433293-5

strategies, and regularly monitoring their infrastructure for faults, cloud providers can maintain reliability. Resource optimization is another essential component of cloud computing since businesses want to utilize their computing resources as effectively as possible to cut costs and improve performance. By leveraging virtualization, which enables numerous virtual machines to run on a single physical server, and by offering flexible pricing structures that allow users to only pay for the resources they really use, cloud providers can maximize resource utilization. An effective cloud computing paradigm must include fault tolerance, dependability, and resource optimization. Cloud providers may offer their clients a highly available and economical computing environment by making sure that their systems can withstand faults, deliver consistent performance, and optimize resource utilization. For both the cloud service providers and their clients, these errors and failures can result in service interruptions, data loss, and revenue losses. Reliability and fault tolerance are hence essential considerations for cloud computing systems. Replication, checkpointing, and failover are a few faults tolerance and reliability approaches that have been suggested in the literature to address these problems. These methods can lessen the effects of errors and failures on cloud systems, but they can also increase the system's resource requirements and costs. Consequently, a fault-tolerant and trustworthy resource optimization model for cloud computing is necessary [1–6].

5.1.1 Cloud Computing and Its Significance in Modern Computing

A methodology for offering computer services over the internet, such as servers, storage, databases, networking, software, analytics, and intelligence, is known as cloud computing. In this model, users don't have to manage the underlying hardware and software; instead, they can access these services as needed from a cloud service provider's infrastructure. Because it provides users with a variety of advantages, such as scalability, cost savings, and flexibility, cloud computing has emerged as an important technology in contemporary computing [7]. Users can use a shared pool of reconfigurable computer resources whenever they need them thanks to the cloud computing approach of providing computing services. Servers, storage, databases, networking, software, analytics, and intelligence are some of these resources. Users can access the services online via a web browser or other client applications, and the cloud service provider owns and operates the infrastructure. Infrastructure as a Service (IaaS), Platform as a Service (PaaS), and Software as a Service (SaaS) are the three primary categories of cloud computing services (Figure 5.1). Users have access to virtualized computing resources including servers, storage, and networking thanks to IaaS. Users may create, manage, and operate apps on a platform thanks to PaaS without having to worry about the underlying infrastructure. SaaS gives consumers access to software programmes that the cloud service provider hosts and manages [8]. Users of cloud computing can take use of its scalability, cost-savings potential, and flexibility. One of the most important advantages of cloud computing is scalability. Depending on their workload, users can scale up or down their computing resources. Users can use this to save money and time by not having to manage their own hardware and software infrastructure. Another important advantage of cloud computing is cost reduction. Pay-as-you-go pricing is a feature offered by cloud service providers, allowing customers to only pay for the resources they really utilize. This eliminates the need for customers to make an initial investment in pricey hardware and software, which can be very expensive. Another key advantage of cloud computing is flexibility. Users can work remotely on any device by using cloud computing services from any location with an internet connection. Users are also better able to work together because they can instantly share data and applications.

Because it provides users with a variety of advantages, such as scalability, cost savings, and flexibility, cloud computing has emerged as a key technology in contemporary computing. Businesses may now scale their computing capabilities up or down as needed without having to worry about managing the underlying infrastructure thanks to cloud computing [9, 10]. Due to this, businesses are now able to be more adaptable and responsive to shifting market conditions, which is crucial in today's hectic business environment. Business collaboration has become simpler thanks to cloud computing. File sharing and real-time collaboration tools provided by cloud computing have made it simpler for companies to collaborate, regardless of

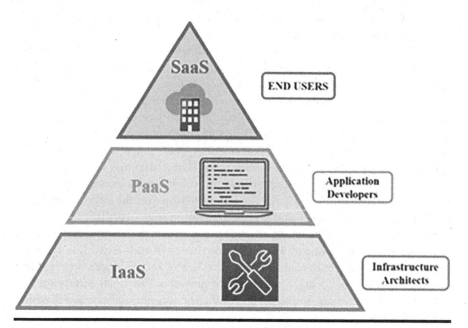

Figure 5.1   Types of services provided by cloud computing.

where they are physically located. Businesses may now access a larger pool of talent and knowledge, which can provide them a major competitive advantage.

5.1.2 *Challenges and Limitations of Cloud Computing*

Although the way we store, access, and share data has been revolutionized by cloud computing, there are still some difficulties and restrictions with this technology. We'll talk about some of cloud computing's biggest obstacles and restrictions in this section (Figure 5.2).

- Security and Privacy

When it comes to cloud computing, security and privacy are two of the main worries. The possibility of unauthorized access, data breaches, and cyber-attacks exists since data is kept on remote servers and accessed via the internet. Cloud service providers must make sure that both their infrastructure and applications are safe, and that they adhere to accepted security procedures. Cloud computing services are susceptible to data breaches, which can happen for a number of reasons, including using weak passwords, making mistakes, or falling victim to cyberattacks. The shared infrastructure that underpins cloud computing services allows several users to share the same resources. This resource sharing could lead to security flaws like information leaks or unauthorized access. Because users have little control over cloud infrastructure, it is challenging to effectively monitor and manage security risks. The handling of sensitive data is subject to stringent laws in several sectors, including healthcare and banking. It may be difficult to employ cloud computing services for sensitive data due to the possibility that they do not adhere to these rules. Data stored by cloud computing services is kept on distant servers, making it challenging for customers to determine who is in charge of and in possession of their data. Users' data may be accessible to cloud service providers, which raises questions regarding privacy and confidentiality. Users of cloud computing services may not be aware of where their data is stored or who has access to it because data may be stored by these services in various places. Users' data may be at risk if cloud service providers do not offer proper data protection measures, such encryption. Because cloud computing services have limited control over the infrastructure, it is challenging to tailor security and privacy controls to suit particular requirements. It may be difficult to evaluate the effectiveness of cloud service providers' security and privacy safeguards due to a lack of transparency in such areas. It is challenging to evaluate the security and privacy practices of these services because their infrastructure is dependent on other service providers. For small enterprises and individuals in particular, implementing sufficient security and privacy measures can be expensive.

- Dependence on Internet Connectivity

Services for cloud computing are very dependent on internet connectivity. Users may encounter performance difficulties or even service outages without a steady and dependable internet connection. For companies that need to be highly available and uptime, this reliance on internet connectivity might be a serious drawback. One major drawback of cloud computing is its reliance on internet connectivity, which limits the user's ability to access and use cloud services. Access to cloud resources, apps, and data requires a steady and dependable internet connection. Here are some specifics on how cloud computing is impacted by internet connectivity dependence:

i) Network Latency: In order to maintain continuous communication between the client and the cloud servers, the cloud computing infrastructure primarily depends on the network connectivity. The performance of cloud services can be impacted by network latency, which is the delay in data transfer over the network. Users may find it frustrating if response times are slow as a result of this.

ii) Bandwidth Limitations: The bandwidth that is available on the internet places a restriction on how much data may be sent through it. The effectiveness of cloud services may be impacted by this, particularly for users with poor internet connectivity. Delays in data transport can affect user experience because of slow internet rates.

iii) Downtime: The functionality of cloud services depends on the accessibility of the internet. Users might not be able to access their data or applications if the internet connection drops if there is a problem with network connections. Downtime might arise from this, which can be expensive for companies that depend on cloud services.

iv) Security Concerns: Security issues with cloud computing can arise due to its reliance on internet access. Cyberattacks frequently target internet connections, and a loss of connectivity might make cloud services vulnerable to intrusion attempts. Data breaches could result from this, endangering the confidentiality of sensitive data.

v) Limited Offline Access: The flexibility to access data and apps from any location with an internet connection is one of the main benefits of cloud computing. However, if users are in a location with poor or no internet connectivity, they might not be able to access their data. This may restrict how useful cloud services are in some circumstances.

- Limited Control over Infrastructure

Users have a limited amount of control over the underlying infrastructure while using cloud computing services. Businesses that need a lot of flexibility or control over their computing environment may find this to be a limitation. For instance, companies might not be able to alter the hardware or network infrastructure to suit their own requirements. Organizations have total control of their IT infrastructure, including servers, storage devices, network hardware, and software, in traditional on-premise computing settings. As a result, they can modify and enhance the infrastructure to suit their unique requirements. However, a large portion of the infrastructure in a cloud computing environment is managed by the cloud service provider. The actual hardware, virtualization layer, network, and storage resources are all included in this. Customers have minimal control over the underlying hardware and network components even if they can configure various components of the infrastructure, such as virtual machines and storage volumes. This loss of control may have the following effects on businesses employing cloud computing:

i) Performance limitations: Customers might not be able to optimize the infrastructure for their particular workloads because of the limited control they have over the underlying hardware and network. Performance restrictions could emerge from this and affect how well an application performs.

ii) Security risks: Additionally, customers have little access to information about the security measures the cloud provider has put in place. Due to this, protecting sensitive data and applications effectively may be challenging.

iii) Vendor lock-in: It can be difficult to move to a new provider or bring the infrastructure back in-house because consumers rely so largely on the cloud provider's infrastructure. Vendor lock-in may come from this, which may reduce the organization's flexibility and agility.

iv) Compliance challenges: Due to their limited influence over the infrastructure, businesses working in regulated industries may encounter compliance issues. For instance, they might be unable to guarantee that the infrastructure complies with all legal standards.

• Data Portability

Data portability refers to the capacity of people or organizations to move or migrate their data from one platform, system, or service provider to another. As more people and businesses rely on digital platforms and services to store and manage their data, this idea has become extremely important in recent years. Data portability has been considerably facilitated by cloud computing, which makes it simple to access computing resources, applications, and data storage through the internet. Data portability in cloud computing has significant restrictions, though, which we shall go over in more depth in the following.

i) Vendor lock-in: Vendor lock-in is one of the main obstacles to data mobility in cloud computing. When a company or person utilizes a certain cloud service provider, they depend on the infrastructure and offerings of that provider. Data migration to another provider or even back to on-premises infrastructure may become challenging as a result.

ii) Data security: Cloud service providers frequently keep data in their data centres, which could be situated anywhere in the world. When the data is sensitive or subject to data protection rules, this may give rise to privacy and data security problems.

iii) Interoperability: Data transmission between different cloud providers or even between on-premises infrastructure and cloud infrastructure can be challenging because cloud service providers frequently employ various data formats, APIs, and architectural styles.

iv) Network restrictions: The network infrastructure, which may not always be universally accessible or dependable in all places, affects data portability. Due to this, moving large amounts of data over long distances may be challenging and may have an impact on the speed and dependability of data transfers.
Cost: Cloud computing's data mobility may result in supplemental expenses like transfer fees or service charges for using third-party migration solutions. Smaller businesses or individuals that want to transfer their data to another cloud provider may find these expenses to be a substantial obstacle.

• Cost

While cloud computing can help businesses save money, it can also significantly increase costs. To secure the security of their data, for instance, corporations may need to invest in additional security measures like encryption or multi-factor authentication. Additionally, using cloud computing services may become more expensive overall if hidden fees, like data transfer fees, are charged by some cloud

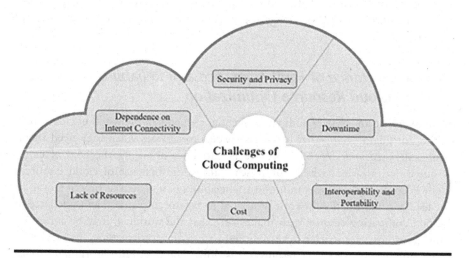

Figure 5.2 Cloud computing challenges.

service providers [11, 12]. Cost management in cloud computing is the process of managing and limiting the costs related to using cloud services. This is a crucial component of cloud computing since it enables businesses to maximize the utilization of cloud resources while cutting expenses.

The price of using cloud services depends on a number of variables. These factors include the kind and quantity of cloud resources used, how long they were used for, and the cloud provider's pricing schemes. Organizations can use cost-cutting techniques like the following to manage these expenses:

i) Cost-Effectiveness: Cloud service providers frequently give a variety of pricing plans, such as pay-as-you-go, reserved instances, and spot instances. Depending on how the organization uses them, each of these possibilities offers benefits and drawbacks. Organizations can select the most cost-efficient pricing strategy by examining their workloads and use trends.

ii) Resource Allocation: Businesses can allocate cloud resources according to their requirements, for as by employing smaller instances or scaling resources up or down as necessary. By doing this, businesses can cut costs on underutilized resources.

iii) Monitoring and Analysis: Businesses can check how cloud resources are used, spot possible waste or underutilized resources, and adjust consumption as needed using cloud monitoring tools.

iv) Automation and Orchestration: Organizations may minimize human error, reduce manual involvement, and maximize cloud usage by automating processes and using orchestration technologies.

Billing and Usage Alerts: Cloud providers offer usage summaries, usage alerts for exceeding thresholds, and usage reports. Organizations can monitor their consumption and proactively control their cloud usage by routinely checking these reports.

5.1.3 Importance of Fault Tolerance and Reliability in Cloud Resource Optimization

Fault tolerance and dependability are essential elements in the world of cloud computing for guaranteeing that users have access to services when they need them. Fault tolerance and dependability are essential for attaining the goal of cloud resource optimization, which comprises making the best use of cloud resources while keeping expenses to a minimum. The ability of a system to function even in the face of a malfunction or error is referred to as fault tolerance. Fault tolerance in a cloud computing environment makes sure that the workload may be automatically transferred to another accessible resource without disturbing the service in the event that one server or resource fails. This guarantees uninterrupted service access for individuals and prevents costly downtime for enterprises. The capacity of a system to consistently carry out its intended purpose is referred to as reliability, on the other hand. Reliability in a cloud computing environment ensures that consumers can access services when they need them and that company operations are not significantly disrupted. For businesses that depend on cloud services to support crucial operations like sales, customer support, and data analysis, reliability is crucial. It is impossible to overestimate the significance of fault tolerance and dependability in the optimization of cloud resources [13]. To guarantee that services are always accessible to users, cloud service providers must make sure that their infrastructure is fault-tolerant and dependable. To ensure that workloads can be swiftly transferred to available resources, a combination of hardware redundancy, software redundancy, and failover techniques is required. Optimizing resource consumption while reducing expenses is another aspect of cloud resource management. Businesses can reduce the risk of downtime and the related expenses of lost income, reputational harm, and higher support costs by designing fault-tolerant and dependable systems. This helps companies to use cloud resources as efficiently as possible while assuring that users can always access services. For the purpose of optimizing cloud resources, fault tolerance and dependability are essential. Businesses can reduce the risk of downtime and guarantee that services are always accessible to users by designing fault-tolerant and dependable systems. As a result, companies can use cloud resources more effectively while spending less money and ensuring that crucial operations are supported [14]. The following justifies the significance of fault tolerance and reliability in cloud resource optimization:

i) High Availability: Users of cloud computing need resources to be readily available. They anticipate that the resources they utilize will always be accessible. Fault tolerance and reliability make sure that users may access cloud resources whenever they need to and that they are always available.

ii) Cost Savings: When it comes to the cloud environment, downtime may be highly expensive for both the supplier and the customer. By ensuring that resources are constantly accessible and that downtime is kept to a minimum, fault tolerance and dependability can aid in lowering the expenses associated with downtime.

iii) User Satisfaction: Cloud users anticipate flawless operation of their apps and resources. Any interruption or downtime can have a negative effect on user satisfaction. Users' satisfaction with cloud environment performance is aided by fault tolerance and reliability.

iv) Reputation Management: Service outages and downtime can hurt cloud companies' reputations. By offering dependable and high-quality services, fault tolerance and reliability serve to guarantee that suppliers maintain a positive reputation.

v) Disaster Recovery: Fault tolerance and dependability can help to ensure that the cloud environment remains operational in the case of a disaster, such as a power loss or a network failure. This is essential for companies whose operations rely on cloud resources.

vi) Scalability: In the cloud context, fault tolerance and reliability are crucial for scaling. Fault tolerance and dependability make ensuring that resources can be added and increased without any disruption in service as resource demand rises.

5.2 Overview of Existing Research on Fault Tolerance and Reliability in Cloud Computing

Recent years have seen a substantial increase in research on fault tolerance and reliability in cloud computing, which is a reflection of the growing significance of these elements in assuring the availability and performance of cloud services. We will give an overview of some of the current studies on fault tolerance and dependability in cloud computing in this part.

- Fault Tolerance Techniques

The creation of methods for identifying, isolating, and recovering from errors in cloud systems is one field of fault tolerance research. Replication, checkpointing, and migration are just a few of the strategies researchers have suggested to make sure workloads can be swiftly transferred to available resources. The ability of a system to continue operating effectively in the face of faults or failures is referred to as fault tolerance. It's critical to have fault tolerance techniques in place in a cloud environment where applications and data are dispersed across various servers and data centres to ensure high availability and reliability. The following list of strategies for fault tolerance is typical in cloud environments:

i) Redundancy: This technology replicates information, software, and services across various servers, data centres, or geographical areas. This guarantees that the workload can be transferred to another server or data centre in the event of a server or data centre failure without interfering with end users. Different methods, including active-active, active-passive, and N+1 redundancy, can be used to achieve redundancy.

ii) Load Balancing: To avoid any one server from getting overwhelmed, load balancing is a technique that divides network traffic among several servers. By ensuring that no single server is in charge of managing all the traffic, this lowers the possibility of failure due to overload. Different methods, such as round-robin, least-connection, and IP-hash, can be used to balance the load.

iii) Data Backup and Recovery: In a cloud context, data backup and recovery methods are essential for fault tolerance. These methods entail periodically backing up data to several different locations and making sure the backups can be quickly retrieved in the event of a problem. As a result, downtime is reduced and data may be restored fast and simply.

iv) High Availability: High availability describes a system's capacity to continue operating even in the face of failures. This is accomplished by making sure that backup components are ready to step in if the primary component fails. Clustering, failover, and hot standby are a few of the different methods that can be used to achieve high availability.

v) Disaster Recovery: Disaster recovery is the process of returning a system to its pre-disaster state following a breakdown or disaster. This calls for having a clear plan in place to respond to emergencies swiftly and make sure the system is operational once again as soon as feasible. Utilising techniques like backup and restore, replication, and active-active data centres, disaster recovery can be accomplished.

• Reliability Metrics

The creation of reliability measures to assess the effectiveness of cloud systems is another field of research. In a cloud setting, availability metrics are used to gauge how well a cloud service provider is doing in terms of uptime, consistency, and availability. In order to guarantee that the services offered are dependable, accessible, and consistent, a cloud service's dependability is crucial. The following reliability measures can be used to assess how well cloud services perform:

i) Uptime: This metric gauges how much of the time a cloud service is functional and accessible. It is determined by deducting the downtime from the overall time and dividing the outcome by the overall duration. An uptime of 99.9%, for instance, indicates that a service is accessible 99.9% of the time.

ii) Mean Time between Failures (MTBF): This metric gauges how long a cloud service typically lasts between two failures. By dividing the total operating time by the total number of failures, it is calculated. A system's dependability and lifespan are predicted using the MTBF.

iii) Mean Time to Recover (MTTR): This metric calculates the typical amount of time needed to recover from a cloud service failure. By dividing the total downtime by the total number of failures, it is calculated. The effectiveness of the recovery procedure is assessed using the MTTR, as is the effect of downtime on the service.

iv) Service Level Agreement (SLA) Compliance: An SLA is a contract that establishes the level of service that a user expects from a cloud service provider. The degree to which the cloud service provider complies with the established

SLA is measured by SLA compliance. Metrics like uptime, response time, and availability are included.

v) Error Rate: Over time, this metric counts the number of errors or service failures in a cloud service. By dividing the total number of requests or transactions by the total number of errors, it is determined. Error rate is used to assess service quality and pinpoint opportunities for development.

vi) Mean Time to Failure (MTTF): This statistic gauges how long it usually takes for a cloud service to experience its first failure after it has begun to run. By dividing the total operating time by the total number of failures, it is calculated. MTTF is employed to forecast a system's life expectancy and gauge its reliability.

- Resource Management

Another topic of cloud computing study is resource management. To increase fault tolerance and reliability, researchers have developed a variety of strategies to optimize resource allocation and scheduling. This includes methods like dynamic resource allocation, fault-tolerant task scheduling, and load balancing. In a cloud context, resource management is effectively assigning and controlling resources like processing power, storage space, and network bandwidth to make sure they are used effectively and efficiently. The goal is to give users the greatest service possible while keeping costs to a minimum. A variety of crucial tasks are involved in managing cloud resources, such as:

i) Resource Provisioning: This process entails assigning resources to satisfy user requests. For instance, the cloud provider allots the necessary resources when a user wants a virtual computer or storage space.

ii) Monitoring Resources: This entails keeping track of how they are being utilised to make sure they are being utilized properly and efficiently. Cloud service providers can find locations where resources are being misused or wasted with the aid of monitoring technologies.

iii) Resource Optimization: This entails making the best use of resources in order to increase efficiency and lower expenses. To maximize resource usage, cloud companies, for instance, can disperse workloads across several servers using load balancing techniques.

iv) Resource Scaling: Resource scaling consists of changing resource allocation in response to demand. To dynamically increase or reduce resource allocation based on workload demands, cloud providers can utilize auto-scaling approaches.

v) Resource Allocation Policies: This entails establishing guidelines for how resources are distributed. Policies may be determined by elements like user profile, cost, or workload prioritization.

In order to effectively manage resources in a cloud environment, a combination of automated technologies, policies, and human skills is needed. To guarantee they are giving their customers the best service at the lowest cost, cloud providers must constantly review and improve the way they allocate their resources.

5.2.1 Testing and Evaluation

Critical areas of research in fault tolerance and dependability also include testing and evaluation. For testing and assessing the operation of cloud systems under various failure situations, researchers have created a number of testing and evaluation techniques. This covers methods including stress testing, performance testing, and fault injection. Any cloud deployment process must include testing and evaluation. To make sure that the cloud services and applications adhere to the appropriate standards of quality, dependability, and security in a cloud environment, testing and assessment are required.

5.2.2 Testing in Cloud Environment

Verifying and validating cloud-based apps and services prior to deployment is part of testing in the cloud environment. There are various types of testing that can be done in a cloud environment:

i) Functional testing: A functional test verifies that an application or service satisfies the stated functional requirements. User interface testing, business logic testing, and data validation testing are all included.

ii) Performance testing: This sort of testing determines whether the application or service operates as efficiently as possible with regard to response time, scalability, and resource utilization. Performance testing aids in discovering performance issues and optimizing the programme.

iii) Security testing: This sort of testing guarantees that the service or application is safe from hacker attacks and data breaches. Penetration testing, vulnerability assessments, and security audits are all types of security testing.

iv) Compatibility testing: This sort of testing makes sure that the service or application is compatible with various browsers, operating systems, and gadgets.

5.2.3 Evaluation in the Cloud Environment

Examining the efficiency and performance of cloud-based applications and services after deployment constitutes evaluation in the cloud environment. Several categories can be used to categorize evaluation in a cloud environment (Figure 5.3):

i) Quality evaluation: This type of review rates the effectiveness, usability, and performance of the application or service. Finding opportunities for improvement and optimization is assisted by quality evaluation.

Figure 5.3   Existing research on fault tolerance and reliability.

ii) Cost evaluation: The cost-effectiveness of the cloud-based application or service is evaluated using this form of evaluation. Cost analysis aids in finding ways to reduce costs and maximize resource utilization.

iii) Risk assessment: In terms of data security, compliance, and legal requirements, this sort of evaluation determines the risk involved with the cloud-based application or service. Evaluation of potential risks enables the implementation of mitigation strategies.

5.2.3.1 Review of Resource Optimization Models for Cloud Computing

Since both businesses and individuals want to use resources as efficiently as possible while keeping costs to a minimum, resource optimization is a crucial issue in cloud computing. For cloud computing, academics have created a number of resource optimization models throughout the years, each with unique advantages and disadvantages. We evaluate a few of the current resource optimization models for cloud computing in this section.

- Cost Optimization Models

Cost optimization is one of the cloud computing topics that has received the greatest attention. To reduce the cost of using cloud resources like virtual computers, storage, and bandwidth, several models have been created. To reduce the overall cost of using cloud services, these models often take workload, resource allocation, and pricing rules into account. The cost of running applications and services in the cloud is minimized while still satisfying the necessary service level goals (SLOs) and performance metrics with the help of the cost optimization model, a sort of resource optimization model for cloud computing. Organizations who seek to lower the cost of their cloud infrastructure without compromising the calibre of their services frequently employ this concept.

The Cost Optimization Model involves several key steps:

i) Define Service Level Objectives (SLOs): The first stage in this paradigm is to specify the necessary SLOs for your apps and services. These SLOs could contain performance indicators like throughput, response time, and availability.

ii) Analyze Usage Patterns: Following the definition of the SLOs, you must examine how your applications and services are used. You can use this to decide how to allocate resources in the best way for each application or service.

iii) Right-Sizing: You can scale the resources allotted to each application or service after analyzing the consumption patterns. To guarantee that each application or service has adequate resources to achieve its SLOs without being over-provisioned, right-sizing entails modifying the amount of CPU, memory, and storage resources allotted to each one.

iv) Implement Cost-Saving Measures: Implementing cost-cutting strategies such as using reserved instances, spot instances, or smaller instance types is the next step. If an application or service's consumption habits change, you might also think about employing auto-scaling to adjust the resources assigned to it.

v) Monitor and Optimize: The performance and cost of your applications and services need to be continuously monitored to make sure they are fulfilling SLOs and that you are getting the most value for your money. Utilize cost optimization tools to find places where costs may be further reduced while using cloud monitoring solutions to keep track of performance indicators.

- Energy Optimization Models

  Another important aspect of cloud computing is energy usage, particularly for huge data centres that need a lot of it. To reduce energy use in cloud computing, researchers have created a number of approaches, including dynamic power management and workload consolidation. The energy usage of cloud computing systems is optimized using energy optimization models, a subset of resource optimization models. these models are designed to reduce energy usage while maintaining the necessary levels of quality of service (QoS). There are various methods for creating energy optimization models, but most models take the following things into account:

i) Resource allocation: This refers to allocating the appropriate physical resources (such as CPUs, memory, storage, and network bandwidth) to each virtual machine (VM) or application running in the cloud.

ii) Workload management: This entails allocating workloads among the available resources to make sure that they are used effectively.

iii) Power management: This is regulating how much energy is utilized by the physical resources. Examples include lowering the CPU clock speed, turning off unused resources, and modifying the cooling system.

iv) Performance management: This entails keeping an eye on the cloud computing system's performance and modifying resource allocation to meet QoS standards.

Energy optimization models employ a number of strategies, including:

i) Dynamic Voltage and Frequency Scaling (DVFS): When the workload is low, this technology lowers the voltage and CPU clock speed to save energy.

ii) Consolidation: This strategy places several virtual machines (VMs) or applications onto fewer physical resources in order to save energy.

iii) Migration: With this strategy, virtual machines (VMs) or applications are moved to physically more energy-efficient resources.

iv) Task Scheduling: Using this method, tasks are scheduled to run on the most energy-efficient resources.

v) Predictive Modelling: This technique forecasts workload demand using predictive models, and then modifies resource allocation accordingly.

In conclusion, energy optimization models are essential for cloud computing systems as they aid in lowering energy usage, which lowers costs and promotes a greener and more sustainable computing environment.

- Performance Optimization Models

In cloud computing, performance optimization is also crucial, especially for companies that depend on cloud services to support crucial operations. In order to improve the performance of cloud services like load balancing and resource scheduling, researchers have created a number of models. In order to maximize system performance, resource allocation and utilization are optimized using performance optimization models in cloud computing. These models use mathematical and statistical models to enable effective cloud resource utilization, lower costs, and increase system performance. The resource optimization model is one of the most often used performance optimization models in cloud computing, while there are other models as well. Based on the system workload needs, this model is made to optimize the distribution of resources in a cloud computing environment. The following stages can be used to categories the resource optimization model:

i) Resource Monitoring and Profiling: Monitoring and profiling cloud resources is the initial step in the resource optimization model. This involves keeping an eye on the cloud's CPU, memory, network, and storage resources. Understanding resource utilization patterns and locating system bottlenecks are both aided by the profiling step.

ii) Workload Characterization: Characterizing the workload in the cloud environment is the second stage. Analyzing system usage patterns and comprehending the requirements of cloud-based apps are necessary for this. The workload characterization assists in determining the applications' resource needs and the best way to allocate resources.

iii) Resource Allocation: The third stage involves allocating resources in accordance with the demands of the workload. Resources are dynamically assigned to applications according to their current demand throughout the resource allocation process. The resource allocation algorithm takes into account the way that resources are currently being used, the system's workload, and the importance of the applications.

Performance Analysis and Optimization: The system's performance is examined and improved upon in the fourth stage. This entails keeping an eye on the system to spot any performance bottlenecks, then optimizing it to increase performance. The system configuration and resource allocation settings are adjusted as part of the performance optimization process.

- Multi-Objective Optimization Models

The goal of multi-objective optimization models is to concurrently improve cost, energy use, and performance. These models often employ Pareto optimization and evolutionary methods to find the best solutions while balancing various goals. A type of mathematical optimization called multi-objective optimization involves simultaneously optimizing several objective functions. For example, maximizing resource utilization while lowering costs, or reducing reaction time while maximizing availability, are common goals of resource optimization models for cloud computing. To discover the optimum solution, multi-objective optimization models can assist in balancing these conflicting aims. There are a number of decision factors that can be changed in a multi-objective optimization model for resource optimization in cloud computing to optimize the system. These deciding factors could be the distribution of virtual machines among real servers, the selection of a cloud service provider, or the network topology setting. A multi-objective optimization model's objective functions stand in for the system's various objectives. For instance, one objective function can represent the system's operating costs, while another might represent resource usage. Each objective function is given a weight that indicates how significant it is in relation to other objectives in the overall optimization issue. The restrictions of the system are reflected in the constraints of a multi-objective optimization model for resource optimization in cloud computing. There can be limitations on the quantity of resources that are accessible or the maximum response time for a certain request, for instance. Pareto optimization is a popular strategy for tackling multi-objective optimization issues. Finding the collection of solutions that best balance the various objectives is the goal of Pareto optimization. In the objective space, these solutions, also referred to as Pareto optimal solutions, form a Pareto front. There are many techniques that may be employed, such as genetic algorithms or particle swarm optimization, to identify the Pareto optimal solutions for a multi-objective optimization model for resource optimization in cloud computing. By iteratively assessing various combinations of choice variables and objective functions, these algorithms look for the set of Pareto optimal solutions. The best answers are then chosen depending on how close they are to the Pareto front.

- Security Optimization Models

Another important concern with cloud computing is security, especially for companies that store sensitive data there. Researchers have created a number of models, such as access control procedures and intrusion detection systems, to optimize security in cloud computing. The security optimization approach (SOM) is a cloud resource optimization approach designed to strike a compromise between security requirements and cloud service performance. The SOM offers a framework for weighing the trade-offs between security and performance and aids cloud service providers in making defensible choices on resource allocation to produce the best outcomes. The SOM considers a number of security factors, including requirements for compliance, availability, confidentiality, and integrity. The performance needs of the cloud services being delivered, such as response time, throughput, and resource utilization, are compared to these criteria. The model then makes suggestions for resource allocation that maximizes security and performance. The following steps make up the SOM:

i) Security Requirements Analysis: In this step, the security requirements of the cloud services being delivered are identified. These requirements include data confidentiality and integrity, access control, and regulatory standard compliance.

ii) Performance Requirements Analysis: In this step, the performance requirements for cloud services are determined. These criteria include reaction time, throughput, and resource usage.

iii) Resource Allocation: The SOM assesses several resource allocation scenarios that strike a balance between security and performance criteria in this step. Based on the findings of the evaluation, the SOM suggests the best possible scenario for resource allocation.

iv) Performance and Security Monitoring: This stage entails continuously checking that the cloud services' performance and security adhere to the set standards. For corrective action, any deviations from the requirements are flagged.

v) Optimization Refinement: Based on the data collected during monitoring, this step comprises improving the resource allocation and performance/security monitoring procedures. This contributes to the ongoing performance and security enhancement of cloud services.

5.2.3.2 Analysis of Fault Tolerance and Reliability Mechanisms in Cloud Environments

Businesses and people can profit greatly from cloud computing, which offers features like flexibility, scalability, and affordability. Cloud environments can, however, also be prone to breakdowns and downtime, which can lead to large financial losses and harm to the service provider's reputation. Therefore, it is crucial to implement fault tolerance and reliability mechanisms in order to guarantee the availability and efficiency of cloud services. We will analyze fault tolerance and reliability techniques in cloud settings in this part.

- Replication

Replication is a common method for achieving fault tolerance and reliability mechanisms in cloud environments. Making numerous copies of data, apps, or services and distributing them among many servers or data centres is the process of replication. Replication is used to make sure that, in the case of a failure, backup copies are available that can take over and keep users' services running uninterrupted. In order to ensure that the workload may be transferred to another server in the event of a server failure, replication is a fault tolerance strategy that involves generating copies of data and services across many servers. Data replication, application replication, and server replication are a few examples of the various levels at which replication can be used. Data replication entails the production of numerous copies of the data and their storage on several servers or data centres. This guarantees that there are backup copies of the data that users may access in case one server fails. Data replication methods include active-active replication, multi-master replication, and master-slave replication. The process of establishing numerous instances of an application and deploying them across several servers or data centres is known as application replication. This makes sure that in the event that one instance of the programme fails, there will still be functioning instances that can continue to serve users.

- Redundancy

In a cloud context, redundancy is the replication of vital parts or systems. By having redundant systems, you can ensure that services continue to be available without interruption if one system malfunctions or experiences an outage because the redundant system can easily take over. Another fault tolerance technique is redundancy, which entails replicating vital parts like power supply, network interfaces, and storage to make sure that if one fails, the system can still function. There are various levels at which redundancy can be applied, including hardware, data, and network redundancy. Duplicating crucial hardware parts like servers, storage, and networking equipment is known as hardware redundancy. The redundant components can take over automatically in the event of hardware failure, guaranteeing that services are still available. Data redundancy entails storing several copies of the same information across various geographical or storage locations. As a result, service continuity is guaranteed in the event that one copy of the data is unavailable and another copy is still available. Duplicating network elements like routers, switches, and firewalls is a form of redundancy. By having redundant network components, you can assure that network connectivity is still available even if one of the components fails.

- Checkpointing

Checkpointing is a reliability technique in which the state of a programme or application is periodically saved to disc so that, in the event of a failure, the programme can be restarted from the most recent checkpoint. There are various levels at which checkpointing can be used, including the process level, virtual machine level, and system level. In order to guarantee the dependability and accessibility of applications and services in cloud computing environments, checkpointing is also employed as a fault tolerance method. It entails routinely saving a checkpoint, or the most recent state of an application or service, to a storage space or memory. The application or service can be resumed after a failure by starting from the most recent checkpoint rather than from scratch. This can save time and lessen the effects of the failure. Process-level, thread-level, and virtual machine checkpointing are a few of the several kinds of checkpointing mechanisms. The whole state of a process, including its memory, registers, and programme counter, is saved by process-level checkpointing. The state of each thread inside a process is saved by thread-level checkpointing. Checkpointing a virtual computer, which can have numerous processes and threads, preserves its current state. Reduced failure impact and quicker recovery periods made possible by checkpointing can increase the dependability and availability of cloud applications and services. The drawbacks include higher overhead and storage needs, as well as the potential for inconsistent checkpointing if the application or service is not correctly structured. The requirements of the application or service, the frequency and granularity of checkpointing, as well as the storage and recovery techniques employed, must all be carefully considered in order to ensure the success of checkpointing in cloud environments. To provide thorough failure protection, it's also crucial to take other fault tolerance and reliability techniques into account, such as replication, redundancy, and monitoring.

- Automatic Failover

When a primary system fails, an automated failover reliability mechanism immediately switches to a backup system. There are various levels at which automatic failover can be performed, including database failover, server failover, and data centre failover.

The performance and availability of cloud services depend heavily on fault tolerance and reliability methods. Replication, redundancy, checkpointing, load balancing, and automatic failover are some of these mechanisms. When choosing a fault tolerance and reliability mechanism for cloud environments, businesses must carefully consider their unique needs. Each of these mechanisms has its own advantages and disadvantages. Businesses may make sure that their cloud services are highly available and dependable even in the face of errors and downtime by putting these methods into place [15].

5.3 Fault Tolerant and Reliable Resource Optimization Model

To guarantee the availability and continuity of cloud services, fault-tolerant and trustworthy resource optimization models are crucial. By effectively managing the available resources, these models are intended to provide high availability, fault tolerance, and dependability of cloud services. To ensure that cloud services can continue to function even in the face of unforeseen occurrences like hardware or software failures, network problems, or cyberattacks [16], fault-tolerant and dependable resource optimization models were developed.

- Dynamic Resource Provisioning

A fault-tolerant and dependable resource optimization strategy called "dynamic resource provisioning" involves automatically allocating more resources to address growing workloads or resource failures in the present resources. This approach is predicated on the notion that a system's resource requirements can alter over time as a result of workload variations, technical difficulties, or other elements. The DRP model uses a feedback control system that continuously evaluates system performance and modifies resource allocation in order to optimize resource allocation in such a dynamic environment. The availability and performance of the cloud services can be maintained using this strategy. Monitoring the demand on cloud resources and automatically supplying more resources as required are both parts of dynamic resource provisioning [17, 18]. Auto-scaling, a cloud service that automatically scales the resources up or down based on the current workload, can be used to achieve this concept. Typically, this model consists of the following elements:

i) Resource Monitor: This element keeps an eye on how the system is using its resources and how busy it is, looking for any changes that might call for adjusting how resources are allocated.

ii) Resource Allocator: This component allocates resources to the system in accordance with the workload and system performance at the time. It chooses the most effective distribution of resources using optimization methods.

iii) Resource Provisioner: This component is in charge of allocating the necessary resources in accordance with the allocation that the resource allocator has provided.

iv) Resource Scheduler: This element plans the provisioned resources to accommodate the system's fluctuating demands.

This model can be used by fault-tolerant and trustworthy resource optimization models to boost system performance, cut costs, and improve reliability. When resources are shared among many users and demand is unpredictable, such as in cloud computing environments, this model is especially helpful.

- Virtual Machine Migration

A fault-tolerant and reliable resource optimization strategy called virtual machine migration (VMM) includes shifting virtual machines from one physical server to another in order to balance the load and prevent overloading any one server. The performance and dependability of cloud services can be increased using this strategy. Virtual machines are moved from overburdened servers to underutilized servers while workload on cloud resources is being monitored. An efficient resource optimization technique that is frequently utilized in cloud computing environments is the virtual machine migration paradigm. This concept aims to maximize resource utilization and reduce downtime by optimizing the distribution of virtual machines (VMs) across a cluster of physical servers. The physical computers in the cluster are continuously monitored for performance by the VMM model, which then dynamically migrates VMs between them as necessary. This makes it possible for the model to react to changes in demand fast and to guarantee that resources are being used effectively. The VMM model offers fault tolerance in addition to resource optimization by seeing and responding to hardware malfunctions or other kinds of system interruptions. The impacted virtual computers can be immediately moved to other machines in the cluster when a physical system fails, minimizing downtime and guaranteeing that services are still available. Tools like VMware vMotion, which enables downtime-free live transfer of virtual machines, can be used to achieve this strategy [19, 20].

- Disaster Recovery

In order to ensure that cloud services can be swiftly restored in the event of a disaster, such as a natural disaster or cyberattack, disaster recovery (DR), a fault-tolerant and dependable resource optimization model, must be implemented. This strategy can be used to guarantee the continuity and availability of cloud services. Making backup copies of data and apps and assuring their availability in the case of a disaster are both parts of disaster recovery. In the event of a disaster or failure, the main goal of DR is to make sure that crucial data and applications can be recovered and restored to a functional form. Backup and recovery strategies for crucial data and applications should be part of a DR plan. To ensure that it is accessible in the case of a disaster, this includes performing regular data backups, using redundant servers, and replicating crucial data across various locations [21, 22]. Some essential components of a DR model for dependable and fault-tolerant resource optimization in the cloud include the ones listed here:

i) Redundancy: A crucial part of a DR paradigm is redundancy. To guarantee the availability of crucial systems, redundant hardware, software, and network components are used. This can entail using various data centres or availability zones in the cloud.

ii) Failover and Recovery: Critical system failover and recovery procedures should be included of a DR plan. This entails the capability to restore the failed system to a functional state as well as the automatic transfer of workloads from a failed system to a backup system.

iii) Testing and Validation: To make sure a DR plan is successful, it should be frequently tested and validated. Testing backup and recovery processes, failover and recovery processes, and other essential DR plan components are included.

Monitoring and Alerting: Vital elements of a DR paradigm are monitoring and alerting. This entails keeping an eye out for malfunctions or faults with crucial systems and components, as well as having the capacity to notify IT workers or administrators of a failure.

- Load Balancing

In order to prevent server overload and to ensure that the burden may be transferred to another server in the event of a failure, load balancing is a fault-tolerant and dependable resource optimization approach. This strategy can be used to guarantee the performance and availability of cloud services. The process of load balancing entails dividing the workload equally among several servers and making sure that they are all in sync and accessible. Load balancing hardware and software are examples of technologies that can be used to accomplish this concept. In cloud computing, load balancing is a crucial component of fault-tolerant and trustworthy resource optimization. In order to prevent any single server or resource from being overloaded, which may result in performance degradation and system failure, the workload must be distributed over several servers or resources [23, 24]. To achieve fault tolerance and reliability in cloud computing, a variety of load balancing strategies can be applied:

i) Round-Robin Load Balancing: In this paradigm, requests are split evenly among the available resources. In order to prevent resource overload, each resource is used in turn.

ii) Weighted Round-Robin Load Balancing: This model is comparable to round-robin, but instead gives each resource a weight based on its capacity. Higher weights and a larger share of the workload are given to resources with greater capabilities.

iii) Least Connections Load Balancing: Requests are routed to the resource that has the fewest active connections in this load-balancing scheme. This guarantees the effective and equitable utilization of resources.

iv) IP Hash Load Balancing: This model chooses the resource to use based on the client's IP address. Each client will always be sent to the same resource thanks to this, which can be helpful for preserving session state.

Redundancy should be considered while designing load balancers in order to provide fault tolerance and reliability. It is recommended to deploy many load balancers and set them up to fail over to one another in the event of a failure. To guarantee that the system can handle shifting demands, resources should also be monitored and scaled up or down as necessary.

5.4 Case Studies and Real-World Applications

To guarantee the availability and continuity of cloud services, fault tolerant and trustworthy resource optimization models are crucial.

5.4.1 Case Studies

These case studies demonstrate the significance of fault tolerance and trustworthy resource optimization in cloud computing (Figure 5.4).

- Netflix

Netflix is a well-known video streaming service that mainly use the cloud. Netflix uses a fault-tolerant design known as the Chaos Monkey to guarantee high availability and dependability. In order to mimic failures and make sure that the system can recover without having an impact on customers, the Chaos Monkey arbitrarily

Figure 5.4 Various case studies.

kills virtual machines in Netflix's cloud architecture. In addition, Netflix makes use of a variety of other fault-tolerant and reliability engineering tools, such as the Simian Army, which comes with a set of tools for assessing and confirming the system's resilience. For its cloud infrastructure, Netflix also employs Amazon Web Services (AWS), which provides a variety of fault-tolerant and dependable services like multiple availability zones, elastic load balancing, and scheduled backups. In order to offer its users high-quality streaming around the globe, Netflix also made use of AWS's worldwide infrastructure. The business caches content closer to users using AWS's content delivery network (CDN), which lowers latency and boosts streaming speed. As the data is delivered from the closest cache rather than the main data centre, this strategy also reduces bandwidth costs. Offering a custom-ized experience for its users is another important advantage of cloud computing for Netflix. Machine learning services from AWS are used by Netflix to analyze user data and offer tailored suggestions to its users. This strategy has significantly increased user engagement and assisted Netflix in keeping its subscribers. Netflix's unique usage of cloud computing is directly related to its success. Netflix has been able to offer top-notch streaming services to its viewers all around the world by utilizing the scalability, flexibility, and international reach of AWS. A personalized experience is another benefit of the company's usage of machine learning, which has significantly increased customer retention and engagement.

- Airbnb

With the help of the well-known online accommodation marketplace Airbnb, people may let tourists stay in their houses, flats, or other places of lodging. The business was established in 2008 and has expanded quickly to rank among the big-gest hotel suppliers worldwide. Airbnb has resorted to cloud computing to handle the enormous volumes of data the site generates. Amazon Web Services (AWS), a cloud-based platform that offers a variety of services and tools for developing and deploying applications, is one of the main ways that Airbnb employs cloud computing. To store and manage its enormous amount of data, including user information, booking information, and financial data, Airbnb employs AWS. With the scalable and dependable storage that AWS offers, Airbnb can effortlessly manage massive volumes of data and cope with unexpected surges in traffic. Additionally, Airbnb's mobile applications and website are powered by cloud computing. AWS offers Airbnb the servers, databases, and other computer resources it needs to run its website and mobile applications. This enables Airbnb to offer its customers a seamless user experience and adapt swiftly to fluctuations in traffic. Additionally, to gain insight into its data, Airbnb uses cloud-based analytics tools. The business stores and analyses its data using the data warehousing provider Amazon Redshift. In order to process and analyze streaming data in real-time, Airbnb also employs Amazon Kinesis, a real-time data streaming service. With the aid of these technologies, Airbnb is able to quickly analyse its data and take informed judgements. Overall, Airbnb has been able to effectively handle its enormous volumes of data and offer a flawless user experience to its consumers because to the usage of cloud computing. Airbnb can concentrate on its core business operations, grow, and innovate by using cloud-based services and technologies.

- Dropbox

Users can save and access their files using the cloud-based Dropbox service from any location with an internet connection. The business is regarded as a pioneer in the application of cloud computing because it mainly relies on cloud-based infrastructure to provide its services to millions of customers globally. The ability to store and exchange information without the use of local servers or physical storage devices is one of the main advantages of utilizing Dropbox. This is made possible by utilizing cloud computing technologies to deliver scalable and dependable processing and storage capacity, such as virtualization and distributed computing. For instance, Dropbox processes and stores its data using AWS. Storage, processing, and database administration are just a few of the many cloud-based services that AWS offers. These services may simply be scaled up or down in response to user demand. Due to this, Dropbox's users always have a smooth and dependable experience, regardless of the volume of files they upload or the number of recipients they share them with. Data protection techniques including encryption and two-factor authentication are also used by Dropbox. Utilizing cloud-based security solutions, which are simple to integrate into the Dropbox platform and offer improved defence against online threats, enables these precautions. Additionally, AWS is used by Dropbox for its cloud infrastructure. AWS provides a number of fault-tolerant and dependable services, including multiple availability zones, elastic load balancing, and automated backups. Dropbox also employs a variety of strategies, including as data redundancy and replication, to guarantee that user data is always accessible and secure from failures. In order to make sure that the system can recover swiftly and without a hitch in the case of a failure, Dropbox also conducts regular disaster recovery testing. The Dropbox case study exemplifies how using cloud computing can allow businesses to offer scalable, dependable, and secure services to users all over the world without the need for costly and intricate on-premise infrastructure. Companies like Dropbox can concentrate on providing value to their users while leaving the technical aspects of infrastructure maintenance to cloud service providers by utilizing the potential of cloud-based technology.

- Uber

Uber is a ride-sharing business whose platform is powered by cloud computing. Uber employs a variety of strategies, such as load balancing, auto-scaling, and failover methods, to ensure high availability and reliability. Uber employs a variety of tools and services from AWS, including Amazon EC2 for computational power, Amazon S3 for object storage, and Amazon RDS for managed databases. These tools and services are meant to be extremely fault-tolerant and scalable. In order to make sure that the system can recover swiftly and without a hitch in the case of a catastrophe, Uber also conducts regular disaster recovery testing. A wonderful illustration of how cloud computing technology may transform a company model is the Uber case study. Uber is a ride-hailing service that uses a smartphone app to connect drivers and riders. Millions of people are served daily by the company, which operates in more than 900 places throughout the world. A big part of Uber's success can be credited to the utilization of cloud computing. Due to the extremely scalable nature of its business model, Uber required a technical infrastructure that could support its expansion. Without having to make substantial upfront hardware investments, cloud computing allows Uber to swiftly deploy more servers and processing resources as needed. Uber did not have to construct and manage its own data centres because of cloud computing. The corporation was able to invest more in other parts of the business since it was able to reduce infrastructure expenditures by millions of dollars. Due to the mission-critical nature of Uber's services, downtime is not an option. A company like Uber needs high uptime and reliability, which cloud computing companies give. Uber was able to experiment with new products and services without having to worry about the underlying technical infrastructure because to cloud computing. As a result, the business was able to develop swiftly and maintain an advantage over rivals.

- NASA

In order to support its scientific goals, NASA uses cloud computing, and in this setting, dependability is crucial. NASA has a fault-tolerant architecture with numerous redundant components and built-in failover mechanisms to provide high availability and dependability. The highly scalable cloud infrastructure used by NASA is also built to support heavy scientific workloads. To make sure that its cloud infrastructure complies with NASA's stringent security and privacy standards, the organization uses a variety of compliance and security solutions. For its cloud infrastructure, NASA employs AWS, which provides a variety of fault-tolerant and dependable services like multiple availability zones, elastic load balancing, and scheduled backups. AWS is used by NASA as part of a case study on cloud computing to analyze and store data for the Mars Rover mission. Large volumes of data from the Mars Rover mission, including pictures, videos, and scientific readings, must be processed, examined, and archived for later use. Historically, NASA has processed and stored this data locally in its own data centres. But as the amount of data increased, NASA started to run into problems with scalability and agility because it was hard to scale up the on-premise infrastructure to handle the escalating amount of data. NASA made the decision to investigate cloud computing as a potential solution to these problems. Because of AWS's scalability, security, and affordability, the government chose to use it. NASA was able to process and analyze data more rapidly and effectively because to the ability to deploy resources on demand using AWS. Additionally, given the sensitivity and significance of the data produced by the Mars Rover mission, AWS offered a secure environment for data storage, which was essential. Additionally, by using AWS rather than spending money on costly on-premise infrastructure that might not be fully utilized, NASA was able to cut costs.

5.4.2 Real-World Applications

To guarantee the availability and continuity of cloud services, fault-tolerant and trustworthy resource optimization models are crucial. We will describe a few of these models' practical applications in the sections that follow (Figure 5.5):

5.4.2.1 E-Commerce Websites

Some of the most popular cloud computing applications are e-commerce websites. To handle enormous user populations, process transactions swiftly and securely, and reduce downtime, they significantly rely on fault-tolerant and dependable resource optimization models. For high availability and reliability, these websites employ a variety of strategies, such as load balancing, auto-scaling, and failover systems. E-commerce websites are using cloud computing more and more to increase scalability, availability, and cost efficiency. These specific instances of cloud computing's use in e-commerce website applications include:

i) Scalability: Cloud computing can assist e-commerce companies in coping with traffic peaks and demand swings. E-commerce websites can handle high traffic counts during peak seasons without having to invest in costly hardware

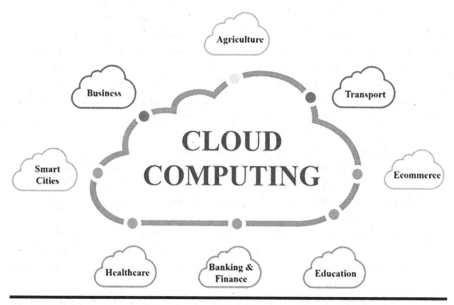

Figure 5.5 **Real-world applications of cloud computing.**

or infrastructure thanks to cloud-based platforms like AWS and Microsoft Azure, which can scale up or down automatically based on traffic levels.

ii) Cost-Effectiveness: By eliminating the need for pricey on-premise servers and hardware, cloud computing can assist e-commerce websites in lowering their infrastructure expenses. Pay-as-you-go pricing models are also available on cloud-based systems like AWS and Azure, enabling e-commerce companies to only pay for the resources they really utilize.

iii) Availability: By offering high availability and disaster recovery options, cloud computing may assist make sure that e-commerce websites are always accessible to customers. E-commerce websites may continue to function even in the case of a hardware or software failure thanks to capabilities like automated failover, load balancing, and data replication offered by cloud-based systems like AWS and Azure.

iv) Security: By offering cutting-edge security features and compliance certifications, cloud computing can aid e-commerce websites in enhancing their security. Encryption, identity and access management, and compliance certifications like PCI DSS and SOC 2 are features available on cloud-based platforms like AWS and Azure.

5.4.2.2 Banking and Financial Services

Cloud computing is also widely used by the banking and financial industries to support their operations. These companies have to make sure that their systems are extremely dependable, secure, and accessible all the time. They employ a variety of strategies, such as data replication, backup and recovery, and redundant infrastructure, to guarantee the continuity of their services and the safety of their customers' data. Due to its capacity to offer scalable and affordable solutions for managing data and applications, cloud computing has grown in popularity across the banking and financial services sectors. The following are some of the main ways that cloud computing is being used in banking and financial services:

i) Data Storage: Cloud computing offers a safe and affordable solution to store significant amounts of data. Anywhere in the world can access the data that financial institutions store in the cloud. In the event of a natural disaster or system failure, cloud storage also offers disaster recovery options, ensuring that data is backed up and safeguarded.

ii) Risk Management: Financial institutions can monitor and control their risks in real-time thanks to cloud computing. Risk management solutions that are cloud-based may analyse data from numerous sources to find potential dangers and give early warning signs.

iii) Customer Relationship Management (CRM): Financial institutions can manage their client connections more effectively with the aid of cloud-based CRM software. Financial institutions can enhance their customer service with the aid of these tools, which can track customer interactions, deliver real-time updates, and produce reports.

iv) Trading Platforms: Financial organizations may be able to access a scalable and adaptable trading platform thanks to cloud computing. Large numbers of transactions can be handled via cloud-based trading platforms, which also offer real-time analytics and reporting.

v) Compliance Management: Financial institutions can handle their compliance needs more efficiently with the use of cloud computing. Tools for compliance management that are hosted in the cloud can offer real-time monitoring, reporting, and auditing features.

vi) Fraud detection: Financial institutions can more effectively detect and prevent fraud with the aid of cloud computing. Large volumes of data can be analyzed in real-time to identify potential fraud and provide early warning signs using cloud-based fraud detection systems.

5.4.2.3 Healthcare

In order to support their operations, healthcare organizations also largely rely on cloud computing. They employ cloud computing for a variety of tasks, like as organizing and storing patient data and executing sophisticated medical simulations. These organizations are responsible for making sure that their systems are extremely dependable, always accessible, and adhere to the highest standards of security and privacy. They employ a variety of strategies to guarantee that patient data is secured from unauthorized access and that their systems are highly available, including data encryption, access controls, backup, and recovery. Healthcare is one of the many industries that loud computing has transformed [25]. The capacity of cloud computing to store, handle, and process enormous volumes of data in real-time without the need for costly hardware and software installations has led to an increase in the adoption of cloud computing by the healthcare sector. Listed here are a few cloud computing applications in healthcare:

i) Electronic Health Records (EHRs): Thanks to cloud computing, healthcare providers can quickly access patient medical records from any location with an internet connection. By doing this, it is made sure that patient information is current and readily available to authorized healthcare professionals.

ii) Telemedicine: Using cloud computing, remote medical treatment can be delivered. Healthcare professionals no longer need to be physically present while conducting virtual consultations with patients thanks to cloud-based telemedicine technology.

iii) Medical Imaging: X-rays, MRI scans, and CT scans may all be stored and shared online thanks to cloud computing. This makes it possible for healthcare practitioners to work in real-time with other healthcare professionals and access these photos from any location.

iv) Healthcare Analytics: Healthcare professionals may analyze vast amounts of data produced by numerous sources, including EHRs, medical equipment, and wearables, thanks to cloud computing. This aids healthcare professionals in spotting trends, forecasting results, and making data-driven choices.

v) Health Information Exchange (HIE): Cloud computing enables the safe exchange of patient data between various hospitals, clinics, and healthcare providers. This improves patient outcomes, encourages coordinated care, and lessens the need for repeated testing and procedures.

5.4.2.4 Government Agencies

Cloud computing is used by government organizations to support their operations and offer services to the public. These businesses must make sure that their systems are extremely dependable, secure, and accessible as well as compliant with all applicable laws and regulations. To ensure that their systems are highly available and that citizen data is secured from unauthorized access, they employ a variety of measures, including data encryption, access controls, backup, and recovery. Government organizations are increasingly relying on cloud computing to boost productivity, cut costs, and offer citizens better services [26]. The following are some ways that government organizations are utilizing cloud computing:

i) Data Management and Storage: Government organizations handle enormous volumes of data, particularly sensitive data. They can securely and effectively store and manage this data thanks to cloud computing.

ii) Disaster Recovery and Business Continuity: Using cloud computing, government organizations may easily restore their data and systems in the case of a catastrophe or other disruption.

iii) Collaboration and Communication: Government agencies may work together more productively even when team members are spread out across multiple places thanks to cloud-based collaboration technologies like email, chat, and video conferencing.

iv) Citizen Engagement: Cloud-based platforms make it possible for government organizations to interact with citizens more successfully via social media, online discussion boards, and other channels.

v) Cost Savings: Government organizations can save money on IT infrastructure and upkeep thanks to cloud computing, freeing up funds for other projects.

5.4.2.5 Social Media Platforms

Cloud computing is crucial to the operation of social media networks. They must make sure that their services are highly available, have the capacity to manage a big volume of consumers' data, and are highly scalable. These platforms employ a variety of strategies, including as load balancing, auto-scaling, and failover methods, to guarantee the availability of their services and the security of the data of their customers. The delivery of social media companies' services to users all around the world depends significantly on cloud computing [27–30]. Social media platforms can handle their expanding user populations and data volumes thanks to the infrastructure, scalability, and flexibility provided by cloud computing. The following are some significant ways that social media networks utilize cloud computing:

i) Data Management and Storage: Every day, social media networks produce enormous volumes of data. These data are stored and managed using cloud storage services like Amazon S3, Google Cloud Storage, and Microsoft Azure. Social media platforms may now simply scale their storage requirements and only pay for the space they really use.

ii) Content Delivery: Social media companies use cloud-based content delivery networks (CDNs) like Amazon CloudFront, Akamai, and Cloudflare to quickly and dependably send material to users all over the world. This is crucial for social media sites with a large global user base since it guarantees that consumers may access material promptly from everywhere.

iii) Computing Power: To power their applications and services, social media platforms also rely on cloud computing. User requests are processed, algorithms are run, and other computationally heavy operations are carried out using cloud-based computing services like Amazon EC2, Google Cloud Compute Engine, and Microsoft Azure Virtual Machines.

iv) Analytics and Insights: To run analytics on their data, social media sites also leverage cloud computing. To analyze user behaviour, track engagement, and obtain insights into trends and patterns, cloud-based analytics services are employed, such as Google BigQuery, Amazon Redshift, and Microsoft Azure Analytics.

5.5 Conclusion and Future Scope

Organizations can increase their operational effectiveness and cut expenses by using the fault-tolerant and dependable resource optimization model that the cloud computing environment offers. Businesses can create fault-tolerant systems that can handle unexpected failures without lowering the quality of service by utilizing the scalability and flexibility of cloud-based infrastructures. Additionally, cloud computing provides organizations with a dependable and strong platform for data processing and storage, ensuring that vital data is always accessible and safeguarded against corruption or loss. In addition, cloud providers provide a variety of tools and services that allow businesses to optimize resource utilization, including load balancing and auto-scaling, which save operating costs and boost performance. Overall, cloud computing has established itself as a vital technology for contemporary companies, offering a dependable and effective resource optimization model that helps them to remain competitive and adaptable in a market that is becoming more complex and dynamic. Given the growing reliance on cloud computing and the need for resource allocation that is more reliable and efficient, this model's future potential is significant. With the incorporation of new technologies like AI and machine learning, we can anticipate additional developments in fault-tolerant and dependable resource optimization models in the future. Additionally, the model's integration with other cloud-based services like networking, security, and data storage can improve the effectiveness and dependability of cloud computing even more. Additionally, the model's use in edge computing and the Internet of Things (IoT) can aid in optimizing resource usage in these environments.

References

[1] Tandon, R., Verma, A., & Gupta, P. K. (2022, November). Blockchain enabled vehicular networks: A review. In 2022 5th International Conference on Multimedia, Signal Processing and Communication Technologies (IMPACT) (pp. 1–6). IEEE.

[2] Tandon, R., & Gupta, P. K. (2022, December). ACHM: An efficient scheme for vehicle routing using ACO and hidden Markov model. In Artificial Intelligence and Data Science: First International Conference, ICAIDS 2021, Hyderabad, India, December 17–18, 2021, Revised Selected Papers (pp. 169–180). Cham: Springer Nature Switzerland.

[3] Tandon, R., Verma, A., & Gupta, P. K. (2022, July). A secure framework based on nature-inspired optimization for vehicle routing. In Advances in Computing and Data Sciences: 6th International Conference, ICACDS 2022, Kurnool, India, April 22–23, 2022, Revised Selected Papers, Part I (pp. 74–85). Cham: Springer International Publishing.

[4] Verma, A., Tandon, R., & Gupta, P. K. (2022). TrafC-AnTabu: AnTabu routing algorithm for congestion control and traffic lights management using fuzzy model. Internet Technology Letters, 5(2), e309.

[5] Tandon, R., & Gupta, P. K. (2019). Optimizing smart parking system by using fog computing. In Advances in Computing and Data Sciences: Third International Conference, ICACDS 2019, Ghaziabad, India, April 12–13, 2019, Revised Selected Papers, Part II 3 (pp. 724–737). Singapore: Springer.

[6] Tandon, R., & Gupta, P. K. (2021). SV2VCS: A secure vehicle-to-vehicle communication scheme based on lightweight authentication and concurrent data collection trees. Journal of Ambient Intelligence and Humanized Computing, 1–17.

[7] Raghavendra, S., Srividya, P., Mohseni, M., Bhaskar, S. C., Chaudhury, S., Sankaran, K. S., & Singh, B. K. (2022). Critical retrospection of security implication in cloud computing and its forensic applications. Security and Communication Networks, 1, 1–17.

[8] Mohbey, K. K., & Kumar, S. (2022). The impact of big data in predictive analytics towards technological development in cloud computing. International Journal of Engineering Systems Modelling and Simulation, 13(1), 61–75.

[9] Heidari, A., & Jafari Navimipour, N. (2022). Service discovery mechanisms in cloud computing: A comprehensive and systematic literature review. Kybernetes, 51(3), 952–981.

[10] Liu, Z., Xu, B., Cheng, B., Hu, X., & Darbandi, M. (2022). Intrusion detection systems in the cloud computing: A comprehensive and deep literature review. Concurrency and Computation: Practice and Experience, 34(4), e6646.

[11] Chakraborty, A., Kumar, M., Chaurasia, N., & Gill, S. S. (2023). Journey from cloud of things to fog of things: Survey, new trends, and research directions. Software: Practice and Experience, 53(2), 496–551.

[12] Nayagi, D. S., Sivasankari, G. G., Ravi, V., Venugopal, K. R., & Sankar, S. (2023). Fault tolerance aware workload resource management technique for real-time workload in heterogeneous computing environment. Transactions on Emerging Telecommunications Technologies, 34(3), e4703.

[13] Liakath, J. A., Krishnadoss, P., & Natesan, G. (2023). DCCWOA: A multi-heuristic fault tolerant scheduling technique for cloud computing environment. Peer-to-Peer Networking and Applications, 1–18.

[14] Sheeba, A., & Uma Maheswari, B. (2023). An efficient fault tolerance scheme based enhanced firefly optimization for virtual machine placement in cloud computing. Concurrency and Computation: Practice and Experience, 35(7), e7610.

[15] Tawfeeg, T. M., Yousif, A., Hassan, A., Alqhtani, S. M., Hamza, R., Bashir, M. B., & Ali, A. (2022). Cloud dynamic load balancing and reactive fault tolerance techniques: A systematic literature review (SLR). IEEE Access, 1, 71853–71873.

[16] Malik, M. K., Singh, A., & Swaroop, A. (2022). A planned scheduling process of cloud computing by an effective job allocation and fault-tolerant mechanism. Journal of Ambient Intelligence and Humanized Computing, 1–19.

[17] Bal, P. K., Mohapatra, S. K., Das, T. K., Srinivasan, K., & Hu, Y. C. (2022). A joint resource allocation, security with efficient task scheduling in cloud computing using hybrid machine learning techniques. Sensors, 22(3), 1242.

[18] Belgacem, A. (2022). Dynamic resource allocation in cloud computing: Analysis and taxonomies. Computing, 104(3), 681–710.

[19] Xu, H., Xu, S., Wei, W., & Guo, N. (2023). Fault tolerance and quality of service aware virtual machine scheduling algorithm in cloud data centers. The Journal of Supercomputing, 79(3), 2603–2625.

[20] Saxena, D., Gupta, I., Singh, A. K., & Lee, C. N. (2022). A fault tolerant elastic resource management framework toward high availability of cloud services. IEEE Transactions on Network and Service Management, 19(3), 3048–3061.

[21] Vinoth, S., Vemula, H. L., Haralayya, B., Mamgain, P., Hasan, M. F., & Naved, M. (2022). Application of cloud computing in banking and e-commerce and related security threats. Materials Today: Proceedings, 51, 2172–2175.

[22] Pallathadka, H., Sajja, G. S., Phasinam, K., Ritonga, M., Naved, M., Bansal, R., & Quiñonez-Choquecota, J. (2022). An investigation of various applications and related challenges in cloud computing. Materials Today: Proceedings, 51, 2245–2248.

[23] Kaur, M., & Aron, R. (2022). An energy-efficient load balancing approach for fog environment using scientific workflow applications. In Distributed Computing and Optimization Techniques: Select Proceedings of ICDCOT 2021 (pp. 165–174). Singapore: Springer Nature Singapore.

[24] Kaur, M., & Aron, R. (2022). An energy-efficient load balancing approach for scientific workflows in fog computing. Wireless Personal Communications, 125(4), 3549–3573.

[25] Vellela, S. S., Reddy, B. V., Chaitanya, K. K., & Rao, M. V. (2023, January). An integrated approach to improve e-healthcare system using dynamic cloud computing platform (pp. 776–782). Tirunelveli: IEEE.

[26] Kaur, M., & Aron, R. (2022). A novel load balancing technique for smart application in a fog computing environment. International Journal of Grid and High-Performance Computing (IJGHPC), 14(1), 1–19.

[27] Hagshenas, N., Mojarad, M., & Arfaeinia, H. (2022). A fuzzy approach to fault tolerant in cloud using the checkpoint migration technique. International Journal of Intelligent Systems & Applications, 14(3).

[28] Yadav, M., & Mishra, A. (2023). An enhanced ordinal optimization with lower scheduling overhead based novel approach for task scheduling in cloud computing environment. Journal of Cloud Computing, 12(1), 1–14.

[29] Tandon, R., & Gupta, P. K. (2023). A hybrid security scheme for inter-vehicle communication in content centric vehicular networks. Wireless Personal Communications, 1–14.

[30] Harnal, S., Sharma, G., Malik, S., Kaur, G., Simaiya, S., Khurana, S., & Bagga, D. (2023). Current and future trends of cloud-based solutions for healthcare. Image Based Computing for Food and Health Analytics: Requirements, Challenges, Solutions and Practices: IBCFHA, 115–136.

Chapter 6

Asynchronous Checkpoint/Restart Fault Tolerant Model for Cloud

Madhusudhan H. S., Satish Kumar T., and Punit Gupta

6.1 Introduction

Over the last decade, cloud computing has been a popular paradigm, and its use has increased significantly [1]. Cloud computing benefits not just individuals, but also big-scale viable businesses and research applications. Users may acquire services from the cloud with minimal effort since it provides ubiquitous, desired retrieve to a common group of computer resources. Hardware, software, and applications are examples of shared resources. Software as a Service, Infrastructure as a Service, and Platform as a Service are the three basic levels of cloud architecture. Although faults can arise on any of these three layers, few algorithms are discovered and used to recover from them.

The capacity of a system to proceed accomplishing its anticipated function looking errors or faults is referred to as fault tolerance [2, 3]. Deprived of fault tolerance capabilities, even the best-designed system through the best services and components cannot be termed dependable [4]. Since a significant amount of delay-sensitive applications should be executed, cloud computing's dependability is crucial. Furthermore, service reliability is essential for the cloud's widespread adoption. Consequently, fault tolerance has received a lot of research interest. Checkpointing, replication, Retry, Self-Healing, Masking, Task migration, Safetybag checks, Task Resubmission, Reconfiguration and other fault tolerance techniques are available to deal with faults at several levels, either reactively or pro-actively [5–8].

DOI: 10.1201/9781003433293-6

6.1.1 Fault Tolerance using Checkpoint/Restart Mechanism

Cloud computing comprises the effective distribution of resources as well as the usage of geographically distributed data centers. The hypervisor, correspondingly identified as the virtual machine monitor (VMM), is a top-level monitoring device that divides and monitors the server's offered resources amongst virtual nodes (VNs) or virtual machines (VMs). Depending on the user's request, a one or several virtual machines are allocated to execute the client application. A virtual machine has the advantage of allowing clients to execute applications on a range of IDEs, software environments and operating systems. Virtual infrastructure management (VIM) is a cloud computing module that supervises resource pooling, virtual and physical resource management, and further tasks in most circumstances [9].

A cluster is made up of a collection of hosts or servers. For greater generality, we regard clusters as server assets. Clusters enable cloud service providers to dynamically allocate virtual machines to virtual clusters based on SLA agreements or user requests. Such previous information is essential for cloud service providers to handle dynamic virtual machine allocation.

This chapter presents an intelligent fault-tolerant system that accomplishes the following goals: Detection of virtual machine failure owing to a node's byzantine fault, higher response time, and performance fault; optimization of the time interval between checkpoints; and modelling cloud service execution, utilizing the asynchronous checkpoint/restart approach. Figure 6.1 depicts the fault tolerance

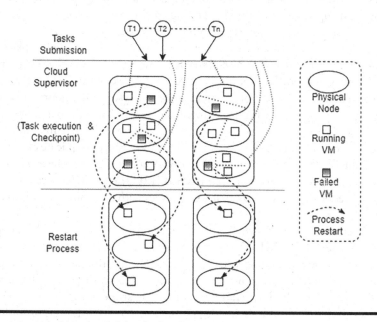

Figure 6.1   Working model for fault tolerance.

mechanism in our cloud model. Users submit tasks at the start of the process. The supervisor in the cloud creates virtual clusters of machines and assigns tasks to VMs, also monitoring virtual machines and hosts. The VMs will begin accomplishing the tasks assigned to them while also checkpointing them at the optimal regular interval of time determined by the optimization method.

If a node's response time exceeds the QOS requirement, the node is paused, and all processes are resumed on a different host. All tasks executing on VMs would be resumed on other VMs from their most stable checkpoints if one fails. As indicated in Section 6.3.1.1, byzantine defects are discovered. When a byzantine defect is identified, the node will be halted and a new virtual machine is begun. To improve the job restart process, a log-based recovery technique is used. It is noted that recognizing diverse varieties of faults and determining the most stable checkpoint point to resume the activities will incur overhead.

The remainder of the chapter is structured as follows: The literature survey is presented in 6.2, fault tolerance approach is addressed in section 6.3 and summary of the chapter is presented in section 6.4.

6.2 Review of Literature

This section incorporates several findings of researchers.

The authors of [10] presented a fault-tolerant virtual machine placement that uses the VM replication approach to accomplish fault tolerance. Various amounts of duplicated copies are employed depending on the needs of the VMs. The mirror copies of the similar virtual machine cannot be deployed on the same PM since each physical machine has its own need or limitation. To manage VM replica placement, the Integer Linear Programming approach is employed. A checkpointing/restart mechanism, as well as a replication strategy, were developed in [11] to improve the system's reliability. The creation of a fault-tolerant system that guarantees service continuity and reliability. Checkpointing is the most vulnerable to a greater failure rate because the checkpointing file becomes unavailable if the machine that holds it crashes, leaving the failed task non recoverable. As a result, a duplicate of the checkpointing file is kept to increase dependability. A fault tolerance approach based on checkpoints and replication has been devised [12]. The study focuses on a cloud-based map reduction framework that leverages proactive established fault tolerance to recuperate from a fault.

Zhou et al. [13] proposed a method for improving cloud service dependability by optimizing VMP. Three algorithms were employed in this work. The first algorithm picks a suitable selection of virtual machine-hosting servers from a large collection of aspirant host servers constructed on the network architecture. The second method generates an acceptable strategy for putting the main and backup virtual machines on the given host servers using k-fault-tolerance assurance. Finally, a heuristic is utilized to tackle the task-to-VM relocation optimization problem that is defined as finding the largest weight similar in bipartite networks. [14] presented a fault tolerance VM allocation for cloud data centers with (m,n) fault tolerance. The quantity of edge switches is m, while the number of host servers is n. To improve the application's or services' reliability, a k-fault-tolerant replication approach was implemented. To begin, reorganize the problem as an ILP and prove it is NP-hard. Next, the differential evolution (DE) approach is used to solve the ILP. In [15], the authors introduced a novel execution time estimate model that includes execution incident that existing multilayer checkpointing models do not. The link between checkpoint/restart overhead, system failure rates, and the duration between successive checkpoints is complex, and establishing the optimal time between checkpoints are challenging. The proposed work discusses how to utilize the model to define checkpoint interim and why these events are important to consider.

[16] Checkpointing is used to provide a fault-tolerant cloud computing service. The fault tolerance service uses semi-coordinated checkpointing, which cuts down on the time consumed in the phase of coordination, lowering energy consumption and overhead. The proposed technique also reduces the cost of a rollback, according to the findings. Authors [17] proposed the fault-tolerant WQR approach, that uses a cluster manager to ensure that a specific amount of copies are present in the domain. Checkpointing increases overhead which may cause the execution time to increase [18, 19]. This cost can be influenced by the checkpointing mechanism, checkpointing storage, and the recovery process [20]. In [21], the authors proposed a fault tolerant system that employs a decision-making system and deadline partitioning mechanism to identify deadline for tasks and the objective is to lower the makespan and enhance efficiency. The authors of [22] presented teaching-learning-based optimization to minimize makespan, failure ratio, and response time to increase performance.

6.3 Fault Tolerance using Asynchronous Checkpoint/Restart Mechanisms

There are three phases to the proposed technique for fault tolerance in cloud datacenters. The first phase aims to identify virtual machine failure. Different algorithms are provided here to identify virtual machine failure caused at the virtualization layer by a higher response time, as well as byzantine faults.

Phase 2 includes the checkpoint interval time calculation procedure, which is part of the proposed method for intelligent fault tolerance mechanism cloud datacenter. Phase 3 discusses asynchronous check-points and an efficient recovery strategy based on logs. The proposed model's operating concept is depicted in Figure 6.2.

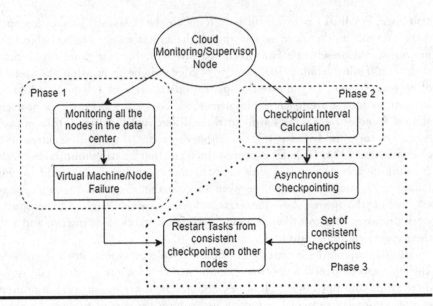

Figure 6.2 Proposed model working phases.

6.3.1 Phase 1: Detection of VM Failure Due to Diverse Faults

6.3.1.1 Checksum Validation to Detect Byzantine Fault

The SHA-2 algorithm was used to identify byzantine faults. SHA-2 is a revolutionary hash function that is utilized in a variety of fields. A 256-bit hash value is used in SHA-256. Eight 32-bit words are used to calculate the hash value. Cloud platforms can also employ the SHA-256 checksum.

When a node connects to another node using the TCP/IP protocol in a cloud environment, an expectancy will be there to create a checksum, hence similar nodes are certainly provisioned with SHA-256. Internodes are nodes that are linked to other nodes via the IP.

Each node of cloud carries the checksum operation. A data block's checksum is all the time unique and wont conflict with the outcome of another data chunk. Thus, if a node receives a message but fails to create the required checksum, node might be flagged as incorrect and vulnerable. Because recreating the initial data using checksum or doing collision analysis are often space-, time-, and cost-restricted processes, spiteful nodes are prevented from manipulating the checksum outcomes. The calculation of SHA-256 checksums on arbitrary data sets is straightforward, easy, and practicable. Due to byzantine fault-induced underestimation, byzantine nodes commonly provide genuine-looking output that is inaccurate. As a result, when a peer node uses the SHA-256 checksum to validate a node, a peer node can compute the checksum and send the message to another node; however, because the responding node for the same message must return the same output, byzantine nodes may fail the test due to their inability to calculate correctly.

6.3.1.2 Checksum Prerequisites

A supervisor node is supposed to automatically transmit the message M to j number of inter nodes and get the checksum $\{C_1,C_2, \ldots C_j\}$ in time $\{T_1,T_2, \ldots T_j\}$. The usual message size for SHA-256 is 512 bits, while the checksum equivalent to 256 bits. In time T, we examine a monitoring node with a pre-computed checksum C. After that, equate set $M\{C\}$ to $N\{C_1,C_2,..C_j\}$.

To equate checksums, let M and N are two sets, and each element of N is also an element of M, then $N \subseteq M$, i.e. N is a subset of M. Therefore

$$N \subseteq M \; if \; \forall y \left(y \in N \to y \in M \right) \tag{6.1}$$

If N is not a subset of M, M's 1 or more components have a processing error, resulting in a variance in the checksum.

A null set {} represented by $\varnothing$ if the set N includes no member of Q. i.e $N \cap M = \varnothing$. It indicates that the whole set of perceived checksums is erroneous, implying that the entire set of perceived nodes is compromised. It might potentially indicate that the monitoring node is vulnerable.

If there is a set of checksums in set N that are generated by incorrect nodes, then,

$$M \, / \, N = \{y : y \in M \mid y \notin N\} \to set \; of \; wrong \; checksums \tag{6.2}$$

Before any cloud application can run, supervisor node chooses message M, produces checksum $M\{C\}$ and delivers it to k nodes automatically and accepts the checksum $Q\{C_1,C_2,..C_j\}$ in time $\{T_1,T_2, \ldots T_j\}$. If $N \subseteq M$ if $\forall \, y \left(y \in N \to y \in M \right)$, then document the response time, that is processing time + transit time as the set $V \{T_1,T_2, \ldots T_j\}$.

6.3.1.3 Algorithms to Identify Diverse Faults

Cloud computing provides services to consumers while preserving the QoS specified in the service level agreement. QoS delay and response time are two QoS measures that are linked with all cloud nodes. Monitoring node keep track of which nodes are meeting the SLA agreement.

Algorithm 6.1: Node failure because of higher response time

Input: Set of operating nodes: N {N1,N2, . . . Nj}
Output: normal node or faulty node
1. for every Nt
2. if node Nt's response time ≥ QoS specified response time

3.   then
4.   capture the checkpoint
5.   call checksum_compare()
6.   else
7.   persist supervise
8.   end if
9. end for

Here, if a node's response time surpasses the QoS response time, the node is check-pointed and the algorithm 6.2 is invoked.

Algorithm 6.2: Byzantine fault detection

Input: A Message M to every active node N
1. for every Nt in N
2.   if C ≠ Ct //denote a byzantine fault
3.   then
4.   stop Nt
5.   initiate new node as Nt from newly found reliable checkpoint
6.   else
7.   call algorithm 6.3
8.   end if
9. end for

The algorithm sends the message M to the operational node; if the operational node generates a checksum that differs from the C, the checksum error denotes a byzantine fault. The method will halt the node and create a new VM if a fault is found. If no faults are found the set W{T1,T2, . . . Ti} is compared to the set V {T1,T2, . . . Tj} using algorithm 6.3.

Algorithm 6.3: delay_deflection_compare()

1. for every operational node Nt
2.   Select Tt from S
3.   Replica equivalent Tt from V
4.   if Tt in V > Tt in S
5. | fault is not detected
6. | call algorithm 6.5
7.   else if Tt in V= Ti in W

8.   fault is not detected
9.   call algorithm 6.5
10.   else if upper limit in V ≤ Tt in W
11.   shutdown Nt
12.   initiate new node as Nt from newly found reliable checkpoint
13.   else
14.   call algorithm 6.5
15.   end if
16.   end if
17.   end if
18. end for

Let f be a function with set V and set W as a subset that is partially ordered, if $W \geq f(V)$ for each r in W, a member w of W represents the upper bound of f. If this holds true for at least one r value, then the variance in the delay observed is extreme or high, indicating a performance failure, and the node is brought down once the workload is transferred to the previous checkpoint.

6.3.1.4 Representation of Checksum Detection Via State Transition

A virtual node's state diagram is shown in Figure 6.3. A node calculates the checksum once the M message is received from the supervisor. The node's initial state is 0 in this case. Identifying an error and the node gets into a byzantine state (i.e., state 1) if it fails to derive the estimated checksum following getting message M. It moves to state 2 with probability p = 1, when the node is halted and a new virtual machine is launched, from the byzantine state. It continues in the same state if no error is discovered. The E represents an error, whereas the NE signifies the absence of an error.

6.3.1.5 Delay Variation Representation via State Transition

There are three kinds of delay variations (Δ): average, high, and extreme. The node's initial state is 0, as seen in Figure 6.4. The node stays in the same state, if variation

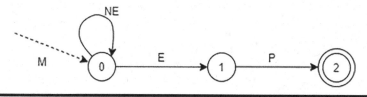

Figure 6.3   **Checksum state transition.**

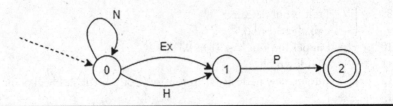

Figure 6.4 Delay variation state transition.

in delay is normal; however, if the variation in delay is extreme (Ex) or high (H), it indicates performance failure or byzantine fault, and the node switches to state 1. Then, the node is moved to state 2, here it is shut down.

6.3.1.6 Delay Sensitive Server Scheduling

The purpose of the delay sensitive server scheduling (DSSS) method is to monitor all the servers in a virtual cluster. DSSS is a simple model that can be linked to a supervisor of the cloud. DSSS maintains track of how many unsuccessful delay-sensitive jobs exceed the QoS delays, in addition to faults produced by Resource contention, virtual machine failures, and other parameters. After each state interval, the count is used to rank the servers, the server having the least fault counts will take top position in the list. Thus, DSSS can assist in dynamic job scheduling depending on the performance of the server. It can also be utilized to rank servers depending on their earlier performance and maintain track of earlier Cluster deployment status. Knowing about former performance would help the model choose the right server for establishing clusters and running important applications in a timely and dynamic way.

Algorithm 6.4: DSSS()

Input: W, V
Output: L_{DSSSss}
1. Split $V = \{J_1, J_2, \ldots \ldots J_m\}$
2. for every s present in W, do
3.   if J_i has been set to s_j then
4.   if L_{DSS} does not contain s_j then
5. $s_j \rightarrow L_{DSS}$
6. $L_{DSSS} = L_{DSSS} + 1$
7.   end if
8.   end if
9. end for

```
10.  for every sⱼ belong to L_DSSS
11.      if Virtual Machine = F_T
12.         FT= FT + 1
13.      else if Virtual Machine = F_VM
14.         FT= FT+1
15.      end if
16.   end if
17. end for
18. sort L_DSSS(s,FT)

19.   for j: 0 to m-1
20.      if s_{j-1·FT} ≥ s_{j·FT} then
21.         exchange (L_DSSS[s_{j-1}], L_DSSS[s_j])
22.      end if
23.   end for
```

Following the choice of an appropriate server to execute the tasks, further process is to implement a fault tolerance mechanism.

6.3.2 Phase 2: Optimizing Checkpoint Interval Time

Keeping checkpoint intervals at the optimal value is a difficult task in checkpoint/ restart optimization. Its goal is to determine the time interval required to take task checkpoints. Let I be the predefined starting interval for monitoring state. Algorithm 6.5 works as follows: the interval value is incremented if a node does not display checksum error or delay variation, which occurs when a node continues in

Table 6.1   DSSS Algorithm Notations

Notation	Meaning
W S R	List of Accessible servers
V	Client Request or Launched Application
Jᵢ	Job or Task
VM	Virtual Machine
FT	Total tasks Failed
F_VM	Virtual Machine (Failed)
L_DSSS	List of servers organized in increasing order

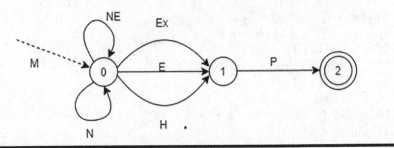

Figure 6.5   State transition for checksum and delay variation.

the state 0 as illustrated in Figure 6.5. The state interval α is reset to initial if a node displays excessive or extreme delay fluctuation and checksum error.

Algorithm 6.5: Checkpoint_Interval_Optimization()

1. Let $\alpha = I$
2. Assign s=0
3. for every Nj node in state 0
4.   if $\Delta C = \{NE \text{ or } N\}$
5. $\alpha \leftarrow \alpha + I$
6.   invoke algorithm 6.3
7.   invoke algorithm 6.2
8.   else if $\Delta C = \{E \text{ or } EX \text{ or } H\}$
9. $\alpha = I$
10.   halt Nj
11.   initiate Nj as new node
12.   end if
13. end for

6.3.2.1 IFTM

The algorithm (Intelligent Fault Tolerant Mechanism; IFTM) proposed in this work incorporates numerous methods which are mentioned in earlier sections of this chapter to accomplish the tasks provided by users.

Algorithm 6.6: IFTM()

1. for every Ji
2. for every VMi

3. do
4. monitor (Delay Variation, Checksum)
5. DSSS()
6. algorithm 6.5
7. Asynchronous_checkpoint
8. algorithm 6.5
9. delay_deflection_compare()
10. if (F_{VM})
11. recovery_alogirthm()
12. end if
13. end for
14. end for

6.3.3 Phase 3: Recovery through Asynchronous Checkpointing

Two types of fault-tolerant virtual machine approaches are frequently used. The first uses checkpoint and log-based rollback mechanisms. The other is centered on the primary–backup model, and includes incremental checkpoints [23].

The asynchronous checkpoint and log-based rollback are used to represent fault tolerance in this work. The tasks or processes that were executing concurrently on the assigned VMs were check pointed separately. These checkpoints are completed independently of one another, with no synchronization between the processes. The global consistent recovery points or checkpoints for various processes are shown in Figure 6.6. Before starting recovery, the recovery procedure essentially looks for the latest checkpoints that are highly consistent.

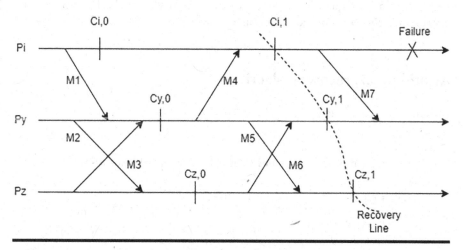

Figure 6.6 Asynchronous checkpointing and recovery.

Processes Pi, Pj, and Pz, take checkpoints at $\{Ci,0\}, \{Ci,1\}, \{\{Cy,0\}, \{Cy,1\}\}$ and $\{\{Cz,0\}, \{Cz,1\}\}$ respectively, as illustrated in Figure 6.6. After the Pi process fails, the system reverts to the last consistent checkpoint $\{Ci,1\}$. When process Pi is rolled back to checkpoint $\{Ci,1\}$ an orphan message M7 is created, forcing Pj to rollback to checkpoint $\{Cy,1\}$. We employed a log-based recovery technique to circumvent the domino effect that asynchronous checkpoints confront during recovery and to maximize recovery.

A few assumptions are taken into consideration during checkpoint and recovery. Communication channels are dependable, with limitless buffers and FIFO delivery of messages. The state of P is represented by the triplet (S, M, and MSG_SENT). When the message M is received by the process at state S, it goes to state S1 then delivers the message out. There are two kinds of log storage: stable log and volatile log. Triplet is logged deprived of any synchronization with other processes when an event is completed. Local checkpoints are a series of reports that are initially kept in the volatile log and subsequently relocated to the stable log. The algorithm 6.7 is utilized during recuperation.

Notations used in the algorithm:

$RC_a \leftarrow_b (CP_a)$: represents the number of messages the process P_a received from P_b, from the start of the computation until checkpoint CP_a.

$SD_a \rightarrow_b (CP_a)$: represents the number of messages the P_a sent to P_b, from the start of the computation until checkpoint CP_a.

Process is recovering after the failure: **R**

Number of processes: **V**

Orphan message: O_c

Depending on the quantity of messages received and sent, checkpoints that are consistent is chosen from the collection of checkpoints.

Algorithm 6.7: recovery_algorithm

Process P_a accomplish:
segment 1
1. if R_a then
2. $CP_a :=$ the most recent event has been saved in a stable location.
3. else
4. $CP_a :=$ most recent event occurred in P_a
5. end if

segment 2
6. for i=1 to V
7.   do

8.   for every nearest process y do
9.   compute $SD_a \rightarrow_b (CP_a)$
10.   send a ROLLBACK $(a, SD_a \rightarrow_b (CP_a))$ message to P_b
11.   end for
12. for each ROLLBACK (b, O_c) message accepted from a nearest b do
13.   if $RC_a \leftarrow_b (CP_a) > O_c$ // designates existence of orphan message
14.   then
15.   detect the recent event e such that $RC_a \leftarrow_b (e) = O_c$
16. $CP_a := e$
17.   end if
18.   end for
19. end for

6.3.4 Checkpoint Model Execution

The mechanism used in checkpointing is deterministic process and the checkpointing cost is purely calculated by how much work has previously been accomplished. W represents the workload, while v is the total checkpoints. WR1,WR2,WR3, . . . , WRv denotes the quantity of work that must be accomplished between every checkpoint holding $\sum_{q=1}^{v} WR_q = \dfrac{wr}{\beta m}$ where m specifies the number of VMs and β denotes the overhead factor $(0 \le \beta \le 1)$. Wq represents the quantity of work completed between checkpoints q-1 and q. $C(F_q)$ denotes the checkpoint cost obtained after completion of the amount of work X_q, here, $X_q = \sum_{i=1}^{q} WR_i$, WRi represents the amount of work that must be accomplished earlier to every checkpoint. R denotes the revive process cost afore qth checkpoint, represented as $R(X_{q-1})$, where $X_{q-1} = \sum_{i=1}^{q-1} WR_i$

During the rollback recovery procedure, there is expected to be no failure. The overall execution time may be calculated as follows:

$$E(P_k) = E(P_{wf}) + \sum_{t=1}^{k} \sum_{q=1}^{v} u_q \cdot E(P_{tf}) \qquad (6.3)$$

Where,
k: *Number of processes*
P_{wf}: *Process without failure*
P_{tf}: *Process with failure and recovery*
$u_q = W_q + C(X_q) + R(X_{q-1})$

6.3.5 Experimental Results and Discussions

A. Experimental setup: The proposed model is evaluated using the CloudSim toolkit simulator. Real-time workload traces from PlanetLab, a ConMon project that includes CPU consumption from over 1000 virtual machines operating on various hosts in over 500 sites across the world. We employed four different sorts of virtual machines: micro, small, medium, and large. There are ten different hosts utilized, all of them are HP ProLiant G4 and HP ProLiant G5. The number of tasks created ranges from 100 to 1000.

The FaultGenerator class in CloudSim is used to produce faults. The VM failure is simulated by halting the virtual machine, the fault through resource contention is simulated by limiting the resource capacity, and the byzantine fault or performance problem is simulated by using a modified FaultGenerator class.

B. Performance Metrics and Results: BFD is employed as a VM placement approach in the proposed method. The active physical machines (hosts) are classed based on its power proficiency, with the most capable hosts being preferred. In BFD, a host is superior to another host if its power competence is higher and its fault counts are lower. The proposed approach is compared to a non-optimization method that uses FCFS. The performance of the proposed and alternative approach is assessed using the metrics listed here.

a. Energy Consumption: It indicates the total amount of energy consumed by all of the physical machines in the datacenter (PMs). PMs' energy usage is calculated using the linear cubic power consumption model. The power consumption host's grows linearly as CPU consumption increases under this power paradigm. The following parameters are taken into account in the power model. When the host k is fully used, the maximum power consumption $= P_k^{max}$

The host k idle power value : P_k^{idle}
Host k's current CPU usage : U_k
The datacenter' total number of hosts : T

The host Pk's power consumption is calculated as follows:

$$P_k = P_k^{idle} + \left(P_k^{max} + P_k^{idle} * U_k^3 \right) \tag{6.4}$$

Our aim is to minimze data center power consumption and it is expressed as:

$$\sum_{k=1}^{T} P_k = \sum_{k=1}^{T} \left[P_k^{idle} + \left(P_k^{max} - P_k^{idle} \right) * U_k^3 \right] \tag{6.5}$$

The power consumption of both approaches is seen in Figure 6.7. For the data set planetlab/20110303 to planetlab/20110420, the proposed approach's average power usage is lower than without the optimization method.

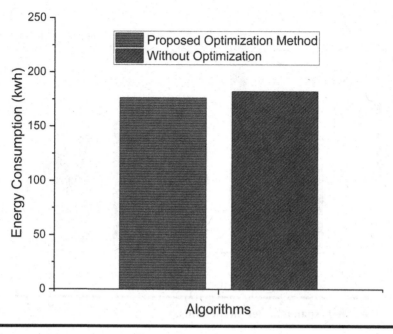

Figure 6.7   Average power consumption.

b. Makespan: It's the overall amount of time it takes to complete all of the jobs. Because the faults are simulated, a few tasks may fail and have to be resumed from the detected checkpoint, taking longer than planned to complete. One of the most important performance indicators for evaluating algorithms and approaches is the Makespan. Figure 6.8 depicts the execution time of the proposed approach vs that of the method without optimization. As indicated in the figure, the proposed method's average execution time utilizing optimization strategy is 25% faster than the method without optimization technique.

Figures 6.9 and 6.10 demonstrate the standard deviation of the proposed method's execution time with and without the optimization approach with VM selection. In the proposed technique, the standard deviation is between 0.005 and 0.012 seconds, while in the method without optimization, it is between 0.009 and 0.021 seconds.

c. Figure 6.11 depicts the number of tasks accomplished by the proposed approach and the non-optimization method by taking the number of tasks between 100 to 1000.

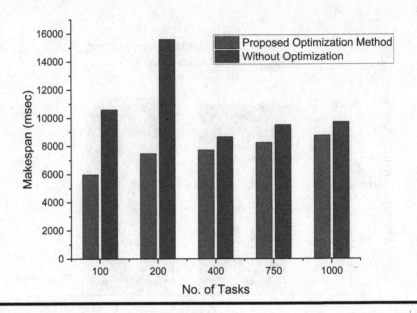

Figure 6.8 **Makespan of different methods.**

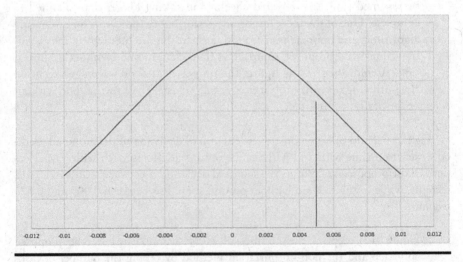

Figure 6.9 **VM selection SD of proposed method execution time.**

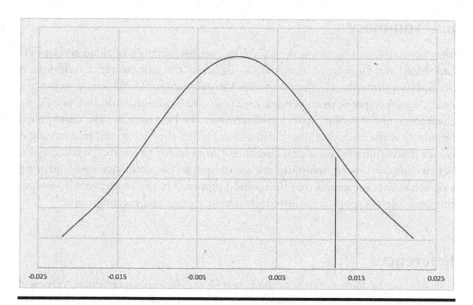

Figure 6.10   VM selection SD without optimization method execution time

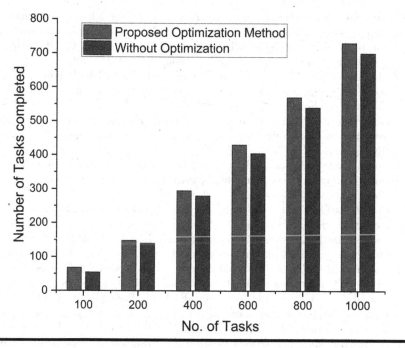

Figure 6.11   Total number of tasks executed.

6.4 Summary

This work aims at improving the reliability and performance of cloud services via fault based and fault aware mechanisms. To begin, the fault tolerance technique is divided into three phases: Phase 1 detects Virtual Machine (VM) failure owing to a node's slower response time, performance fault and byzantine fault. In Phase 2, the checkpoint optimization algorithm determines the best time to take checkpoints frequently while executing jobs. Finally, after failure, the backup and recovery algorithms determine the best global checkpoint from which to restart the failed tasks. When compared to the non-optimization technique, the simulation result utilizing a real-time data set reveals that the method proposed in this work provides a superior fault-tolerant solution while reducing energy usage and execution time.

References

[1] Mukwevho, Mukosi Abraham, and Turgay Celik. "To-ward a smart cloud: A review of fault-tolerance methods in cloud systems." IEEE Transactions on Services Computing 14, no. 2: 589–605, 2018.

[2] Ahmed, Waseem, and Yong Wei Wu. "A survey on reliability in distributed systems." Journal of Computer and System Sciences 79, no. 8: 1243–1255, 2013.

[3] Hernández, Sergio, Javier Fabra, Pedro Alvarez, and Joaquin Ezpeleta. "Using cloud-based resources to im-prove availability and reliability in a scientific workflow execution framework." In The Fourth International Conference on Cloud Computing, GRIDs, and Virtualization, Cloud Computing, pp. 230–237, 2013.

[4] Cheraghlou, Mehdi Nazari, Ahmad Khadem-Zadeh, and Majid Haghparast. "A survey of fault tolerance architecture in cloud computing." Journal of Network and Computer Applications 61: 81–92, 2016.

[5] Bala, Anju, and Inderveer Chana. "Fault tolerance-challenges, techniques and implementation in cloud computing." International Journal of Computer Science Issues (IJCSI) 9, no. 1: 288, 2012.

[6] Saikia, Lakshmi Prasad, and Yumnam Langlen Devi. "Fault tolerance techniques and algorithms in cloud computing." International Journal of Computer Science & Communication Networks 4, no. 1: 01–08, 2014.

[7] Essa, Youssef M. "A survey of cloud computing fault tolerance: techniques and implementation." International Journal of Computer Applications 138, no. 13, 2016.

[8] Taskeen Zaidi, Rampratap. "Modeling for fault tolerance in cloud computing environment." Journal of Computer Sciences and Applications 4, no. 1: 9–13, 2016.

[9] Essa, Youssef M. "A survey of cloud computing fault tolerance: techniques and implementation." International Journal of Computer Applications 138, no. 13, 2016.

[10] Gonzalez, Christopher, and Bin Tang. "FT-VMP: Fault-Tolerant Virtual Machine Placement in Cloud Data Centers." In 2020 29th International Conference on Computer Communications, and Networks (ICCCN), pp. 1–9. IEEE, 2020.

[11] Meroufel, Bakhta, and Ghalem Belalem. "Optimization of checkpointing/recovery strategy in cloud computing with adaptive storage management." Concurrency and Computation: Practice and Experience 30, no. 24: e4906, 2018.

[12] Raghuwanshi, Monika, and Deepak Kumar Gour. "Checkpoint and replication based fault tolerance for map reduce framework in cloud environment." Inter-national Journal of Engineering Science 18097, 2018.

[13] Zhou, Ao, Shangguang Wang, Bo Cheng, Zibin Zheng, Fangchun Yang, Rong N. Chang, Michael R. Lyu, and Rajkumar Buyya. "Cloud service reliability enhancement via virtual machine placement optimization." IEEE Transactions on Services Computing 10, no. 6: 902–913, 2016.

[14] Zhou, Ao, Shangguang Wang, Ching-Hsien Hsu, Myung Ho Kim, and Kok-seng Wong. "Virtual machine placement with (m, n)-fault tolerance in cloud data center." Cluster Computing 22, no. 5: 11619–11631, 2019.

[15] Dauwe, Daniel, Sudeep Pasricha, Anthony A. Maciejewski, and Howard Jay Siegel. "An analysis of multilevel checkpoint performance models." In 2018 IEEE International Parallel and Distributed Processing Symposium Workshops (IPDPSW), pp. 783–792. IEEE, 2018.

[16] Meroufel, B. A. K. H. T. A., and G. H. A. L. E. M. Belalem. "Service to fault tolerance in cloud computing environment." WSEAS Transactions on Computers 14, no. 1 (2015): 782–791.

[17] Bansal, Jyoti, Shaveta Rani, and Paramjit Singh. "A fault tolerant scheduler with dynamic replication in desktop grid environment." International Journal of Emerging Trends & Technology in Computer Science 3, no. 1: 170–175, 2014.

[18] Yang, Bo, Feng Tan, and Yuan-Shun Dai. "Performance evaluation of cloud service considering fault recovery." The Journal of Supercomputing 65, no. 1: 426–444, 2013.

[19] Di, Sheng, Yves Robert, Frédéric Vivien, Derrick Kondo, Cho-Li Wang, and Franck Cappello. "Optimization of cloud task processing with checkpoint-restart mechanism." In Proceedings of the International Conference on High Performance Computing, Networking, Storage and Analysis, pp. 1–12, 2013.

[20] Al-Kiswany, Samer, Matei Ripeanu, Sudharshan S. Vazhkudai, and Abdullah Gharaibeh. "stdchk: A check-point storage system for desktop grid computing." In 2008 The 28th International Conference on Distributed Computing Systems, pp. 613–624. IEEE, 2008.

[21] Farid, Mazen, Rohaya Latip, Masnida Hussin, and Nor Asilah Wati Abdul Hamid. "A fault-intrusion-tolerant system and deadline-aware algorithm for scheduling scientific workflow in the cloud." PeerJ Computer Science 7: e747, 2021.

[22] Devi, K., and D. Paulraj. "Multilevel fault-tolerance aware scheduling technique in cloud environment." Journal of Internet Technology 22, no. 1: 109–119, 2021.

[23] Zhang, Wei, Xiao Chen, and Jianhui Jiang. "A multi-objective optimization method of initial virtual machine fault-tolerant placement for star topological data centers of cloud systems." Tsinghua Science and Technology 26, no. 1: 95–111, 2020.

Chapter 7

Fault Prediction Models for Optimized Delivery of Cloud Services

Shivani Jaswal and Manisha Malhotra

7.1 Introduction

Cloud computing has revolutionized the IT industry by offering scalable, on-demand resources and services to businesses and individuals. However, as cloud environments grow increasingly complex and dynamic, ensuring fault tolerance and optimizing cloud services becomes crucial. Fault prediction plays a significant role in achieving these goals by enabling proactive detection of potential failures or performance degradation in cloud systems [1]. There are many benefits associated with fault prediction in cloud computing. Some of them are listed here:

Enhanced Reliability: Fault prediction allows cloud service providers to identify and address potential faults before they cause service disruptions. By proactively detecting and mitigating faults, cloud providers can significantly improve the reliability and availability of their services, leading to increased customer satisfaction.

Performance Optimization: Fault prediction models help optimize cloud services by identifying and addressing performance bottlenecks. By predicting and mitigating potential faults that can impact system performance, cloud providers can ensure optimal resource utilization and deliver consistent service levels to users.

Cost Efficiency: Fault prediction enables effective resource management in cloud environments. By accurately predicting faults, cloud providers can allocate

DOI: 10.1201/9781003433293-7

resources more efficiently, avoiding unnecessary provisioning of additional resources or over-provisioning, which can result in cost savings.

Service-Level Agreements (SLAs) Compliance: Fault prediction helps cloud providers meet their SLAs by minimizing service disruptions and maintaining agreed-upon performance levels. Proactive fault detection and mitigation ensure that cloud services remain within the specified SLA boundaries, avoiding penalties and maintaining customer trust.

Proactive Maintenance and Scalability: Fault prediction models assist in identifying potential points of failure, allowing cloud providers to plan proactive maintenance activities and scalability measures. By understanding potential risks in advance, providers can take necessary actions to prevent service interruptions and ensure seamless scalability as demand grows.

Improved Resource Allocation: Fault prediction models can guide resource allocation decisions in cloud environments. By anticipating potential faults, providers can allocate resources to mitigate the impact of failures, ensuring high availability and performance for critical applications and services.

7.2 Challenges Associated with Fault Identification and Mitigation

As there are many benefits related to fault prediction in cloud computing. In the same way, there are challenges which are associated with it. Some of the challenges with fault identification and mitigation have been explained:

Complex and Dynamic Infrastructure: Cloud environments are characterized by their complex and dynamic nature, with multiple interconnected components and services distributed across various physical and virtual resources. Identifying and mitigating faults in such a dynamic infrastructure can be challenging due to the sheer scale and complexity of the system.

Lack of Visibility: Cloud providers often face limited visibility into the underlying infrastructure and components of the cloud environment, especially in the case of Infrastructure as a Service (IaaS) or Platform as a Service (PaaS) models. This lack of visibility makes it challenging to detect and isolate faults effectively.

Scalability and Resource Management: Cloud environments are designed to scale horizontally by adding or removing resources dynamically. However, managing faults and ensuring fault tolerance becomes more challenging as the number of resources and the scale of the environment increase. Efficient resource management and fault detection mechanisms are crucial to maintaining service availability and performance.

Heterogeneous Technologies and Dependencies: Cloud environments typically involve a mix of hardware, software, and networking technologies from different vendors [2]. These heterogeneous technologies and dependencies can introduce complexities when it comes to identifying and mitigating faults. Different technologies may have varying fault detection and reporting mechanisms, making it challenging to have a unified approach.

Evolving Threat Landscape: Cloud environments are subject to evolving security threats and vulnerabilities. Identifying and mitigating faults caused by malicious activities or cyber-attacks requires robust security measures and proactive monitoring to detect anomalous behaviour and potential threats.

Data Volume and Variety: Cloud environments generate a massive amount of data from various sources, such as monitoring logs, system metrics, and user activities. Analyzing and extracting meaningful insights from this vast volume and variety of data can be challenging. Effective fault prediction models must be able to handle and process large-scale data efficiently.

Real-time Fault Detection and Response: Cloud environments require timely fault detection and response to minimize service disruptions. Traditional fault detection mechanisms may not be suitable for the dynamic nature of cloud systems, where faults can arise and spread rapidly. Real-time fault detection and response mechanisms are essential to ensure quick mitigation and minimize the impact of faults.

Interdependencies and Cascading Failures: Faults in one component of a cloud system can have cascading effects on other interconnected components. Identifying and mitigating faults in such interdependent systems requires a comprehensive understanding of the dependencies and potential propagation paths of failures.

In summary, fault prediction in cloud computing is of paramount importance as it helps enhance reliability, optimize performance, achieve cost efficiency, comply with SLAs, enable proactive maintenance and scalability, and improve resource allocation. By leveraging fault prediction models, cloud service providers can proactively address potential faults, optimize resource utilization, and deliver robust and dependable services to their customers. Addressing these challenges requires a combination of proactive fault prediction models, advanced monitoring and analytics tools, effective resource management strategies, robust security measures, and continuous improvement in fault detection and response mechanisms. Cloud providers need to invest in comprehensive fault management approaches to ensure high availability, reliability, and optimal performance of their cloud services. This chapter has been divided into various sections. Section 7.3 illustrates the related work shown in the field of fault tolerance and predictions in cloud computing. Section 7.4 explains the process involved in predicting fault occurrences in cloud services. The sections 7.5 depicts various fault predicting techniques that can be used in this area. The section 7.6 and 7.7 proposes a framework along with its performance evaluation. The section 7.8 shows various comparison analysis of proposed framework. The last section shows the conclusion of the chapter along with future work.

7.3 Related Work

Lee et al. (2015) [3] The FRAS framework (Fault Tolerant and Recuperation Agent System) is a fault tolerant and recovery framework that is proposed in this study.

This framework is based on specialists and includes four different types of operators. After an unfortunate event, the recovery operator does a move back recovery. Data specialists speculate about learning and data in an activity free of setbacks. The facilitator oversees specialist communications, and the rubbish collector collects trash for information. It is suggested to calculate operator recovery in order to maintain a system's steady state and foresee domino effects.

Dipankar et al. (2014) This study successfully presented and put into practice a framework that allows businesses to test risk variables and different compliances using research on multiple compliance models as an interface. The tool that was created creates SLA documents for organizations, aiding in the identification of the proper services that must be obtained from cloud service providers in order to certify compliance.

Sagar et al. (2014) It has suggested a fault-tolerant method that can manage multiple failures by moving different machines away from a failing computer to a new place. Due to this, the idea of virtual data centers (VDCs), where allocation can be carried out on virtual machines, has emerged. Additionally, by utilizing the proper allocation algorithms, numerous VDCs may be physically housed on a single data center.

Nuygen et al. (2013) [4] The tremendous challenge of fault tolerance, which immediately identifies the defective system components, has been elaborated in this study. When an anomaly is found in a system, a Black Box online fault localization system, also known as F-Chain, can successfully identify the problematic parts right away. This model is used when infrastructure as a service is offered, and it is independent of any anomalies that have been discovered or that have yet to be discovered. Additionally, an integrated fault localization scheme that takes into account fault propagation patterns and other functional dependencies has been implemented, aiding in the achievement of higher pinpointing inaccuracy.

Sun et al. (2013) [5] The dynamic adaptation to internal failure process (DAFT), which has been developed in this paper, revolves around the standards and semantics of cloud adaptation to non-critical failure. An investigation of the relationship between different failure rates and the two different non-critical failure method adaptations, registration and replication, has been performed. By combining the two adaptations to non-critical failure models, which increase serviceability, a dynamic flexible model has been developed.

Bala and Chana (2012) [6] In order to identify diverse task failures for scientific workflow applications, this study presents a notion of intelligent task failure detection models. The model's operation is divided into two modules as well. Task failures are discovered using various machine learning techniques in the first module, and real-time failures are established in the second module following the execution of workflows in cloud testing. Different machine learning techniques, including native Bayes, ANN, random, and regression, are used to forecast failures of tasks quickly and intelligently.

Other than scheduling, fault tolerance has been regarded as one of the most crucial issues in workflow management. To address system flaws, authors in Yehuda et al. (2013) [7] and Arockiam et al. (2012) [8]) adopted the replication technique. This method can be applied in a system where tasks are completed by a deadline. Authors have been given 50 approaches that strike the right balance between replication and resubmission in (Palaniammal and Santhosh (2013) [9]). However, by employing all of these methods, performance is diminished and SLA compromise increased.

Checkpointing is an alternative to replication and resubmission that can be utilized as a strategy. Authors have employed the checkpointing technique, which generates checkpoints sporadically between running tasks, in (Zhang et al. (2010) [10], Nguyen at al. (2012) [11], and Egwutuoha at al. (2012) [12]. The method put out in Ramkrishnan et al. (2008) employs synchronized checkpointing in two phases, which actually raises system overheads. The concept of independent checkpointing, which causes a domino effect, is used by the authors.

Belalem and Limam (2014) [13], A checkpoint mechanism that is adaptive in nature was demonstrated in a published study. In this, unnecessary checkpoints are removed, and the additional checkpoints that are needed in the present cloud environment are added.

An algorithm to choose a unique fault tolerance technique for each virtual machine was proposed by Zheng et al. in 2012 [14]. These methods of replication, such as multi-version and parallel, are all possible. It is suggested to use replication-based fault tolerance, which actually shortens service times and eventually boosts system availability. Additionally, there is less chance of errors developing in this way. It is accomplished by not assigning scheduled tasks to servers with a low success rate.

7.4 Process Involved in Predicting Fault Occurrences in Cloud Services

In cloud computing, data collection for training fault prediction models is of paramount importance. Cloud environments are complex and dynamic, consisting of numerous interconnected components, such as virtual machines, storage systems, network devices, and load balancers. Data collection is vital for training fault prediction models in cloud computing, as it enables the models to learn from historical data, detect patterns and anomalies, provide early warnings, enhance system reliability, optimize resource allocation, and continuously improve their predictive capabilities. By collecting data on various metrics, such as CPU usage, memory utilization, network traffic, and response times, fault prediction models can identify patterns and anomalies that precede system failures or performance degradation. These models can learn the normal behaviour of cloud systems and detect deviations that indicate potential fault. Also, timely identification of potential faults is vital in cloud computing to prevent service disruptions and minimize downtime. Data collection enables fault prediction models to learn from historical data and proactively detect warning signs that may lead to faults. By providing early warnings, the models can trigger appropriate actions, such as scaling resources, reallocating workloads, or initiating maintenance activities. Fault prediction models trained with comprehensive datasets can help improve the reliability of cloud systems. By analysing historical data on system failures, errors, and performance degradation, these models can identify the root causes and contributing factors of faults. This information can then be used to implement preventive measures, optimize system configurations, and enhance overall system reliability. Data collection for fault prediction models can also provide insights into resource utilization and demand patterns. By analyzing this data, the models can identify underutilized or overloaded resources, predict resource demands, and suggest resource allocation strategies to optimize the cloud infrastructure. This helps ensure efficient resource utilization, cost-effectiveness, and improved performance. Data collection facilitates continuous learning and improvement of fault prediction models. As new data is collected over time, the models can be periodically retrained to incorporate the latest system behaviour and fault patterns. This enables the models to adapt to evolving conditions, learn from new fault instances, and refine their predictions, ultimately leading to more accurate and reliable fault detection.

Pre-processing collected data is an essential step to clean, normalize, and transform it into a suitable format for fault prediction modelling in cloud computing. Here are the key pre-processing steps involved:

Data cleaning: Data cleaning focuses on identifying and handling missing values, outliers, and noise in the collected data. Missing values can be filled using techniques like imputation (e.g., mean, median, or regression-based imputation) or removing incomplete records. Outliers, which are extreme values that deviate significantly from the normal range, can be addressed through methods such as truncation or Winsorization. Noise, which refers to random fluctuations or errors in the data, can be reduced by applying smoothing techniques like moving averages or median filters.

Data normalization: Data normalization is necessary to bring different features or variables onto a common scale. This step ensures that no single feature dominates the modeling process due to differences in measurement units or scales. Common normalization techniques include min-max scaling (rescaling values to a range between 0 and 1), z-score normalization (transforming values to have a mean of 0 and a standard deviation of 1), or logarithmic scaling for skewed data distributions.

Feature selection: Feature selection involves identifying the most relevant and informative features for fault prediction modeling. This step helps reduce dimensionality, improve model performance, and avoid the curse of dimensionality. Techniques such as correlation analysis, mutual information, or statistical tests can be employed to assess the relationship between features and the target variable. Features that contribute the most to the prediction task can be selected, while redundant or irrelevant features can be removed.

Feature engineering: Feature engineering involves creating new derived features from the existing ones to capture additional information or improve model performance. This can include aggregating features over time intervals (e.g., mean, maximum, or standard deviation of a metric over a specific time window), creating lagged variables (using previous values of a feature), or constructing statistical measures (e.g., moving averages, exponential smoothing, or cumulative sums). Feature engineering aims to extract meaningful patterns and relationships that can aid in fault prediction.

Data transformation: Data transformation techniques can be applied to achieve a more suitable data distribution, normalize skewness, or reduce heteroscedasticity. Common transformations include logarithmic, exponential, or Box-Cox transformations. These transformations help meet assumptions required by certain modeling algorithms and improve the performance and interpretability of the models.

Data splitting: The final pre-processing step involves splitting the pre-processed data into training, validation, and testing sets. Typically, a portion of the data is reserved for training the fault prediction model, another portion for tuning model parameters using the validation set, and a separate portion for evaluating the final model's performance using the testing set. Proper data splitting helps assess the model's generalization ability and prevents overfitting.

By performing these pre-processing steps, the collected data is cleaned, normalized, and transformed into a format that is suitable for fault prediction modeling in cloud computing. This ensures that the data is consistent, informative, and compatible with the chosen modeling techniques, leading to more accurate and reliable predictions of faults.

7.5 Fault Prediction Techniques

Several fault prediction techniques are commonly used in cloud computing to anticipate and mitigate potential failures. Here are some of the commonly employed techniques:

7.5.1 Threshold-based monitoring: This technique involves setting predefined thresholds for various performance metrics, such as CPU utilization, memory usage, or network latency. When the monitored metrics exceed the thresholds, it indicates a potential fault or performance degradation. Threshold-based monitoring is simple and effective for detecting abrupt changes or violations in system behaviour but may not be suitable for complex or subtle faults.

7.5.2 Machine learning algorithms: Machine learning techniques are widely used for fault prediction in cloud computing. Supervised learning algorithms, such as decision trees, random forests, support vector machines (SVM), or neural networks, can be trained on historical data to learn patterns and make predictions about future faults. These models can capture complex relationships between different system metrics and identify fault patterns that may not be apparent through manual rule-based approaches.

7.5.3 Time series analysis: Time series analysis methods are employed to analyze historical data collected over time and identify temporal patterns associated with faults. Techniques like autoregressive integrated moving average (ARIMA), seasonal decomposition of time series (STL), or exponential smoothing can be used to model and forecast future system behaviour. Time series analysis is particularly useful for predicting recurring or cyclic faults in cloud systems.

7.5.4 Anomaly detection: Anomaly detection techniques aim to identify abnormal or outlier behaviour in system metrics that may indicate the presence of a fault. Statistical methods, such as the Mahalanobis distance, Gaussian mixture models, or the Isolation Forest algorithm, can be used to detect deviations from normal behaviour. Unsupervised machine learning algorithms, like clustering or density-based methods, can also be employed to identify anomalous patterns in the collected data.

7.5.5 Data mining techniques: Data mining approaches can be applied to analyze large volumes of historical data and discover hidden patterns or associations related to faults. Techniques such as association rule mining, sequential pattern mining, or classification and regression tree (CART) analysis can uncover interesting relationships between system events and subsequent faults. These techniques can aid in understanding the causes and factors contributing to faults in cloud computing.

7.5.6 Hybrid approaches: Hybrid fault prediction techniques combine multiple methods, such as machine learning, statistical analysis, and expert rules, to leverage the strengths of each approach. For example, a hybrid approach may use machine learning algorithms for general fault detection and prediction, while employing expert rules or thresholds for specific fault types or critical system components. Hybrid techniques can provide more robust and accurate fault prediction by combining complementary approaches.

It is important to note that the choice of fault prediction technique depends on the specific characteristics of the cloud system, the available data, the type of faults to be predicted, and the desired accuracy and timeliness of predictions. A combination of multiple techniques or customized approaches may be necessary to effectively address the complexities of fault prediction in cloud computing environments.

7.6 Proposed Framework

Based on the values of trust that the broker agent displays to the cloud user, the user chooses the cloud services. When determining the ultimate trust value of any cloud service provider, these trust values take a number of factors into consideration. Now, it is the exclusive responsibility of the cloud service provider to offer the service consumer a fault-free service. This proposed framework aids in both early defect detection and issue resolution, preventing time waste from occurring. The framework aids with this by causing a checkpoint to be triggered at the appropriate moment, allowing a fault to be handled promptly. This framework's many levels take into account factors for fault tolerance and trust. The multiple layers such as service consumer layer, administrative layer, trust evaluation layer and fault tolerance layer embedded in service provider layer only. Figure 7.1 shows the proposed framework.

This fault tolerance layer becomes active in nature when a service provider completes the service consumer's request. Actually, it is work based on virtualization. As seen in Figure 7.1, each host displayed in the service provider layer has a collection of several virtual machines installed for the fulfilment of service requests. A physical machine is located in this at the very bottom of the virtual machine. Located over this physical machine is a hypervisor. A hypervisor facilitates the use of guest operating systems on computers. Also, a virtual machine monitor (VMM) helps in creating set of nodes as requested by the user. A VMM can run several virtual machines and can be either hardware, software, or firmware. The primary layer of fault tolerance sits above all of this. defect tolerance layer manages all defect types, whether they are software or hardware-related. It initially keeps the system functioning until the problem can be tolerated 100%, and then it starts looking for a new system that is fault-free.

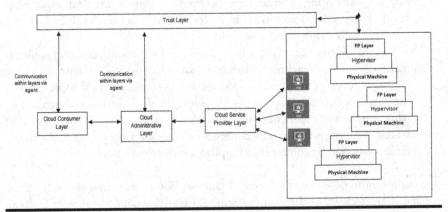

Figure 7.1 Proposed framework.

7.7 Performance Evaluation

There are numerous simulators that may be used to simulate cloud services. One of the most effective simulators is Cloud Sim. Cloud Sim makes simulation simple, and the only simulator that can truly generate the likelihood that problems would occur is that one. This involves the creation of additional classes into which packages are imported. These classes can be used to construct new fault-based algorithms that monitor different virtual machines in order to find and fix faults.

The trust value has been assessed using these criteria:

$$\textbf{Trust Value}(\underline{\textbf{Ti}}) = \Sigma_{i=1}^{n} \frac{Ti}{n}$$

$$\text{where Ti} = \{(pi * a) + (pi * \beta) + (pi * \sigma) + (pi * \mu) + (pi * \gamma)\}$$

where pi represents are the feedbacks submitted by provider agent along with the parameters i.e., availability, reliability, data integrity, turnaround efficiency and response time and analysed by the feedback collector existing in the trust evaluation layer. The proposed mechanism has been put up against the OCI, or optimal checkpoint interval. The checkpoints happen in this at regular intervals. The outcomes of the simulation were contrasted with OCI. Throughput, availability, and checkpoints overhead are the variables considered. The checkpoints in this are triggered based on the cloud service provider's most recent ranking. The less checkpoints are used and vice versa if the rating exceeds the threshold.

In general, event-driven and time-evolved methodologies are taken into consideration for failure detection. It operates according to the stochastic process theory. The random variables of time periods in the cloud system are taken into account in a semi-marked procedure with the following distribution. It is anticipated that the Poisson distribution will be used in this model. It means that the occurrence of faults is unrelated to the passage of time. As a result, the following equation must be taken into account:

The failure probability distribution of the VM at the specified time is provided by:

$$\text{Fp (Nn)} = (e^{\wedge}(-\mu) \ \mu^{\wedge}n)/n! \ 0 < \text{Fp (N)} <= 1 \text{ and } n = 0, 1, 2 \ldots$$

where N (n0, n1, n2 . . . .) represents failures and μ represents the average number of failures.

The values of μ is given by:

$$\mu = fn/(Ti/\tau jn)$$

where fn: number of failures and Ti represents the time period at which fn occurred.

τjn: Estimated time at which at which request occurred.

The likelihood that one error will occur is shown by:

$$Fp\ (N1) = [\![\mu e]\!]^{\wedge}(-\mu)$$

Last but not least, the rank of VM is determined by taking into account the ranker component. Its value is taken from a database of statuses. the equation is as a result

$$Rp = [\![\mu e]\!]^{\wedge}(-\mu) \times Pi$$

where Pi is the profit margin achieved when VM is used properly.

7.8 Performance Validation

The findings are shown in this part, and graph curves demonstrate superior availability and throughput for the suggested architecture. Additionally, compared to OCI, the checkpoint overheads have been significantly decreased.

7.8.1 Throughput

The x-axis in this graph displays the total number of requests, and the y-axis the throughput results, which are expressed in requests per hour. Figure 7.2 demonstrates that the suggested framework produces superior outcomes than OCI. It is because every service's ranking is taken into account before it is provided due to the produced trust value. As the CSP's rating rises, its throughput value rises as well, producing better outcomes than the competition.

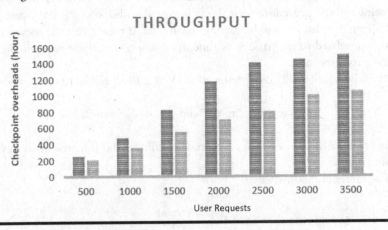

Figure 7.2 Throughput comparison.

7.8.2 Checkpoint Overheads

As demonstrated in Figure 7.3, user requests are represented on the x-axis and throughput on the y-axis in this. The result graphs demonstrate a significant decrease in checkpoint overheads. In this instance, checkpoints are activated when needed. As a result, checkpoints that are not necessary will not be used, which has actually decreased checkpoint overhead.

7.8.3 Availability

As ranking and trust values are used to deliver cloud services. As a result, the concerned cloud service provider's availability will be substantially greater than OCI, as illustrated in Figure 7.4.

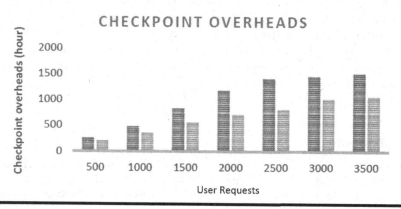

Figure 7.3   Checkpoints overheads comparison.

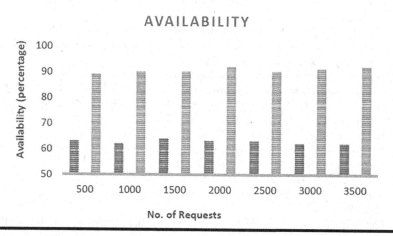

Figure 7.4   Availability comparison.

7.9 Conclusion and Future Work

Cloud computing has several benefits, including scalability, elasticity, high availability, and many others. The cloud computing concept has altered the IT sector since it offers numerous advantages to people, researchers, enterprises, and even nations. Although the cloud system offers many benefits, it is also prone to errors. Because of the size of the operation, failures are unavoidable in cloud computing. To handle errors in the cloud environment effectively, fault tolerance policies are frequently adopted. Techniques for fault tolerance assist in both preventing and accepting system flaws, which can result from either hardware or software failure. To accomplish failure recovery, high reliability, and improved availability, fault tolerance techniques are mostly used in cloud computing. This chapter has discussed various benefits, implications, processes and techniques involved with fault prediction in cloud environment. Various techniques are there such as checkpointing, time-series, ARIMA, threshold monitoring. Also, the proposed framework also shows better results in respect to various parameters in performance evaluation and validation. The future work insights on covering various other parameters and techniques for predicting the fault occurrence in cloud environment.

References

[1] Dasgupta, D., & Rahman, M. (2014, October). A framework for estimating security coverage for cloud service insurance. In Proceedings of the Seventh Annual Workshop on Cyber Security and Information Intelligence Research, Oak Ridge, Tennessee, USA: ACM, p. 40.

[2] Jaswal, S., & Malhotra, M. (2022). AFTM-agent based fault tolerance manager in cloud environment. The International Arab Journal of Information Technology, 19(3), 396–402.

[3] Lee, H., Chung, K., Chin, S., Lee, J., Lee, D., Park, S., & Yu, H. (2015). A resource management and fault tolerance services in grid computing. Journal of Parallel and Distributed Computing, 65(11), 1305–1317.

[4] Nguyen, H., Shen, Z., Tan, Y., & Gu, X. (2013). Fchain: Toward black-box online fault localization for cloud systems. In Distributed Computing Systems (ICDCS), 2013 IEEE 33rd International Conference on, Philadelphia, PA, USA: IEEE, July, pp. 21–30.

[5] Sun, D., Chang, G., Miao, C., & Wang, X. (2013). Analyzing, modeling and evaluating dynamic adaptive fault tolerance strategies in cloud computing environments. The Journal of Supercomputing, 66(1), 193–228.

[6] Bala, A., & Chana, I. (2012). Fault tolerance-challenges, techniques and implementation in cloud computing. International Journal of Computer Science Issues (IJCSI), 9(1), 288.

[7] Ben–Yehuda, O., Schuster, A., Sharov, A., Silberstein, M., & Iosup, A. (2013). ExPERT: Pareto–efficient task replication on grids and a cloud. In IEEE 26th International Parallel & Distributed Processing Symposium (IPDPS), Shanghai, China, 21–25 May 2013, pp. 167–178.

[8] Arockiam, L., & Francis, G. (2012). FTM–A middle layer architecture for fault toler-ance in cloud computing. IJCA Special Issue on Issues and Challenges in Networking, Intelligence and Computing Technologies, ICNIT, No. 2, pp. 12–16.

[9] Palaniammal, P., & Santhosh, R. (2013). Failure prediction for scalable checkpoints in scientific workflows using replication and resubmission task in cloud computing. International Journal of Science, Engineering and Technology Research (IJSETR), 2(4), 985–991.

[10] Zhang, M., Jin, H., Shi, X., & Wu, S. (2010). VirtCFT: A transparent VM–level fault-tolerant system for virtual clusters. In IEEE Proceeding of the 16th International Conference on Parallel and Distributed Systems (ICPADS), 8–10 December 2010, Shanghai, pp. 147–154.

[11] Nguyen, T., & Desideri, J-A. (2012). Resilience issues for application workflows on clouds. In Proceeding of the 8th International Conference on Networking and Services (ICNS2012), March 2012, Sint–Maarten (NL).

[12] Egwutuoha, I., Chen, S., Levy, D., Selic, B., & Calvo, R. (2012). A proactive fault tolerance approach to high performance computing (HPC) in the cloud. In Second International Conference on Cloud and Green Computing (CGC2012), 1–3 November 2012, Xiangtan, pp. 268–273.

[13] Limam, S., & Belalem, G. (2014). A migration approach for fault tolerance in cloud computing. International Journal of Grid and High Performance Computing, 6(2), 24–37, April/June 2014.

[14] Zheng, Z., Zhou, T. C., Lyu, M. R., & King, I. (2012). "Component ranking for fault-tolerant cloud applications," IEEE Transaction on Services Computing, 5(4), 540–550.

Chapter 8

Secured Transactions in Storage Systems for Real-Time Blockchain Network Monitoring Systems

Satish Kumar T., Ashwini N., and A. V. Krishna Mohan

8.1 Introduction

Stream processing plays a significant role within the financial industry due to the enormous sums of information created by monetary exchanges. Stream processing allows financial services [1–3] companies to ingest, process, and analyze this data in real-time to gain insights into their customers' behavior and preferences, identify fraudulent transactions, optimize trading strategies, and make data-driven decisions. Fraud detection, trading analytics, risk management, and customer insights are a few particular use cases of stream processing in the financial services industry [4–6]. By analyzing data from multiple sources, stream processing can provide traders with a comprehensive view of the market. In risk Management systems, Stream processing can be used to monitor and analyze risk factors in real-time. By processing and analyzing data from multiple sources, stream processing can provide a comprehensive view of an organization's risk exposure. Stream processing has become a critical tool for financial services companies to gain real-time insights into their operations, customers, and markets.

Pravega [7, 8] is an open-source distributed storage system designed exclusively for streaming data. It was developed by Dell EMC, and is now it is LF Edge organization under the Linux Foundation. Pravega allows for the storage and processing of

DOI: 10.1201/9781003433293-8

large-scale continuous and unbounded streams of data with strong consistency guarantees, durability, and scalability. It provides features such as data retention policies, automatic scaling, and flexible querying. Pravega is used in various industries such as finance, healthcare, telecommunications, and more, for applications such as real-time analytics, event-driven applications, and IoT data processing. In Pravega, the multiple reader and writer problem can occur when multiple clients or applications attempt to simultaneously read and writes data to the same stream. Primarily, it is designed for high-throughput streaming workloads, it supports concurrent access to streams by multiple readers and writers. As the need for event streaming in financial services are increasing day by day, continuous real-time data integration and processing needs a constant upgradation. Pravega is deployed for various financial services and critical applications, very recently big-data analytics has joined the race.

Blockchain is a distributed technology that allows for secure, transparent, and decentralized transactions [9–12]. It was developed for use in cryptocurrencies such as Bitcoin, but has since been applied to a wide range of industries and applications. A blockchain is a growing collection of documents, or blocks, that are connected together and safeguarded by encryption. Each block includes transaction information, a timestamp, and a cryptographic hash of the one before it. It is incredibly secure and impervious to manipulation since once a block is included in the chain, it cannot be changed without altering all succeeding blocks. One of the key benefits of blockchain is its decentralized nature. Rather than being stored on a single central server or database, the blockchain is stored across a network of computers, each with a copy of the chain. This means that no single entity has control over the data, and transactions can be made directly between individuals without the need for intermediaries such as banks. Blockchain has the potential to revolutionize many industries, from finance and banking to healthcare and supply chain management. It offers increased security, transparency, and efficiency, and has the potential to reduce costs and streamline processes. Blockchain technology relies heavily on consensus algorithms [13] because they let many users in a decentralized network agree on the legitimacy and chronological sequence of transactions.

The work carried out in this research is an attempt to integrate blockchain and Pravega to benefit the banking and other applications by incorporating the features provided by these technologies. Pravega built for scalability and increase high throughput, whereas blockchain guarantees the order and structure of a sequences also provides the security during transactions.

8.2 Related Works

8.2.1 Blockchain

Blockchain technology is used in cloud computing to enhance security, privacy, and efficiency. There are several ways in which blockchain is integrated with cloud computing. Blockchain creates a decentralized storage network that is distributed across multiple nodes, providing greater security and resilience compared to traditional centralized storage systems. Since it lowers the possibility of data breaches and hackers, this may be especially helpful for keeping sensitive data and files on the cloud. Smart contracts can be used in cloud computing to automate tasks, such as data backups and disaster recovery, and to streamline processes, such as payments and invoicing. Blockchain can be used to create a decentralized identity management system, enabling users to control their own identity and personal data. This can enhance security and privacy in cloud computing, as users can control who has access to their data and what information is shared. Blockchain can be used to create a transparent and secure supply chain management system, enabling real-time tracking of goods and reducing the risk of fraud and counterfeiting. This can be particularly useful in cloud-based supply-chain management systems, where multiple parties are involved in the supply chain process.

8.2.2 Blockchain in Stream Processing for Banking Applications

[13–16] Blockchain in stream processing for banking applications combines the benefits of blockchain technology with the real-time data processing capabilities of stream processing. In the context of banking, stream processing refers to the continuous analysis and processing of streaming data, such as customer transactions, account balances, and financial market data. By integrating blockchain with stream processing, banking applications can achieve enhanced security, transparency, and efficiency. Blockchain provides a decentralized and immutable ledger that records and verifies every transaction, ensuring trust and eliminating the need for intermediaries. This enables secure and tamper-resistant recording of financial transactions in real time.

Stream processing allows for the continuous analysis of incoming banking data streams, enabling immediate detection of anomalies, fraud, or suspicious activities. Blockchain technology complements this by providing a trusted and auditable record of these transactions, ensuring the integrity and accuracy of the processed data. Additionally, blockchain in stream processing can streamline and automate various banking processes, such as payment settlements, identity verification, and regulatory compliance. Smart contracts, built on blockchain, can be used to enforce predefined rules and automate complex workflows, reducing the need for manual intervention and improving operational efficiency.

Furthermore, the combination of [17] blockchain and stream processing enables real-time auditing and reporting, allowing banks to have a comprehensive view of their financial operations and comply with regulatory requirements more effectively. Overall, blockchain in stream processing for banking applications offers increased security, transparency, efficiency, and automation. It has the potential to transform traditional banking processes, improve customer experiences, and enable new innovative financial services.

8.2.3 Pravega

Pravega is an open-source, distributed stream storage system designed for continuous and real-time data streaming applications. It provides a scalable and fault-tolerant platform for storing and processing high-volume, high-throughput data streams. Pravega is specifically built to address the unique requirements of streaming workloads, such as event-driven architectures, real-time analytics, and data-intensive applications.

The primary features of Pravega are its ability to handle unbounded data streams, which can be generated from various sources like IoT devices, social media feeds, financial transactions, or sensor data. Pravega offers durable storage and allows for both sequential and random access to the data streams, enabling efficient processing and analysis. Pravega provides strong consistency guarantees, ensuring that data is accurately and reliably processed across distributed systems.

Another notable feature of Pravega is its support for stream scaling and elasticity. It allows for dynamic addition or removal of stream processing resources based on the workload demands, enabling efficient utilization of resources and accommodating varying data ingestion rates. Pravega also offers advanced stream processing capabilities, such as support for exactly once processing semantics, automatic stream rollups for time-based aggregation, and integration with popular stream processing frameworks like Apache Flink and Apache Spark. Recently, [18] attempts to bundle blockchain technology with Apache Kafka to build robust financial system across cloud. The research carried out in this work is an attempt to integrate blockchain with Pravega.

8.3 Integrating Blockchain into Pravega

Pravega is able to process enormous amounts of data in real-time, making it the perfect platform for applications that need fast throughput and low latency. Blockchain technology can be used with Pravega to provide enhanced security and privacy for streaming data. One way that blockchain can be integrated with Pravega is by using blockchain as a secure ledger to record all transactions and data exchanges in the Pravega system. Each Pravega message is hashed and added to the blockchain, providing a secure and tamper-proof record of all data transactions. This can be particularly useful in applications where data privacy and security are critical, such as financial transactions or healthcare data.

Another way that blockchain shall be used with Pravega is through the creation of smart contracts. They can be deployed on a blockchain network, enabling

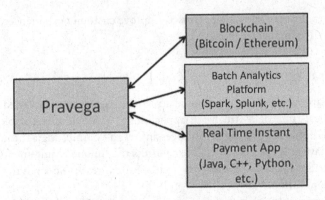

Figure 8.1 Pravega and blockchain.

automated and secure execution of transactions between parties. Smart contracts are used with Pravega to automate tasks, such as data backups and disaster recovery, and to streamline processes, such as payments and invoicing. The integration of blockchain with Pravega can provide enhanced security, privacy, and efficiency for streaming data applications. However, there are still challenges to be addressed, such as scalability and interoperability, before blockchain-based Pravega systems can be widely adopted. Figure 8.1 shows the build-up of Pravega and blockchain.

A fantastic (but extremely difficult) blockchain solution is Hyperledger Fabric, which is powered by Pravega. 'Consensus algorithm' is what you could know as 'ordering' on Hyperledger Fabric, which is a blockchain. It ensures the legitimacy of transactions.

There are several similarities between Pravega and Hyperledger Fabric. As a result, this pairing makes sense. A fault-tolerant, very scalable, and effective architecture is made possible by using Pravega for transaction ordering.

The architecture diagram representing the **Pravega and blockchain for banking application** in Figure 8.2, consists of several components, each of which performs a specific function. The primary components are Pravega, blockchain, and the banking application. Pravega serves as a messaging platform for the banking application, allowing multiple producers to write messages and multiple consumers to read those messages. The producers can include applications that generate events, such as user transactions, and the consumers can include applications that process those events, such as fraud detection and risk analysis. Blockchain serves as a distributed ledger to store all the transaction records securely. The blockchain can be permissioned or public, depending on the specific use case and regulatory requirements. In the case of a permissioned blockchain, only authorized parties can access the network, while in a public blockchain, anyone can join and participate in the network. The banking application is responsible for managing user accounts, handling transactions, and interacting with the Pravega and blockchain components.

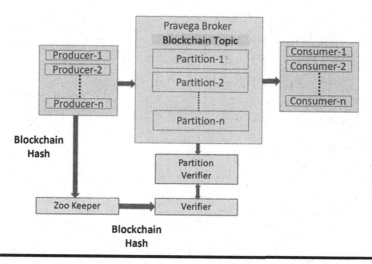

Figure 8.2 Architectural diagram: Pravega and blockchain for banking application (courtesy: www.kai-waehner.de).

The application receives user events from Pravega and writes them to the blockchain for secure storage. The application also reads data from the blockchain to retrieve transaction history and account balances. The diagram shows multiple producers and consumers connected to Pravega, which is responsible for collecting user events and writing them to the blockchain. The blockchain component stores all the transaction records securely, and the banking application interacts with the blockchain and Pravega to manage user accounts and transactions.

The data ingestion and processing is shown in Figure 8.3, the multiple applications act as producers and generate events, such as user transactions or account changes. For example, an ATM machine or a mobile banking app could act as a producer to send transaction events to Pravega. It acts as a messaging platform and collects all the events generated by the producers. Pravega is distributed and scalable, allowing multiple producers and consumers to connect and interact with the messaging system. Further, Pravega organizes messages into topics, which represent a particular stream of data. For example, the transaction events could be stored in a "Transaction" topic, while account changes could be stored in an "Account" topic. Data is transferred between Pravega and other systems using the connectors. The blockchain nodes can be run by different organizations, such as banks or financial institutions, and each node can maintain a copy of the ledger. A consensus protocol is used to ensure that all nodes agree about the status of the blockchain. Different consensus protocols can be used, depending on the specific use case and requirements. Smart contracts can be used to define the rules and logic for specific transactions. For example, a smart contract could be used to define the rules for a loan agreement. The banking application is responsible for managing user accounts,

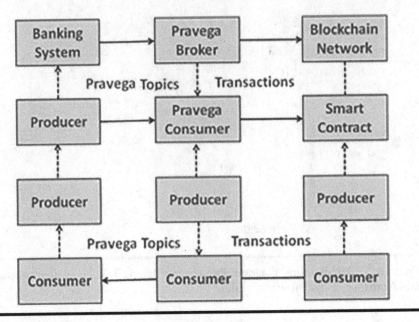

Figure 8.3 Data ingestion and processing.

handling transactions, and interacting with Pravega and the blockchain. The combination of Pravega and blockchain provides a scalable, secure, and reliable architecture for banking applications with multiple producers and consumers.

8.3.1 Role of Blockchain in Pravega for Online Bank Transactions

The role of blockchain in Pravega for online bank transactions can be critical in ensuring secure and reliable transactions for customers and financial institutions. One of the main advantages of using blockchain with Pravega for online banking is the ability to maintain data integrity and security. A safe and impenetrable record of every transaction may be provided by the blockchain ledger, which can be validated by all parties engaged in the transaction. This can help in preventing fraud, cyber-attacks, and other security threats.

Another important role of blockchain in Pravega for online bank transactions is the capability to create a decentralized and trustless environment. As a result, it is possible to execute online transactions without the use of middlemen or reliable third parties, which can lower transaction costs and increase system efficiency.

Blockchaining in Pravega for online bank transactions has a number of benefits. Online banking transactions may be made safer by combining Pravega with the blockchain. The blockchain technology can provide a tamper-proof and transparent record of all transactions, which can be verified by all parties involved in the transaction. This can help in preventing fraud, cyber-attacks, and other security threats.

8.3.2 Modeling Blockchain in Pravega

The steps mentioned here provide a general outline of some mathematical concepts and equations that are commonly used in blockchain and Pravega systems:

1. Consensus Algorithm:
   - For Proof of Work (PoW), the equation for mining a block can be represented as:
     - Find a Nonce (n) that, when combined with other block data (D), results in a hash (H) with a specific number of leading zeros: $H = SHA256 (n + D)$.
   - For Proof of Stake (PoS), the equation for selecting a block validator can be based on a participant's stake (S):
     - Probability of being selected as a validator = S/Total stake in the network.
2. Data Structures:
   - Block Hash Calculation:
     - $H = SHA256(Block\_Header)$, where Block_Header includes the previous block hash, transaction data, timestamp, and other relevant block information:
   - Merkle Tree Calculation:
     - Calculate the hash of each transaction, then pair and hash those hashes until a single Merkle root hash is obtained.
3. Communication Protocol:
   - Pravega Message Ordering:
     - Assign a sequence number or timestamp to each message to ensure correct ordering during replication and consumption.
4. Security and Cryptography:
   - Digital Signature Verification:
     - Use the sender's public key (PubKey) and the message's hash (H) to validate a digital signature (Sig): Verify (Sig, PubKey, H).
   - Hash Function:
     - $H = SHA256(Data)$, where Data represents the input data to be hashed.

These steps provide a simplified representation of certain concepts and operations in blockchain and Pravega. The actual implementation and equations can vary depending on the specific blockchain and Pravega frameworks being used. Additionally, more complex equations and algorithms may be involved depending on the specific requirements and cryptographic techniques employed in the system.

8.4 Consensus Algorithm in Blockchain

The consensus algorithm playing a pivotal role in ensuring the integrity, security, and trustworthiness of the distributed network. With no central authority, the consensus approach lets users to collectively vote on the legitimacy and order of transactions in a decentralized environment. Decentralization is a crucial component of the consensus algorithm. By allowing multiple participants to validate and agree on transactions, consensus algorithms eliminate the need for intermediaries or central authorities, promoting a transparent and trustless environment. This decentralization ensures that no single entity has control over the network, preventing censorship, manipulation, or single points of failure. Security is another critical aspect that consensus algorithms address. By reaching a consensus on the validity of transactions, the algorithm prevents fraudulent activities such as double-spending or tampering with transaction records. The algorithm makes sure that only legitimate transactions are put to the blockchain, producing an immutable and tamper-evident record, using cryptographic techniques and consensus procedures. PoW is the most well-known consensus algorithm, popularized by Bitcoin. It requires participants, known as miners, to solve complex mathematical puzzles to validate transactions and create new blocks. Proof of Stake (PoS) is an alternative to PoW that selects validators based on their stake or ownership of cryptocurrency. Validators are chosen to create new blocks and validate transactions based on their stake, eliminating the need for energy-intensive mining. Delegated Proof of Stake (DPoS) is a strategy were in the participants elect a group of delegates who are in charge of verifying transactions and constructing blocks. DPoS combines the benefits of PoS with faster transaction confirmations and scalability. Practical Byzantine Fault Tolerance (PBFT) is a consensus algorithm designed for permissioned Blockchain networks. It requires a predetermined set of validators to reach agreement on transactions through a series of rounds of voting. Raft, again is a consensus algorithm used for fault-tolerant distributed systems, including some blockchain implementations. It elects a leader to manage the consensus process and replicate logs across nodes. Proof of Authority (PoA), here in this algorithm the authorities are a group of authorized validators who are in charge of approving transactions and building blocks in PoA. Validators are selected based on their reputation or identity, providing fast transaction processing but with limited decentralization. Each algorithm has its own trade-offs in terms of security, scalability, decentralization, energy efficiency, and suitability for different blockchain use cases. The unique needs and objectives of the blockchain network determine the consensus algorithm to be used.

8.5 Experimental Evaluation and Metrics Evaluation

The hardware platform on which the experiment was conducted is a workstation equipped Intel(R) Core(TM) i7–10510U CPU @ 1.80GHz 2.30 GHz, 32GB RAM and 256GB SSD. The software platforms were Ubuntu 20.04 LTS. We created a container for Pravega and constructed four topologies that process each data of private network. The comparison data is based on blockchain.

When referring to a blockchain, the term "latency" describes the amount of time it takes for a transaction or activity to be completed and verified on the network. It is a vital measure that affects how effective and quick blockchain systems are. Blockchain networks are intended to be decentralized, which means that before a transaction can be added to the blockchain, it must first be approved by a number of network nodes. This validation procedure adds latency and requires time. The specific latency experienced in a blockchain system can be influenced by factors such as network communication, consensus mechanisms, block size and time, smart contract execution, and scalability. Minimizing latency is a key goal in blockchain development, as faster transaction processing enables quicker and more seamless interactions on the network. Various optimization techniques and improvements are being explored to reduce latency, such as implementing faster consensus algorithms, optimizing network protocols, and enhancing scalability. By addressing latency concerns, blockchain technology can become more effective and helpful for real-world applications that require swift and reliable transaction processing.

Throughput in blockchain refers to the measure of the number of transactions or operations that can be processed within a given time frame. It represents the system's capacity to handle and execute transactions efficiently. Blockchain networks aim to achieve high throughput to accommodate a large volume of transactions and support scalability. However, the throughput of a blockchain system can be influenced by various factors. These include the consensus algorithm used, network bandwidth, block size, block time, and the complexity of the transactions or smart contracts being executed. Some consensus algorithms, such as PoW, may have lower throughput due to the computational requirements for mining new blocks. On the other hand, consensus mechanisms like PoS or DPoS can offer higher throughput as they do not rely on intensive mining computations. Improving the throughput of a blockchain system often involves optimizing these factors and exploring techniques such as sharding, parallel processing, or off-chain scaling solutions. Enhancing throughput enables blockchain networks to handle a greater number of transactions, making them more suitable for applications requiring high transaction processing capabilities. Figure 8.4, shows the graph presenting the comparison of five consensus algorithm. It is clearly evident that DPoS out performs the rest of the algorithms in the system.

It's vital to note that several factors, including as the hardware infrastructure, network circumstances, system setup, and the complexity of the processing logic provided by the clients, can affect both throughput and latency in Pravega. In a Pravega implementation, optimizing these variables and the system configuration can assist increase throughput and decrease latency. The loss in throughput and increase in latency with blockchain incorporation with Pravega are clearly seen in both graphs, Figures 8.5 and 8.6.

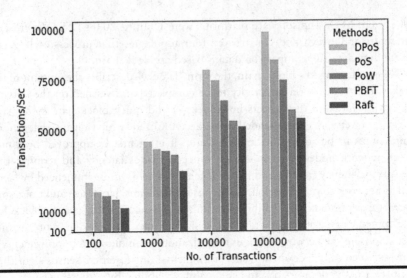

Figure 8.4   Throughput of different consensus algorithms.

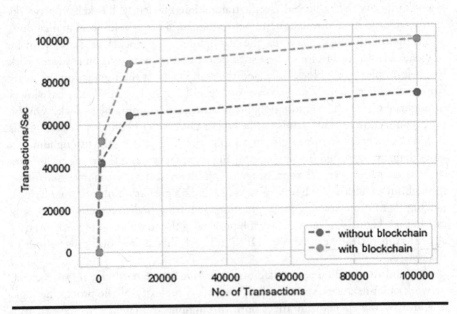

Figure 8.5   Average throughput of with and without blockchain.

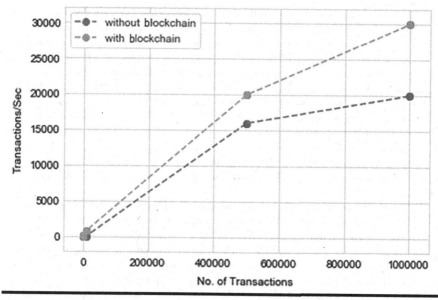

Figure 8.6   Average latency with and without blockchain.

8.6 Conclusion and Future Work

By offering a decentralized and secure platform for transactions and data sharing, blockchain technology has the potential to revolutionize a number of businesses and sectors. In conclusion, combining blockchain technology in Pravega brings several benefits and considerations. The integration of blockchain with Pravega, a stream storage system, offers enhanced security, immutability, and decentralized data management capabilities. Pravega's integration with blockchain technology will benefit all of the company's bespoke business applications, such as CRM and big data analytics. Further, utilizing blockchain will provide safe communication across different organizations.

Overall, combining blockchain technology in Pravega holds promise for applications requiring secure, auditable, and decentralized data management. However, careful analysis, planning, and implementation are essential to maximize the benefits and address the considerations specific to the use case at hand.

References

[1] Gedik, Bugra, et al. "SPADE: The System S declarative stream processing engine." *Proceedings of the 2008 ACM SIGMOD International Conference on Management of Data.* Association for Computing Machinery, 2008.

[2] Hwang, J-H., et al. "High-availability algorithms for distributed stream processing." *21st International Conference on Data Engineering (ICDE'05)*. IEEE, 2005.

[3] Sahal, Radhya, John G. Breslin, and Muhammad Intizar Ali. "Big data and stream processing platforms for Industry 4.0 requirements mapping for a predictive maintenance use case." *Journal of Manufacturing Systems* 54 (2020): 138–151.

[4] Omair, Badr, and Ahmad Alturki. "Taxonomy of fraud detection metrics for business processes." *IEEE Access* 8 (2020): 71364–71377.

[5] Aral, Atakan, Melike Erol-Kantarci, and Ivona Brandić. "Staleness control for edge data analytics." *Proceedings of the ACM on Measurement and Analysis of Computing Systems* 4.2 (2020): 1–24.

[6] Shakya, Subarna, and Smys Smys. "Big data analytics for improved risk management and customer segregation in banking applications." *Journal of ISMAC* 3.3 (2021): 235–249.

[7] Sanjay Kumar, N. V., and Keshava Munegowda. "Distributed streaming storage performance benchmarking: Kafka and Pravega." *International Journal of Innovative Technology and Exploring (IJITEE)* 9 (2019).

[8] Munegowda, Keshava, and N. V. Sanjay Kumar. "Design and implementation of storage benchmark kit." *Emerging Research in Computing, Information, Communication and Applications: ERCICA 2020, Volume 2*. Singapore: Springer Singapore, 2021.45–62.

[9] Chang, Shuchih E., and Yichian Chen. "When Blockchain meets supply chain: A systematic literature review on current development and potential applications." *IEEE Access* 8 (2020): 62478–62494.

[10] Cao, Bin, et al. "When internet of things meets blockchain: Challenges in distributed consensus." *IEEE Network* 33.6 (2019): 133–139.

[11] Schmitz, Jana, and Giulia Leoni. "Accounting and auditing at the time of Blockchain technology: a research agenda." *Australian Accounting Review* 29.2 (2019): 331–342.

[12] Li, Jennifer, and Mohamad Kassem. "Applications of distributed ledger technology (DLT) and Blockchain-enabled smart contracts in construction." *Automation in Construction* 132 (2021): 103955.

[13] Zhang, Shijie, and Jong-Hyouk Lee. "Analysis of the main consensus protocols of Blockchain." *ICT Express* 6.2 (2020): 93–97.

[14] Baiod, Wajde, Janet Light, and Aniket Mahanti. "Blockchain technology and its applications across multiple domains: A survey." *Journal of International Technology and Information Management* 29.4 (2021): 78–119.

[15] Patki, Aarti, and Vinod Sople. "Indian banking sector: Blockchain implementation, challenges and way forward." *Journal of Banking and Financial Technology* 4.1 (2020): 65–73.

[16] Raddatz, Nirmalee, et al. "Becoming a blockchain user: understanding consumers' benefits realisation to use Blockchain-based applications." *European Journal of Information Systems* 32.2 (2023): 287–314.

[17] Han, Hongdan, et al. "Accounting and auditing with Blockchain technology and artificial Intelligence: A literature review." *International Journal of Accounting Information Systems* 48 (2023): 100598.

[18] www.kai-waehner.de/blog/2020/07/17/apache-kafka-Blockchain-dlt-comparison-kafka-native-vs-hyperledger-ethereum-ripple-iota-libra/

Chapter 9

Service Scaling and Cost-Prediction-Based Optimization in Cloud Computing

Punit Gupta, Sanjit Bhagat, and Dinesh Kumar Saini

9.1 Introduction

A cloud system provides on demand, pay-per-use services from and individual to a large organization without any need of physical existence at their end. It's a 24/7 seven service that can scale the services according to the user requirements. In today's world, the cloud needs no introduction, as most of the data has moved and moving onto the cloud. With increasing numbers of data service providers and service holders, managing the data and maintaining the quality of services is quite challenging. A service can be software specific or platform specific, or a complete infrastructure can be given as a service. Scalability of service is an important factor to consider for the quality of service (QoS) and cost as providing resources according to the user requirement maintains QoS and optimizes the cost for both user and service provider. Scaling of resources/services can be vertical or horizontal: a vertical scale upgrades the current system with more power or reduces the existing power (a horizontal scaling is bound to the capacity of server) while horizontal scaling adds more resources to the existing service, like adding more servers to transfer loads for balancing. Scaling up and down services at proper time and according to the user requirement is very challenging with this large amount of data and large number of users.

DOI: 10.1201/9781003433293-9

Sometimes users may require more resources and sometime less resources. Thus, to determine the right amount of memory, processing, storage, and scaling (Up/Down), we must consider factors like CPU load, memory usage, response time, number of requests, etc. It is quite difficult for and individual to keep a record of these factors and act accordingly. There are various machine learning models available for the prediction to manage cloud scaling. In this chapter we are going to discuss service scaling and cost prediction models for better optimization in cloud services.

9.1.1 What is the Cloud?

Cloud computing is a scalable on demand service mechanism works on pay-as-you-go terminology. Resources are always available online so it is usable 24/7. Cloud technology is categorized according to the use and the services it provides, which is discussed later. Cloud growth is evolutionary as most of the organizations are moving onto the cloud and this number is expected to increase in upcoming years. With moving onto the cloud, complexities are also increasing like migration issues, proper resource utilization, and security risks. So, it is also a big challenge for the service providers to maintain service-level agreements (SLA) while providing QoS.

The resources provided by the cloud are on demand and can be scaled up and down. Users only need to pay for only the resources being used. The infrastructure services are managed by provider while user can install, configure and manage its all the software.

9.2 Service Scaling in the Cloud

Scalability is the ability to increase resources to manage the resource according to the change in demand. Resource scalability is the primary component of cloud

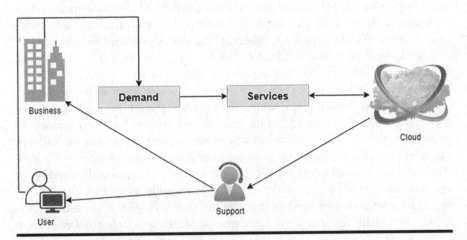

Figure 9.1 Cloud computing model.

services. In cloud computing infrastructure data storage, services, networks, processor etc., can be scaled up/down. Scaling can be horizontal, vertical, or diagonal. Nowadays there are well built infrastructure by cloud service providers to scale resources which took weeks to scale on premise physical structure. Scalability is the core reason to migrate to the cloud. Sudden increase and decrease in the demand in terms of traffic or workload, cloud provides cost efficient and quick solutions to the businesses. (Figure 9.2).

Cloud scalability with this ease is only possible by virtualization [virtualization is a mechanism that creates a virtual environment to represent resources (i.e., Storage, Network, Server etc.) on a single domain]. Owning a physical server comes with the need of good experience to manage and scale the servers when required. On the other hand, virtual machines are very flexible, easily scalable, and can be moved onto different servers or can be hosted on multiple servers. It is easy to shift services on large VMs. Most of the service providers already have their hardware and software resources installed in a manner that can easily scale up or

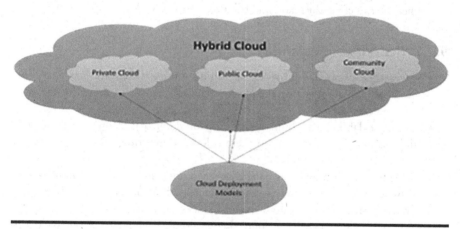

Figure 9.2 Cloud computing hybrid model

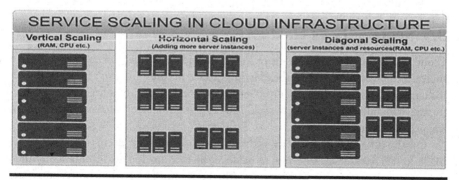

Figure 9.3 Service scaling in cloud infrastructure.

down according the business needs. Cloud scalability services are also important because it's not possible for a single business to scale up/down so easily and in a cost-efficient manner.

- **Horizontal Scaling:** Horizontal scaling allows us to connect multiple servers together. Increase in server helps to maintain workload balancing in multiple servers. This method is complex to implement and time taking process, so down time may be higher in comparison of vertical scaling. We can handle multiple workloads and large traffic in easy and efficient manner.
- **Vertical Scaling:** Vertical scaling binds the user within a single server. We can increase resources (i.e., memory, storage etc.) within the limit/capacity of the server. Scaling within a single server is quite easy and quick if we do not exceed the maximum capacity of the server. Scaling in a single server helps to reduce latency and extra management.
- **Diagonal Scaling:** Diagonal scaling is the hybrid modal of horizontal and vertical scaling. In this method if we exceed the limit of vertical scaling (single server), then we can clone the server and balance workload within multiple servers.

9.2.1 Benefits of Scalability

- Saves time of service provider, as adding more services are just few clicks away, instead of setting up the physical environment to increase the hardware resources.
- Cloud scalability can quickly scale up or down based on the demand of the business or individual. So there is lower down time and better resource utilization.
- Scalability is cost saving as businesses need not purchase the equipment (that may become outdated in few years) to increase the power/speed of the organization; instead pay-as-you-go service reduces the cost and waste of resources.
- With the help of a scalable cloud, there is no requirement of secondary maintenance of data, thus reducing the recovery costs.

9.3 Scalability vs Elasticity

Cloud scalability is different from cloud elasticity. Namely, it is the ability to increase the workload size in the existing infrastructure. It doesn't impact the performance. Cloud scalability is pre-planned with extra resources for future requirements. Scalability can scale up or scale out to prevent lack of resources to maintain the performance.

On the other hand, elasticity is the ability to increase or decrease the resources of cloud infrastructure as needed to balance the workload in an automatic manner, thus maximizing resource utilization. All the resources (i.e., hardware, software,

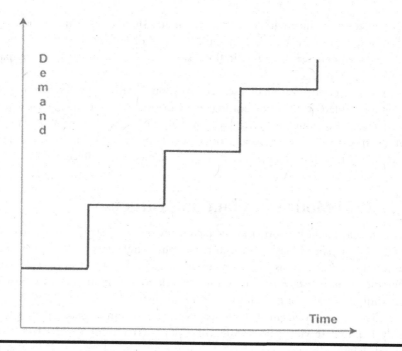

Figure 9.4   Cloud scalability.

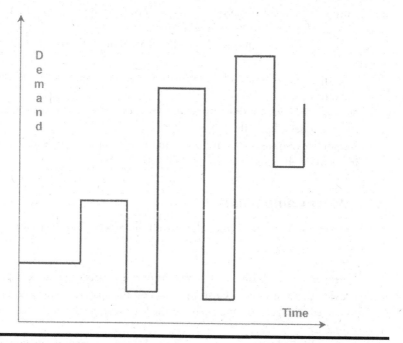

Figure 9.5   Cloud elasticity.

QoS, policies, connectivity, and other resources) should be elastic for elasticity services. The performance of certain application totally depends on the environment. Elasticity is more useful in public cloud services where a system works on pay-per-use or pay-as-you-go.

For better optimization of resources and cloud scaling, the service provider must monitor the factors affecting scaling, such as response time, memory usage, CPU load, etc. So horizontal or vertical scaling can be managed accordingly. Automation of scaling can reduce the workload of the service provider. It can determine a threshold point where scaling takes place, so performance is not affected.

9.4 Cost Models in Cloud Infrastructure

Cost management is another prime factor in cloud infrastructure. Almost 50% of organizations spend more than required amount only based on their guess on cloud expenditure. Guess basis services increase the cost on metered services due to either overuse or underuse of resources. Effective cloud cost management is required to maximize the value of money and minimum cost.

Cloud cost management is the concept of managing cloud expenses by using only required services and eliminating unnecessary resources used as a part of cloud. Cloud cost management helps in the analysis of memory, storage, traffic, servers etc., to find optimal economical models for a business. Cost management can be used to increase the productivity of businesses and reduce financial overhead, as well as unnecessary resource/features.

Cost management strategies may include different methods, such as:

- Selecting the right size of cloud instance that is economical and suitable for the business.
- Managing power by shutting down unnecessary resources or shutting down the resources when idle.
- Removing resources that are not being used, as that may lead to an increase in cost as well as security vulnerabilities.

9.4.1 Main Components

There are three major factors to compute overall costs of cloud computing services. These are:

1. **Storage:** Storage is one of the most important parts of cloud services. Clouds provide this as a service. Customers pay on the basis of storage utilization. For managed storage, customers pay for the total storage allotted instead of storage utilized.
2. **Networking:** Networking charges are different according the volume of data transfer. Ingress is transferring data into the cloud and egress is transferring

data out of the cloud. VPN, load balancers, and special gateways entail additional charges for the customers.

3. **Computing:** There is a range of computing services for customers. Every resource has some type of CPU, memory, or hardware. Customers pay according to the utilization of these resources, in terms of number of instances and duration of use.

9.4.2 Cloud Cost vs Traditional Cost

Cloud systems have advantages over maintaining infrastructure on premises (Traditional Approach). On premises infrastructure includes:

- **Capital Cost:** It includes infrastructural development cost of physical/virtual resources such as software, hardware, network, storage environments, and backup.
- **Operational Cost:** Includes maintaining the hardware and operating software, as well as support to the infrastructure and manpower training costs, etc.
- **Indirect Business Cost:** It includes unexpected downtime and recovery of the infrastructure.

9.4.3 Cloud Cost Includes

- **Direct Cost:** It is easy to estimate and calculate as it includes hardware, software, and all other physical resource facilities. It is a straightforward cost so it is easy to estimate.
- **Indirect Cost:** It includes all the indirect costs such as loss of customer trust due to migration onto the cloud, server downtime etc. These costs are difficult to estimate and predict.

There are various cost models available in cloud infrastructure; these models are dynamic in nature as different user groups have different requirements. There are three major approaches for cloud pricing model: the value-based pricing model based on the demand by user, cost-based model based on supply of resources, and market-based model, which is based on supply and demand.

- **Service-Based Model:** This product-oriented pricing model focuses on value delivery for the client, and service can be measured in levels, per device, customer, and priority. The cost of the service is predefined without any current market survey. Cost is based on the production cost.

Service based cost model may include software services, hardware services, personnels to install and operate these hardware and software or other external services

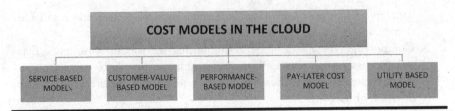

Figure 9.6 Cloud cost-based service models.

Figure 9.7 Service-based model different stages.

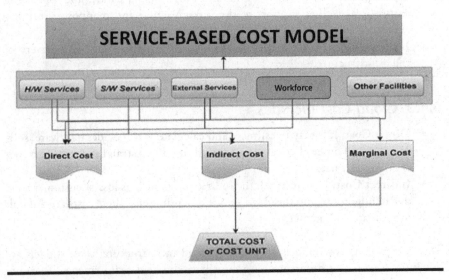

Figure 9.8 Service-based cost model.

with facilities. This pricing model includes direct cost, indirect cost and marginal cost for other facilities and extra services. We can calculate overall cost and performance of this model.

- **Customer-Value-Based Pricing Model:** This model optimizes profit and market share for the business. This model considers perception, sociology, economics, and utility.

Figure 9.9 Customer-based model, different stages.

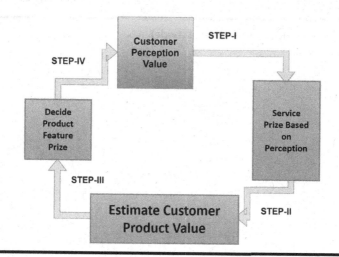

Figure 9.10 Customer-based model, different stages.

Businesses first estimate the price customers are willing to pay and propose the price in the market for survey. After customer feedback (how much they are willing to pay) is received, the price of product is decided. In the next step customer value for the product is checked. Then the price for the differentiated feature of product is decided. This model charges for the product and services primarily based on customer perception and secondarily on production cost.

- **Performance-Based Cost Model:** According to M. McNair's definition, "it is a contract in which the seller is compensated based on the exact performance of a cloud service or model. It's linked to the business results of a client, which is based on certain performance criteria." In this model the provider is paid according to the actual performance of the cloud model.

The performance-based model does not include any predefined package for consumer, so there is no feature limitation. It's easy to access full featured services with a low budget. There is more testing and integration timing with services provided under this strategy. You can scale up and down or stop services anytime you want.

- **Utility-Based Service Model:** These are metered price models where services are monitored and paid for as necessary. Customers demand cloud models

Figure 9.11 **Performance-based cost model.**

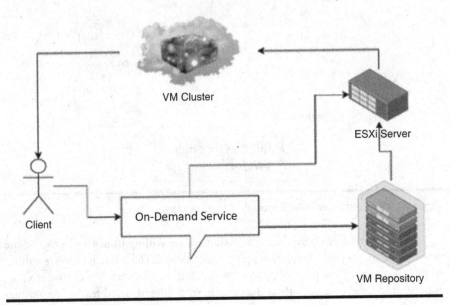

Figure 9.12 **Utility-based service model.**

and reject outdated hardware-based pricing. Several benefits are provided to the user to draw their attention. Computing resources, infrastructure management, and technical services available to the customers on demand. It helps to maximize resource utilization while minimizing the cost. It is a more flexible and cost-cutting service model as personal interaction is very low. That said, data security is a major issue in this service model.

- **Free upfront and pay later cost model:** some service providers provide free upfront and pay later services to promote their product. These services draw attention from new clients and generate revenue from premium clients. In this strategy customers have the ability to pay for services later in fixed installments. It is more suitable for the customers who don't have enough to pay; the businesses accepting buy now, pay later services have almost 30% uplift in sales volume. As the financer is a third party, you receive full payment with a minor fee. There is no risk of fraud. This method reaches more customers and provides a better customer experience.

Though cost and scaling are major factors affecting cloud services, there are various strategies available for better optimization, but it is a challenging task to implement these strategies in a real-world scenario. Automation made the task a little easier as there is no need to monitor everything on a daily basis. In the next section we are going to discuss existing work to date on this subject.

9.7 Related Work

Cloud computing systems have evolved very quickly. Innovation in AI and ML has improved the efficiency and QoS of the cloud system. Though we have not yet achieved a fully optimized cloud system, we have gone so far in different fields of cloud (i.e., Cost, Scaling, Resource, Energy, etc.) optimization. In this section we discuss the scaling and cost-based research to date.

Qian, H. et al.[1] proposed a model to optimize operational cost over dynamic time duration. They considered that the demand can be changed during any time duration, thus turning off/on data centres according to the demand. The proposed method was able to reduce operational costs in comparison to static capacity allocations. This experiment was on a small dataset but can be applied on large-scale datasets with heuristic algorithms.

Shahidinejad, A. et al.[2] proposed hybrid ICA-K-Means to cluster the workload according to the QoS. They have performed their work under NASA and FIFA real workload traces. In their experiment there was a significant amount of improvement in terms of cost, CPU utilization, response time, and elasticity.

Buyya, R. et al.[3] proposed a resource management framework SCOOTER that has the ability to manage resources automatically. This framework can self-heal, self-optimize, and minimize execution cost and execution time. It performs better than other existing autonomic resource management techniques.

Patel, E. et al.[4] worked on pCNN-LSTM, a hybrid approach to predict CPU utilization at multiple consecutive times. It was able to learn different CPU loads at different scales. This model achieved up to 16% improvement in load prediction over other existing techniques.

Xu, M. et al.[5] found an *e*fficient supervised learning-based *D*eep *N*eural Network (*esDNN*) approach to predict workload balance on the cloud. The experiments were conducted on realistic data from Google data centres. It was able to predict accurately with the least mean square error. This method was able to reduce the active hosts, thus optimizing the overall cost.

Saxena, D. et al.[6] proposed the novel Online virtual machine Failure Prediction and Tolerance Model (OFP-TM). This model could predict vulnerable VMs so necessary actions could be taken before failure. It monitored power usage and resource usage to predict the failure in advance. A failure unit decides the faulty VMs and allocates tasks to new servers. This approach was able to maximize service availability and minimize performance degradation.

Gupta, P. et al.[7] proposed the ANN based BB-BC model to predict a cost-efficient solution in a constant time. The proposed model tends to achieve better resource scheduling with optimized cloud costs within optimal cloud resources under overload and underload conditions.

Nabi, S. et al.[8] proposed a modified and adaptive PSO-based resource-and deadline-aware dynamic load-balanced (PSO-RDAL) algorithm. It was designed to achieve optimal solution for workload with lower time and cost. The overall experimental results accuracy was 89% in terms of resource utilization, response time, and total execution time.

Hosseini Shirvani, M. et al.[9] presented a hybrid bi-objective optimization based on simulated annealing and task duplication algorithm (BOSA-TDA). This approach resulted in 18.5% average improvement in comparison to other approaches considering the cost, speed up, SLR, and efficiency matrix as parameters.

Manikandan, N. et al.[10] proposed a Whale optimization (WOA)-based bee algorithm. It is a hybrid approach where whale optimization is enhanced by bee's algorithm. The algorithm was able to optimize execution time, resource utilization, and computational cost. This algorithm converged faster than other approaches for large-scale scheduling problems.

Mangalampalli, S. et al.[11] introduced a cat swarm optimization algorithm for task scheduling. Parameters considered for evaluation were migration time, energy consumption, and total power cost at data centres. This approach was able to improve the performance 20% more than other existing approaches.

Imene, L. et al.[12] proposed a non-dominated sorting genetic algorithm (NSGA-III) for improved task execution and resource optimization. NSGA-III outperformed the existing nondominated algorithms in terms of execution time, power consumption, and cost.

Yu, D. et al.[13] proposed a hybrid fog and cloud environment and presented a live environment to migrate on VM with effective load balancing. Their algorithm was almost 20% more cost effective than other existing approaches.

Askarizade Haghighi, M. et al.[14] proposed a KMGA approach to reducing the power consumption while improving the resource utilization. A micro genetic algorithm was used to reduce power consumption and k-means cluster for better resource allocation. This approach was able to achieve its goals while maintaining SLA.

Gill, S. S. et al.[15] proposed a cuckoo optimization-based energy-reliability aware resource scheduling technique (CRUZE) to optimize all the cloud resources including networks, servers, storage, and other resources. It reduced the power consumption by 21% and lowered cost while maintaining the QoS.

Shahidinejad, A. et al. [16] introduced the hybrid Imperialist Competition Algorithm (ICA) and K-means algorithm to reduce the overall cost by optimizing the resource and CPU utilization. This approach reduced overall costs up to 7% and increased response time up to 7%, compared to other existing approaches.

Sanaj, M. S. et al. [17] proposed a chaotic squirrel search algorithm (CSSA) to provide cost-effective multi-task scheduling in Infrastructure as a Service environments. It was more effective for optimal multi-task scheduling while minimizing the overall cost of the infrastructure.

Ma, X. et al.[18] introduced a deadline and cost-aware algorithm to minimize the executional cost. Tasks were divided into different levels according to the structure. Strings were used to code the genes and HEFT was used to generate individual with minimum completion time and cost. Finally, novel approaches were used for crossover and mutation. This approach was able to reduce overall cost and time.

Prem Jacob, T. et al. [19] combined cuckoo search (CS) and Particle swarm optimization (PSO) To reduce deadline violation and the cost of the system. The experiment was performed on a CloudSim toolkit and it was able to outperform PBACO, ACO, MIN-MIN, and FCFS.

Zhang, C. et al.[20] proposed a Model Ark (Mark) system to maintain SLA with better cost effectiveness. To achieve this, they first dynamically created batches of requests, and served them to the hardware to reduce cost ratio. In the next step they used predictive autoscaling to reduce the cost and delay. This system was able to achieve better latency performance in comparison of other existing approaches.

Mapetu, J. P. B. et al.[21] proposed Binary Particle Swarm Optimization to lower the time complexity and cost while task scheduling and load balancing. It is a realistic approach which achieved task scheduling and load balancing better than existing heuristic and metaheuristic algorithms.

9.8 Summary

In this chapter we have discussed various cloud scaling approaches and the difference between scaling and elasticity. Scaling is a progressive process where resources can only be scaled up to the server (vertical) or out of the server (horizontal) or both, but in increasing order only. In elasticity, resources can be scaled up or down according to a pay-as-you-go concept. It is more suitable for public cloud services. Scalability and elasticity are prime components of a cost-efficient cloud system with proper resource utilization. We then discussed various cost management techniques to optimize overall cost for the user as well as for the service providers. Every cost

Table 9.1 Comparative Study of Related Work

S. No	Objective	Technique	Achievements	Remark
1	To reduce operational cost in limited time durations.	Metaheuristic Optimization Model	Overall cost reduction over dynamic time duration and demand.	Experiment was performed on a small dataset, so it is questionable over a large dataset.
2	To maintain SLA, cost, CPU utilization, and elasticity.	Hybrid ICA-K-Means Approach	Improvement in terms of cost, CPU utilization, response time, and elasticity.	Energy efficiency; overall power consumption is still a challenge.
3	To achieve automatic resource management.	Resource Management Framework SCOOTER	This framework can self-heal, self-optimize, and minimize execution cost and execution time.	Power efficiency is considerable.
4	To obtain CPU utilization at multiple consecutive times.	pCNN-LSTM, a hybrid prediction approach	It was able to learn different CPU loads at different scales.	Cost and resource utilization can be improved.
5	To predict workload balance on cloud.	Efficient Supervised Learning-Based *Deep* Neural Network (es*DNN*) Approach	Reduced active hosts to optimize overall cost.	Other factors for cost and resource optimization can be considered.

6	To maximize service availability by predicting task failure.	A novel Online Virtual Machine Failure Prediction and Tolerance Model (OFP-TM)	Able to predict failure in advance, hence maximizes service availability and minimizes performance degradation.	Accuracy can be improvised with other parameters.
7	To achieve better resource scheduling with optimized cost.	ANN-based BB-BC Model	It was able to perform optimally under overload and underload conditions.	Energy efficiency may be considered.
8	To achieve optimal solutions for workload with lower time and cost.	PSO-based Resource- and Deadline-Aware Dynamic Load-Balanced (PSO-RDAL) Algorithm.	Improvised resource utilization, response time, and total execution time.	Cost and energy parameters can be improvised.
9	To improve cost, speed up, and SLR.	Bi-Objective Optimization Based on Simulated Annealing and Task Duplication Algorithm (BOSA-TDA).	This approach has 18.5% average improvement in comparison to other approaches.	Should be tested in a multi-cloud environment with larger dataset.
10	To optimize execution time, resource utilization, and computational cost.	WOA (Whale Optimization Algorithm)-based BEE algorithm	It significantly optimized the computational cost and time with proper resource utilization.	Should be implemented on larger datasets with unlabelled, unstructured data.

(Continued)

Table 9.1 (Continued) Comparative Study of Related Work

S. No	Objective	Technique	Achievements	Remark
11	To improve energy consumption and power cost at data centres.	Cat Swarm Optimization Algorithm	It improves the performance 20% more than other existing approaches.	Worked on overall computational cost only.
12	To improve task execution and resource optimization.	Non-Dominated Sorting Genetic Algorithm (NSGA-III)	Outperformed the existing non dominated algorithms in terms of execution time, power consumption and the cost.	Energy efficiency was less improved in comparison to other approaches.
13	To achieve effective load balancing while maintaining cost.	Hybrid Fog And Cloud Environment Approach	It was almost 20% more cost effective than other existing approaches.	Worked on load balancing only; power and energy can be considered.
14	To reduce power consumption and better resource allocation.	KMGA (K-Means Genetic Algorithm) Approach	It was able to reduce the power consumption while improving the resource utilization.	Should be tested on larger realistic unstructured data.
15	To optimize all cloud resources including networks, servers, storage, and other resources.	Cuckoo Optimization-Based Energy-Reliability Aware Resource Scheduling Technique (CRUZE)	It reduced power consumption by 21% and lowered cost while maintaining the QoS.	Overall cost optimization can be improvised.

16	To reduce the overall cost by optimizing resource and CPU utilization.	Hybrid Imperialist Competition Algorithm (ICA) and K-means algorithm	This approach reduced overall cost up to 7% and increased response time up to 7%.	Should be tested on a larger unstructured dataset while considering power and energy.
17	To provide cost-effective multi-task scheduling in IaaS.	Chaotic Squirrel Search Algorithm (CSSA)	In a multi-task scheduling environment, it minimized overall cost of the infrastructure.	Only for IaaS; should be implemented on other types with larger datasets.
18	To minimize executional costs.	Deadline and Cost-Aware Algorithm	This approach was able to reduce overall cost and time.	Limited parameters; can be tested on realistic larger datasets.

model has its own advantage and disadvantage. Service-based models provide services to the customer on pre-defined cost, you can decide the services under your budget. Value-based services are customer value based where a survey is conducted in the market to estimate the price of the product and service. Based on the survey, the price of product is decided and provided to the customers. It is more customer oriented than product oriented. We have discussed related work for better scalability and resource optimization to improve cost. A lot of data is being migrated onto the cloud every day, so it is becoming more challenging to maintain the QoS and SLA while maintaining costs and providing better services. Much more research is going on and is needed for optimization of resources and sustainable use of energy.

References

[1] Qian, H. and Medhi, D., 2011, March. Server operational cost optimization for cloud computing service providers over a time horizon. In *Hot-ICE*.

[2] Shahidinejad, A., Ghobaei-Arani, M. and Masdari, M., 2021. Resource provisioning using workload clustering in cloud computing environment: a hybrid approach. *Cluster Computing*, 24(1), pp. 319–342.

[3] Gill, S.S. and Buyya, R., 2019. Resource provisioning based scheduling framework for execution of heterogeneous and clustered workloads in clouds: from fundamental to autonomic offering. *Journal of Grid Computing*, 17, pp. 385–417.

[4] Patel, E. and Kushwaha, D.S., 2022. A hybrid CNN-LSTM model for predicting server load in cloud computing. *The Journal of Supercomputing*, 78(8), pp. 1–30.

[5] Xu, M., Song, C., Wu, H., Gill, S.S., Ye, K. and Xu, C., 2022. esDNN: deep neural network based multivariate workload prediction in cloud computing environments. *ACM Transactions on Internet Technology (TOIT)*, 22(3), pp. 1–24.

[6] Saxena, D. and Singh, A.K., 2022. OFP-TM: an online VM failure prediction and tolerance model towards high availability of cloud computing environments. *The Journal of Supercomputing*, 78(6), pp. 8003–8024.

[7] Gupta, P., Kaikini, R.R., Saini, D.K. and Rahman, S., 2022. Cost-aware resource optimization for efficient cloud application in smart cities. *Journal of Sensors*, 2022.

[8] Nabi, S. and Ahmed, M., 2022. PSO-RDAL: Particle swarm optimization-based resource-and deadline-aware dynamic load balancer for deadline constrained cloud tasks. *The Journal of SuperComputing*, pp. 1–31.

[9] Hosseini Shirvani, M. and Noorian Talouki, R., 2022. Bi-objective scheduling algorithm for scientific workflows on cloud computing platform with makespan and monetary cost minimization approach. *Complex & Intelligent Systems*, 8(2), pp. 1085–1114.

[10] Manikandan, N., Gobalakrishnan, N. and Pradeep, K., 2022. Bee optimization based random double adaptive whale optimization model for task scheduling in cloud computing environment. *Computer Communications*, 187, pp. 35–44.

[11] Mangalampalli, S., Swain, S.K. and Mangalampalli, V.K., 2022. Multi objective task scheduling in cloud computing using cat swarm optimization algorithm. *Arabian Journal for Science and Engineering*, 47(2), pp. 1821–1830.

[12] Imene, L., Sihem, S., Okba, K. and Mohamed, B., 2022. A third generation genetic algorithm NSGAIII for task scheduling in cloud computing. *Journal of King Saud University-Computer and Information Sciences*, 34(9), pp. 7515–7529.

[13] Yu, D., Ma, Z. and Wang, R., 2022. Efficient smart grid load balancing via fog and cloud computing. *Mathematical Problems in Engineering, 2022,* pp. 1–11.

[14] Askarizade Haghighi, M., Maeen, M. and Haghparast, M., 2019. An energy-efficient dynamic resource management approach based on clustering and meta-heuristic algorithms in cloud computing IaaS platforms: Energy efficient dynamic cloud resource management. *Wireless Personal Communications, 104,* pp. 1367–1391.

[15] Gill, S.S., Garraghan, P., Stankovski, V., Casale, G., Thulasiram, R.K., Ghosh, S.K., Ramamohanarao, K. and Buyya, R., 2019. Holistic resource management for sustainable and reliable cloud computing: An innovative solution to global challenge. *Journal of Systems and Software, 155,* pp. 104–129.

[16] Shahidinejad, A., Ghobaei-Arani, M. and Masdari, M., 2021. Resource provisioning using workload clustering in cloud computing environment: a hybrid approach. *Cluster Computing, 24*(1), pp. 319–342.

[17] Sanaj, M.S. and Prathap, P.J., 2020. Nature inspired chaotic squirrel search algorithm (CSSA) for multi objective task scheduling in an IAAS cloud computing atmosphere. *Engineering Science and Technology, an International Journal, 23*(4), pp. 891–902.

[18] Ma, X., Gao, H., Xu, H. and Bian, M., 2019. An IoT-based task scheduling optimization scheme considering the deadline and cost-aware scientific workflow for cloud computing. *EURASIP Journal on Wireless Communications and Networking, 2019*(1), pp. 1–19.

[19] Prem Jacob, T. and Pradeep, K., 2019. A multi-objective optimal task scheduling in cloud environment using cuckoo particle swarm optimization. *Wireless Personal Communications, 109,* pp. 315–331.

[20] Zhang, C., Yu, M., Wang, W. and Yan, F., 2019, July. MArk: Exploiting cloud services for cost-effective, SLO-aware machine learning inference serving. In *USENIX Annual Technical Conference* (pp. 1049–1062).

[21] Mapetu, J.P.B., Chen, Z. and Kong, L., 2019. Low-time complexity and low-cost binary particle swarm optimization algorithm for task scheduling and load balancing in cloud computing. *Applied Intelligence, 49,* pp. 3308–3330.

Chapter 10

Cost- and Network-Aware Metaheuristic Cloud Optimization

Punit Gupta, Sanjit Bhagat, and Dinesh Kumar Saini

10.1 Introduction

Cloud computing is an essential service for almost every business. Most businesses have migrated their data onto the cloud or are in the process of migrating onto the cloud. Managing data and maintaining cost is a prime concern for every organization. Improper use and management of resources may lead to increases in cost with lower resource utilization. Resource optimization is essential to increasing utilization of resources with better cost efficiency. Cost optimized services ensure efficient resource allocation to each workload or application. A properly allocated resource manages cost, performance, compliance, and security in an optimal and appropriate manner for business requirements. There is much more research required to gain full advantage of the cloud. Resource scheduling is the prime component of cloud systems because of its large solution space, and thus it falls under NP (nondeterministic polynomial time)-Hard problem. It takes a long time to find an optimal solution for scheduling using normal techniques. Metaheuristic approaches have been proven to provide nearly optimal solutions in limited time durations. With the evolution of cloud systems, the architecture of the cloud is also improvising and becoming more complex, especially in a hybrid environment. In this chapter, we are going to discuss various metaheuristic methods for cloud environments. There are various metaheuristic approaches available, such as ant colony optimization (ACO), genetic algorithm (GA), and particle swarm optimization (PSO). All approaches

DOI: 10.1201/9781003433293-10

have their benefits and limits. To achieve the full benefit of cloud services it is necessary to have full access to cloud services in a cost- and time-efficient manner without the need for a service provider. This way, organizations can build a highly efficient and reliable network infrastructure. These infrastructures may become complex and costly, and cloud networking helps to build a cost-effective, reliable, and secure network infrastructure.

10.1.1 What Is Cloud Networking?

Cloud networking is a part of cloud computing. It is an IT infrastructure where networking services of an organization is hosted on the cloud. It can be hosted on a private or public cloud, managed by an organization or by the service provider. These services are similar to other cloud services that are available on demand. Networking infrastructure can be built on the premises of the organization (private cloud) or can use cloud resources (public or hybrid) for networking. The network resources include routers, firewalls, bandwidth, virtual private networks (VPN), DNS, and network management software.

There are different types of cloud networking:

1. **Cloud Networking:** This type of network includes connectivity between all the resources of on premises or over cloud services (IaaS, PaaS, SaaS). Due to networking on a single cloud system, it is secure and less time consuming. This network reduces risk of data and application breach. Lifecycle of network is very simple and easy to manage, it provides a better user experience.

2. **Multi-Cloud Networking:** This is an advanced cloud network architecture that has the capability to maintain workload between applications and integration with multiple public cloud platforms. It automatically manages multiple cloud environments whether it is public or on premises. This network provides easy and optimized access across IaaS, PaaS, and SaaS. MSDN (multi-cloud software defined network) are used for better automation between on

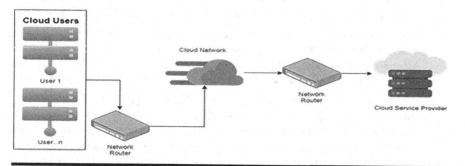

Figure 10.1   Simple cloud network.

Figure 10.2 Multi cloud network.

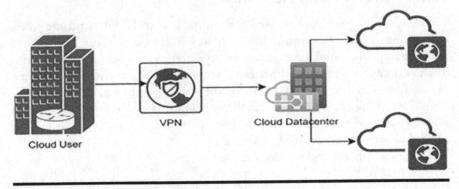

Figure 10.3 Hybrid cloud network.

premises and virtual environment. A multi-cloud system interacts with at least two different clouds. However, this multiple interaction with different clouds makes it, inefficient to manage, risky with security, and inconsistent in infrastructure. The main benefit of this network is that we can use the same resource to manage across different clouds and increase application portability opportunities.

3. **Hybrid Cloud Networking:** As its name indicates, this is a combination of cloud and multi-cloud networking. It is similar to the multi-cloud environment; the only difference is that in multi-cloud environments each cloud has independent workloads, while in hybrid clouds workload can be distributed among different clouds. This network transfers data and workload between private, public, and on-premises clouds. This architecture consists of public and private cloud servers and networks to connect them. Automatic management of workload helps to improve performance and adjusts bandwidth accordingly. This flexible environment makes cloud cost efficient, feasible, and scalable. It has removed the physical existence of servers and other tools on organizations' premises.

4. **Cloud-Enabled Networking:** In this architecture some part of the network physically exists on the user's premises. Core infrastructure, routers, management software, and security services are managed locally at the user end. All the remaining networking services exists on the cloud.

5. **Cloud-Based Networking:** In this architecture, completed infrastructure is hosted over the cloud network. All the resources and applications are connected and deployed over the cloud only; there no end-user management.

10.1.2 Benefits of Cloud Networking

1. **Reliability:** Multiple cloud interactions reduce the total downtime of the server. There are minimal or no requirements to shut down the server for upgrades. Load balancing helps to make the cloud more reliable and highly available.
2. **Easy and Quick Deployment:** Users need not configure or install networking tools to access applications and services.
3. **Scalable:** Cloud networking creates a scalable environment, so new users can be added or removed at run time without any downtime.
4. **Flexible:** Cloud networking helps to provide a flexible cloud environment and gives users a choice between private, public, or hybrid clouds for deployment.
5. **Security:** Firewalls, encryption support, authentication, and many other tools are available over the cloud for data protection and security.
6. **Low Cost:** Organizations need not buy physical networking equipment and software. Networking services are similar to cloud service's pay-per-use basis.

10.2 Metaheuristic Algorithms

These algorithms are designed to find optimal solutions or nearly optimal solutions for task scheduling, resource optimization, or cost optimization. It is a searching process designed to find good solutions in a deterministic time duration. These algorithms are capable of solving complex optimization problems in polynomial time. The metaheuristic approach is able to find optimal solutions of NP-Hard problems with less computational effort in comparison to other optimization algorithms.

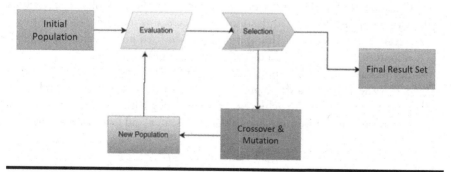

Figure 10.4   Basic GA (genetic algorithm) metaheuristic approach.

We are going to discuss some metaheuristic algorithms with their achievements. Metaheuristic algorithms can be applied on different complex problems. These algorithms are problem-independent, which means the same algorithm can be used to solve a variety of problems. According to their working mechanism of finding solutions, we can divide metaheuristic algorithms into three categories

1. Iterative Approach (Local Search): The best solution set is found by iteratively performing the fitness operation over data.
2. Constructive Approach: Problems are divided into several sub problems, each of them having partial results that are finally merged into a single final solution at the end.
3. Population-Based Matrix: This method improvises a group of potential solutions to a given problem by refining the results using the fitness method.

10.3 Related Work

Aktan, M. N. et al.[1] proposed a hybrid metaheuristic task scheduling algorithm DESA, DE & GA. DESA performed better for large task groups while DE&GA performed better in smaller task groups. It improved average execution time and scheduling time over the network, although energy efficiency might be considered.

Farzai, S. et al.[2] presented a multi-objective optimization model to improve power efficiency and resource utilization by preventing resource wastage, as well as to reduce data transfer rate over DC's network. This approach was significantly better than existing approaches.

Kiani, M. et al.[3] proposed the Virtual Machine Placement (VMP) algorithm to improvise power consumption over heterogenous cloud networks. Further they applied CRO (chemical reaction optimization) as a metaheuristic approach to improve power efficiency on VMs.

Venkata Subramanian, N. et al.[4] proposed the Network-Aware Dynamic Cuckoo Search (NDCS) optimization algorithm, the main objective of which was to improve resource utilization while decreasing total migration time over a secure cloud network. This approach proved itself power efficient, better at resource utilization, and an overall efficient migration model.

Abdel-Basset, M. et al.[5] proposed an energy-aware metaheuristic algorithm called the Harris Hawks Optimization based on Local Search (HHOLS). This model was able to achieve energy efficiency with low carbon emission, but it was time-consuming due to the local search and less cost efficient.

Gupta, P., et al.[6] proposed the nature-inspired Biogeography Based Optimization (BBO) algorithm to improvise network delay, resource utilization, and finish time. The proposed model significantly improved network cost and total execution time. It was able to improve network delay in multi-cloud, multi-user environments.

Keshavarznejad, M., et al.[7] proposed the Multi Objective Optimization model to improve power efficiency and response time. Results were satisfactory in terms of power and time efficiency. Downtime due to task failure was not considered. Machine learning algorithms can be applied to improvise the algorithm.

Kakkottakath Valappil, J. et al.[8] proposed the improvised hybrid Ant-Lion Optimization (ALO) and Particle Swarm Optimization (PSO) algorithms to optimize cost, load, and workload scheduling. This method improved cost efficiency and load balancing in comparison to GA, RR, PSO, ALO etc. It also reduced energy consumption and increases reliability.

Parvizi, E. et al.[9] designed a non-deterministic sorting genetic algorithm (NSGA-III) to compete with Multi Objective Virtual Machine Placement (MOVPM) to minimize resource wastage and improve power efficiency. It outperformed MOVPM in time complexity, thus reducing resource wastage and increasing power efficiency.

Singh, H., et al.[10] worked on a crow search-based load balancing algorithm designed for better resource utilization and load balancing. This algorithm optimally worked for equal and effective distribution of resources. Although distribution was not vast and dynamic, it was an effective method compared to the load balancing of other approaches.

Ibrahim, G. J. et al.[11] created the hybrid Shuffled Frog Leaping Algorithm and Genetic Algorithm (SFGA) to improve response time while reducing power utilization and cost. This energy-aware mechanism was more feasible than other methods.

Mohammadzadeh, A. et al.[12] proposed a hybrid of the Antlion Optimization (ALO) and Grasshopper Optimization Algorithm (GOA) models to improve workflow scheduling in multi-objective environments. The main objective of hybridization was to increase throughput and minimize cost and energy consumption. This approach performed well in comparison to current methods.

Nithyanantham, S. et al.[13] presented the Multivariate Metaphor-Based Metaheuristic Glow Worm Swarm Map-Reduce Optimization (MM-MGSMO) to satisfy multiple objectives (cost, bandwidth, energy, and storage) in cloud networking environments. This approach improved scheduling, storage, cost, and power efficiency.

10.4 Comparative Study

Table 10.1 Summary Table of Related Work

S. No	Objective	Proposed Method	Achievement	Remark
1.	To improve completion time and load balancing over virtual machines in the cloud.	Hybrid metaheuristics algorithm DESA	Proposed method outperformed other algorithms for longer task batch.	It proposed scheduling in an acceptable time period; cost and energy factors might be considered.
2.	To improve resource utilization and reduce high rate of data transfer over DC network.	Multi-Objective Optimization Model	This approach achieved efficient power management, reduction of resource waste, and total data transfer rate.	It might not be cost efficient, but it can be implemented on multi cloud network.
3.	To improve power efficiency and compute power consumption of cloud network.	Virtual Machine Placement (VMP)	This novel method calculated average power consumption over network and able to reduce overall power consumption.	Cost and time factors might be considered. This approach was applied on a heterogenous network.
4.	To improve power efficiency and maximum resource utilization over secure network.	Network-Aware Dynamic Cuckoo Search (NDCS)	It identified a secure network while reducing power consumption and resource waste.	Could be improved over different SLA parameters while maintaining lower cost.

S. No	Objective	Proposed Method	Achievement	Remark
5.	To achieve an energy-efficient model with low power consumption in cloud environments.	Harris Hawks Optimization based on Local Search (HHOLS)	It shows reduction in carbon emission and power consumption.	Limited to independent tasks. Cost and time were less optimized. Can be implemented on dependent tasks.
6.	To improvise network delay and total execution time over a multi-cloud environment.	Biogeography Based Optimization (BBO)	BBO outperformed algorithms like PSO and ACO in terms of network delay and total execution time.	This algorithm can be revised with power efficiency as a computational matrix.
7.	To reduce overall power consumption and calculate probability of offloading.	Multi Objective Optimization Algorithm	It produced a satisfactory trade-off between offloading and power consumption.	Need to investigate node failure and downtime; can be implemented with other metaheuristic algorithms for better results.
8.	To reduce overall cost, makespan, and load workflow.	Hybrid Multi Objective ALO and PSO Algorithm	It was able to achieve better workflow scheduling, reliable and energy efficient scheduling with lesser cost.	It was proposed on IaaS; can be tested on other platforms with different QoS criteria.

(Continued)

Table 10.1 *(Continued)* Summary Table of Related Work

S. No	Objective	Proposed Method	Achievement	Remark
9.	To reduce resource wastage and time complexity, and increase power efficiency.	Non-Deterministic Sorting Genetic Algorithm (NSGA-III)	This method reduced the time complexity while minimizing the resource wastage and power consumption.	In the future, this could be tested on multi VMs or may be targeted for a single VM placement.
10.	To improve load balancing and resource distribution over a cloud network.	Crow Search-Based Load Balancing Algorithm	It provided significant improvement in effective resource distribution.	Applying different learning approaches to the method can increase dynamicity of the algorithm.
11.	To improve response time, cost, and power efficiency.	Hybrid Shuffled Frog Leaping Algorithm and Genetic Algorithm (SFGA)	It outperformed PSO, GA, PSOGA, CA algorithms in terms of response, cost, and power.	In future work it can be combined with new heuristic approaches for energy-aware evaluation.
12.	To increase throughput and minimize cost and energy consumption.	Hybrid model of Antlion Optimization (ALO) and Grasshopper Optimization Algorithm (GOA)	This approach performed well in comparison of current methods.	In future work it can be applied on different performance matrices over a multi-cloud environment.
13.	To improve cost, power, and bandwidth efficiency.	Multivariate Metaphor-Based Metaheuristic Glow Worm Swarm Map-Reduce Optimization (MM-MGSMO)	This approach improved scheduling, storage, cost, and power efficiency. It decreased the false positivity rate and increased storage efficiency.	Objective can be expanded for data security and large data handling in efficient and effective ways.

10.5 Summary

In this chapter, we have discussed networking services in cloud infrastructures. Networking is one of the major components of the cloud environment. We covered types of cloud networking, where private networking can be built on premises, while public networks are available at the provider's end. Security has been a major concern about the public cloud network, so a hybrid model was proposed. In this model, confidential data and configuration was stored at the user end while rest of the data and configuration was taken from the public cloud network. Increases in data and migration of enterprises over the cloud have spiked in recent years. It is a challenging task to handle all the data over the cloud network while maintaining SLA, minimum downtime, and better resource utilization while minimizing cost and power consumption. Many heuristic and metaheuristic approaches exist, and we have discussed some of them. Every approach has its advantages and limitations. The evolutionary process will improvise the algorithm to satisfy awider range of objectives. In the future, we will see much improved multi-objective metaheuristic approaches in the multi-cloud environment.

References

[1] Aktan, M.N. and Bulut, H., 2022. Metaheuristic task scheduling algorithms for cloud computing environments. *Concurrency and Computation: Practice and Experience, 34*(9), p.e6513.

[2] Farzai, S., Shirvani, M.H. and Rabbani, M., 2020. Multi-objective communication-aware optimization for virtual machine placement in cloud datacenters. *Sustainable Computing: Informatics and Systems, 28*, p. 100374.

[3] Kiani, M. and Khayyambashi, M.R., 2021. A network-aware and power-efficient virtual machine placement scheme in cloud datacenters based on chemical reaction optimization. *Computer Networks, 196*, p. 108270.

[4] Venkata Subramanian, N. and Shankar Sriram, V.S., 2022. An effective secured dynamic network-aware multi-objective cuckoo search optimization for live VM migration in sustainable data centers. *Sustainability, 14*(20), p. 13670.

[5] Abdel-Basset, M., El-Shahat, D., Elhoseny, M. and Song, H., 2020. Energy-aware metaheuristic algorithm for industrial-Internet-of-Things task scheduling problems in fog computing applications. *IEEE Internet of Things Journal, 8*(16), pp. 12638–12649.

[6] Gupta, P., Goyal, M.K., Mundra, A. and Tripathi, R.P., 2020. Biogeography-based meta-heuristic optimization for resource allocation in cloud for E-health services. *Journal of Intelligent & Fuzzy Systems, 38*(5), pp. 5987–5997.

[7] Keshavarznejad, M., Rezvani, M.H. and Adabi, S., 2021. Delay-aware optimization of energy consumption for task offloading in fog environments using metaheuristic algorithms. *Cluster Computing*, pp. 1–29.

[8] Kakkottakath Valappil Thekkepuryil, J., Suseelan, D.P. and Keerikkattil, P.M., 2021. An effective meta-heuristic based multi-objective hybrid optimization method for workflow scheduling in cloud computing environment. *Cluster Computing, 24*, pp. 2367–2384.

[9] Parvizi, E. and Rezvani, M.H., 2020. Utilization-aware energy-efficient virtual machine placement in cloud networks using NSGA-III meta-heuristic approach. *Cluster Computing, 23*(4), pp. 2945–2967.

[10] Singh, H., Tyagi, S. and Kumar, P., 2021. Cloud resource mapping through crow search inspired metaheuristic load balancing technique. *Computers & Electrical Engineering, 93*, p. 107221.

[11] Ibrahim, G.J., Rashid, T.A. and Akinsolu, M.O., 2020. An energy efficient service composition mechanism using a hybrid meta-heuristic algorithm in a mobile cloud environment. *Journal of Parallel and Distributed Computing, 143*, pp. 77–87.

[12] Mohammadzadeh, A., Masdari, M. and Gharehchopogh, F.S., 2021. Energy and cost-aware workflow scheduling in cloud computing data centers using a multi-objective optimization algorithm. *Journal of Network and Systems Management, 29*, pp. 1–34.

[13] Nithyanantham, S. and Singaravel, G., 2021. Resource and cost aware glowworm mapreduce optimization based big data processing in geo distributed data center. *Wireless Personal Communications, 117*(4), pp. 2831–2852.

Chapter 11

The Role of SLA and Ethics in Cost Optimization for Cloud Computing

Rohit Verma, Vaishali Chourey, and Dheeraj Rane

11.1 Introduction

Offering scalable and on-demand access to computing resources, cloud computing has revolutionized the way organizations manage their IT infrastructure [1]. Cost optimization is one of the most important aspects of cloud computing, as organizations strive to maximize the return on their cloud investments. Multiple variables, such as resource utilization, service quality, and maintenance requirements, affect the cloud environment's cost implications, which are complex [2]. As the cloud has become the platform of choice for software implementations, the need for effective cost optimization strategies has become of the utmost importance.

The function of service level agreements (SLAs) in the cost optimization of cloud computing and ethics in SLA are examined in this chapter. The chapter's goal is to provide a comprehensive analysis of how cost optimization, SLAs, and ethical standards interact. By filling in this research gap, the authors intend to add to the knowledge available in cloud economics and provide beneficial information for cloud service providers, customers, and researchers.

The chapter's introduction highlights the importance and driving forces behind cloud optimization. As cloud services become more commonplace [3], organizations are faced with the dilemma of cost optimization while maintaining the appropriate level of service quality and performance. This calls for further effectiveness and resource utilization through research and innovation in the area of cloud optimization. It is essential to understand the elements or aspects that affect cost fluctuations [4] in order to optimize cloud expenses. These elements, which significantly affect cost variance, include input/output (IO) activities, storage needs, and data transport. Businesses can learn how to optimize resource allocation, data management, and process scheduling by analyzing these aspects, which will help them cut costs without compromising service quality.

In recent years, numerous optimization strategies, such as machine learning (ML), deep learning (DL), and statistical analysis, have emerged as valuable tools for cloud optimization [5]. These techniques allow for the forecasting and monitoring of resource utilization, enabling organizations to allocate resources proactively and optimize cost management [6]. By leveraging the power of these optimization techniques, businesses can make informed decisions and take proactive steps to optimize cloud costs.

In addition, the role of a cloud broker in optimizing costs cannot be ignored. Brokers in the cloud serve as intermediaries between cloud service providers and customers, facilitating the selection of cost-effective service offerings [7]. They play a vital role in performance optimization by assisting businesses in identifying the optimal service configurations that meet their cost and performance requirements. In addition, cost optimization metrics such as resource utilization, scalability, and service-level agreements provide organizations with quantifiable benchmarks for evaluating and optimizing their cost performance in the cloud.

The chapter also discusses the importance of SLAs and ethical considerations within the context of cost optimization. Compliance and conformance with SLAs guarantee that service providers fulfil their contractual obligations, which has a direct effect on cost optimization [8]. The behaviour of cloud service providers is guided by ethical principles, ensuring equitable and transparent cost structures and pricing models [9]. Examining the role of SLAs and ethics in cost optimization enables organizations to develop strategies that promote ethical practises, foster trust between service providers and consumers, and optimize costs in an ethically responsible manner.

Finally, the chapter concludes with a comprehensive introduction to the role of SLAs and ethics in cloud computing cost optimization. This chapter lays the groundwork for a more in-depth examination of cost optimization strategies in the cloud environment by examining the importance and motivation for cloud optimization, identifying key parameters and optimization techniques, discussing the role of cloud brokers, and highlighting the importance of SLAs and ethics. Understanding the complexities of cost optimization and its relationship to SLAs and ethics becomes crucial as organizations strive to maximize their cloud investments while maintaining cost-effectiveness.

11.2 The Need for Cloud Optimization

Cloud optimization, also known as the process of optimizing cloud computing resources, is essential for ensuring maximum value extraction, efficient resource utilization, and financial viability [10]. This study's second section examines the significance and driving factors of cloud optimization, as well as a variety of parameters and methodologies implemented for improving cloud performance, resource allocation, and cost management.

11.2.1 The Importance and Justification of Cloud Optimization

Cloud computing is a central pillar in the ever-changing landscape of digital technology, supporting numerous applications and services on which businesses and consumers rely daily. The inherent flexibility, scalability, and on-demand nature of the cloud make it an ideal platform for providing these services. To realize its full potential, optimization is essential; it is a multifaceted process that aims to satisfy service level agreements (SLAs), meet user demands, and maximize resource utilization. This section will examine the significance and justification of cloud optimization in greater detail, focusing on its role in ensuring optimal response time, throughput, latency, bandwidth management, and energy consumption [11].

Users expect rapid, reliable, and consistent access to applications and data in today's digital environment. This places a tremendous amount of pressure on cloud service providers to deliver services with minimal response time, high throughput, and low latency. The inherent dynamism and complexity of the cloud environment pose significant obstacles to achieving these goals. Consequently, effective cloud optimization strategies are required to preserve a seamless user experience.

Response time, or the interval between a user's request and the system's response, is a crucial metric for measuring user satisfaction. This must be minimized by balancing resources and adjusting capacity in real time to accommodate fluctuating demand without causing service delays or interruptions. Similarly, high throughput, which refers to the system's capacity to concurrently process multiple requests, is essential for sustaining optimal system performance. This requires effective load balancing and resource scheduling to evenly distribute work across the system and prevent bottlenecks [12].

Latency, or the delay before a data transfer begins, is an additional crucial factor that has a direct effect on the user experience. Reducing latency necessitates not only efficient routing and load balancing, but also the geographical distribution of data centres in order to bring services closer to users [13, 14]. Cloud service providers must continuously monitor and analyses network performance metrics in order to promptly identify and resolve any latency issues.

Management of bandwidth is another essential aspect of cloud optimization. Given the increasingly data-intensive nature of contemporary workloads, such as streaming services and big data analytics, it is crucial to effectively manage network bandwidth. Strategies for bandwidth allocation must be adaptable to the varying requirements of various tasks and processes. In addition, traffic shaping techniques can be used to priorities specific data types, ensuring that critical services are not impacted during peak load times.

Optimizing the makespan, the total time required to complete a given set of tasks or processes, is essential for achieving high levels of productivity and efficiency. By utilizing sophisticated scheduling algorithms and predictive analytics, cloud service providers can reduce makespan, thereby decreasing wait times and increasing system throughput [15, 16].

In addition to these performance parameters, the increasing emphasis on sustainability in the IT industry has elevated the optimization of energy consumption. Given the enormous energy footprint of data centres, implementing energy-efficient practises is not only an environmental necessity, but also a crucial factor in lowering operational costs. Dynamic voltage and frequency scaling (DVFS), server consolidation, and the use of renewable energy sources can significantly reduce the cloud infrastructure's energy consumption.

In summary, cloud optimization is a necessity in the current digital era. By ensuring optimal response time, throughput, and latency, as well as efficient bandwidth and energy management, cloud service providers can deliver high-quality services that satisfy user requirements and SLAs. In addition, these practises can result in substantial cost savings, thereby making cloud services more affordable and accessible to a wider range of users. The significance and justification of cloud optimization cannot be overstated, as it is the foundation of the reliable, efficient, and sustainable operation of cloud services.

11.2.2 Optimization Considerations

The constantly changing landscape of cloud computing presents both opportunities and challenges [10, 11, 17]. The optimization of cloud services is a crucial factor in realizing its potential. Several variables and parameters directly affect the performance, dependability, and cost-effectiveness of cloud services are involved in this complex task. This section aims to provide a thorough examination of the fundamental considerations that guide cloud-based optimization strategies.

In the field of cloud computing, performance optimization is a complex endeavour. It includes load balancing, resource allocation, network configuration, and data management. Load balancing is the process of distributing network traffic evenly across multiple servers to prevent any one server from becoming overloaded, thereby ensuring high availability and dependability [10]. Resource allocation, on the other hand, refers to the efficient distribution of computational resources to different tasks based on demand, thereby preventing resource waste and ensuring timely task completion.

Additionally, network configuration has a substantial impact on cloud performance. Adjusting network parameters such as bandwidth, latency, and packet loss rate to optimize data transmission. In addition to data placement, replication, and caching, data management is an essential component of performance optimization. Optimized data management enables rapid data access, thereby reducing latency and enhancing the overall performance of cloud services.

Cloud optimization must also take into account the dependability of cloud services, including their availability and dependability [13]. The percentage of time that services are operational and accessible to users is referred to as their availability. Utilizing redundancy at multiple levels, including hardware, software, and data, along with robust disaster recovery mechanisms, ensures high availability. Reliability, on the other hand, refers to the system's ability to perform its required functions under given conditions for a specified period of time. Techniques such as fault tolerance, automatic error detection and correction, and system health monitoring are used to maintain it.

In optimizing cloud services, cost-effectiveness plays a crucial role. Frequently, cloud service providers must strike a delicate balance between performance and cost [18]. The cost-effectiveness of cloud services is significantly impacted by factors including server utilization, energy consumption, data transfer costs, and storage costs.

Server utilization is the proportion of time that servers are in use. Server utilization optimization reduces computational resource waste and lowers operational costs. In cloud services, energy consumption in data centres is a major cost driver. Utilizing energy-efficient technologies and procedures, such as virtualization, dynamic power management, and renewable energy, can significantly reduce energy costs [19].

Costs are associated with transferring data into and out of the cloud. Data deduplication, compression, and caching are techniques that can help reduce these costs. The costs associated with storing data in the cloud can be minimized using techniques such as tiered storage and thin provisioning. These techniques involve storing data in different classes of storage based on its importance and frequency of access.

Optimizing cloud services is a complex endeavour that necessitates careful consideration of a multitude of factors. To provide high-quality cloud services, it is necessary to optimize performance, dependability, and cost-effectiveness. By comprehending and appropriately addressing these optimization considerations, cloud service providers can not only improve service quality but also gain a competitive edge in the dynamic and challenging cloud market. In the following subsections, some of these factors are discussed:

11.2.2.1 Parameters of Quality of Service (QoS)

Quality of service (QoS), which includes the vital parameters of availability and dependability, is the foundation of proficient cloud computing [11]. These elements, which are essential to delivering a consistent and seamless service, contribute to a user experience that exceeds expectations and a robust operational framework with minimal disruptions and downtime. In the broader context of cost optimization for cloud services, maintaining these QoS parameters while delivering a cost-effective and efficient service can be a difficult but necessary task.

In this context, SLAs are essential. SLAs, as legally enforceable documents, establish mutual expectations between cloud service providers and their clients. They specify the benchmarks for service provision, which may include uptime, reliability, and service availability, among others. Typical SLAs quantify system reliability as a percentage of operational uptime over a specified period of time, such as a year. An SLA could, for instance, guarantee an availability of 99.999% (commonly referred to as "five nines"), implying a maximum acceptable downtime of approximately five minutes per year.

SLAs play multiple roles within the context of cloud optimization [20]. On the one hand, they establish evaluation and optimization criteria for service performance. This feature is essential, as it safeguards service quality despite efforts to improve operational efficiency. SLAs serve as a balancing mechanism, ensuring that cost-reduction efforts do not compromise service quality and consistency. In many cases, they also stipulate penalties for providers who do not meet the agreed-upon service standards, providing a financial incentive to maintain high levels of availability and reliability. This mechanism is essential for achieving cost optimization and service quality commitments in harmony.

On the other hand, achieving the SLA-required high availability and reliability is frequently an expensive endeavour. To ensure high availability, providers must implement both physical and software redundancies (such as backup servers and failover systems) to maintain service continuity in the event of system failures. To maintain service dependability, providers may need to invest in resilient and robust systems, which typically consist of premium hardware, well-designed software, and ongoing system maintenance. Consequently, the pursuit of high QoS standards can incur additional expenses, making cost optimization more difficult.

The dynamic nature of cloud services is a further aspect of QoS optimization in the cloud. Cloud computing is inherently designed to be scalable and flexible, adapting to user needs [21]. Maintaining high QoS levels in this dynamic environment therefore requires accurate demand forecasting and efficient resource allocation. Machine learning (ML) and other predictive analytics tools can play a crucial role in ensuring that high QoS levels are maintained while costs are minimized.

Furthermore, QoS is not a static notion. As technology evolves, user expectations and metrics for measuring QoS also change. As more services migrate to the cloud, latency and data transfer speeds, while always important, are becoming increasingly crucial. For cloud service providers, keeping up with these trends and incorporating them into both QoS standards and SLAs is an ongoing challenge.

In a nutshell, the role of QoS in cloud optimization is extensive and intricate, particularly with regard to the parameters of availability and dependability. SLAs play a crucial role in defining the expected service standards, ensuring that the requirements for high availability and dependability are aligned with objectives for cost-effectiveness. Despite the fact that adherence to SLAs can incur additional expenses, these agreements help to create a balanced and effective cloud optimization strategy. The challenge for cloud service providers is to continuously adapt and innovate in order to maintain high QoS levels, meet changing user expectations, and achieve cost optimization; this challenge is at the core of cloud computing's ongoing evolution.

11.2.2.2 Cost Optimization

In the field of cloud computing, cost optimization is crucial for maximizing resource utilization and service quality. Consistently difficult is the task of balancing the costs associated with providing superior cloud services with an affordable pricing model. This section will explore the complexities of cost optimization, focusing in particular on efficient scheduling, dynamic resource provisioning, and intelligent storage cost management. When handled skillfully, these factors contribute significantly to achieving an optimal performance-to-cost ratio, fostering business growth, and maintaining market competitiveness [5].

Effective resource scheduling is an essential aspect of cloud computing. The allocation of appropriate computing resources to various tasks and processes based on their requirements constitutes efficient scheduling. This method ensures that the system operates efficiently, minimizing downtime and maximizing resource utilization. Nevertheless, effective scheduling requires the capacity to anticipate and adapt to the dynamic nature of workload demands. Tools for predictive analytics can be useful for predicting future demand, aiding in the accurate allocation of resources, and preventing waste due to over- or under-provisioning.

Incorporating SLAs into scheduling decisions further complicates the undertaking. SLAs typically stipulate specific performance benchmarks that must be met to maintain the agreed-upon service quality. This requirement requires cloud service providers to consider these performance metrics when scheduling in order to meet their SLA obligations without incurring unnecessary costs.

The capacity to adjust resources based on demand is central to dynamic resource provisioning, a crucial element of cost optimization. Computing in the cloud is inherently scalable, allowing resources to be scaled up or down based on user requirements. Effective resource provisioning guarantees optimal system performance without incurring additional costs due to unused resources. This requires the implementation of intelligent algorithms capable of analyzing current workloads, anticipating future requirements, and allocating resources accordingly. During this process, providers must also consider their SLA obligations. Overprovisioning resources to meet SLA commitments can result in waste, whereas under-provisioning can cause service degradation. Therefore, a balanced strategy is necessary for cost-effective resource provisioning.

The management of storage costs is another pillar of cloud cost optimization. As data volumes continue to grow exponentially, it becomes increasingly important to effectively manage storage costs. Intelligent data placement ensures that data is stored in the most cost-effective manner. However, these strategies must also take data accessibility and security into account. Compressing data, for example, can reduce storage costs but increase retrieval computation costs. Similarly, while deduplication can save storage space, if not handled properly it can introduce security risks.

In addition to these technical considerations, cloud cost optimization also involves ethical issues. For instance, outsourcing certain services or storage to lower-cost providers can reduce costs, but it can also raise ethical concerns regarding data privacy and security, particularly if these providers do not adhere to the same standards as the original provider. Therefore, cloud service providers must strike a balance between cost optimization and ethical considerations, ensuring that their pursuit of cost savings does not compromise their ethical obligations.

Cost optimization in cloud services is, therefore, a multifaceted endeavour requiring efficient scheduling, dynamic resource provisioning, and intelligent storage cost management. These strategies, along with the constant consideration of SLAs and ethical concerns, play a crucial role in the delivery of affordable, high-quality cloud services. The challenge for cloud service providers is to find innovative and efficient ways to optimize costs without sacrificing service quality or ethical standards. This balancing act is essential for the cloud computing industry's sustainable and responsible growth.

11.2.3 Optimization Techniques

To improve performance, reliability, and cost-effectiveness in the cloud computing environment of today, sophisticated methodologies are required. Adopting the dynamic capabilities of ML, DL, and advanced statistical analysis techniques is essential for ensuring cloud optimization success [5, 6, 22]. This section will explore how these modern approaches enhance the overall cloud optimization process.

Machine learning, a fundamental subfield of artificial intelligence, enables systems to autonomously learn from existing data and adapt their performance over time. Consequently, ML has proven to be an extremely effective tool for cloud optimization. The benefit of ML in implementing optimizations in cloud is manyfold for instance—optimal resource allocation through historical analysis of usage patterns and timely deciding on the future resource requirements. This adequately reduces the illicit allocation of resources and optimizes the costs fairly.

Simple linear regression models for workload prediction, complicated decision trees, and clustering algorithms are just a few of the methods available for ML-based cloud optimization. Reinforcement learning (RL), a subset of ML noted for its adaptive reactions to environmental changes, is given special attention. It is useful for controlling resource allocation dynamically in response to fluctuating workloads.

DL is the most advanced form of machine learning. DL models, particularly neural networks, offer the capacity to comprehend complex relationships within vast data sets, to self-learn from multi-dimensional and hierarchical data structures, resulting in extremely accurate and robust predictive capabilities. In the context of cloud optimization, DL models are employed to predict workloads, manage energy consumption, optimize task scheduling, and even mitigate security risks.

DL algorithms excel at real-time processing of large volumes of data, a requirement for managing data-intensive cloud applications. DL models such as autoencoders, convolutional neural networks (CNNs), and recurrent neural networks (RNNs) are gaining popularity in cloud computing, providing a deeper understanding of data and significantly assisting in optimizing resources and improving performance.

The integration of statistical analysis techniques with ML and DL provides a solid basis for cloud optimization. Certain techniques, such as regression analysis, time-series forecasting, and probability theory, aid businesses in making data-driven decisions, thereby streamlining their cloud operations.

Regression analysis, an integral statistical technique, models the relationship between resource utilization and a variety of influencing factors, thereby supplying crucial insights for resource provisioning and cost management. Multivariate regression analysis can be particularly useful in the context of cloud optimization, as it permits the simultaneous examination of the effect of multiple variables on resource consumption, thereby enabling more precise resource allocation.

Another valuable statistical technique, time-series forecasting, predicts future workloads based on past trends, facilitating anticipatory resource allocation. It is particularly useful in cloud computing in events of extremely fluctuating workloads, whereby an accurate and precise demand of particular resources can be forecasted to enhance system performance and cost-effectiveness dramatically.

Hardware failures and network bottlenecks are just two examples of the kinds of events that can be estimated using methods from probability theory, the area of mathematics that deals with the analysis of random phenomena. By offering a framework for evaluating uncertainty and tackling risk optimization, it enables the development of resilient and effective cloud systems.

Integrating ML, DL, and sophisticated statistical analysis methods offers a data-centric, cutting-edge method for optimizing cloud computing. A fine balance of intelligent techniques like these enable responsive decision making and in turn improves cost effectiveness, dependability and performance. In the constantly evolving world of cloud computing, these devious, versatile approaches prove essential for establishing both a competitive edge and operational excellence.

11.2.3.1 Forecast: Predictive Analytics in Cloud Optimization: Future Projection

Predictive analytics is a pioneering data analytics approach that encompasses processing data with statistical algorithms, and machine learning approaches to evaluate the likelihood of future outcome. These predictions are critical in the context of cloud optimization. Its elementary objective is to estimate future resource requirements, network traffic motives, and workload variations, all of which are critical techniques for improving cloud performance. As the world advances greater into the age of digitization, the ability to reliably anticipate future needs allows organizations to better organize their resources, improve service delivery, and realize significant cost reductions. This section presents an in-depth examination of the use of predictive analytics in cloud optimization.

Cloud services are exceptionally unpredictable in nature, and demand for these services can fluctuate dramatically dependent on variables such as user behavior, market trends, and specific events. Predictive analytics, using ML and DL, may extract significant conclusions from past data to decipher these patterns and trends. Predictive models may discover nuanced patterns by analyzing massive amounts of historical usage data.

Predictive analytics may enhance the functionality of cloud services dramatically. As an exemplar, organizations can prevent system downtimes or failures by precisely forecasting server demand during peak usage periods and allocating resources appropriately. Similarly, predictive analytics may identify low usage periods, allowing firms to save resources (hibernating) and lower the energy consumption during these times.

Predicting network traffic patterns is a crucial factor that predictive analytics can significantly control. Network congestion is a prevalent problem in cloud computing environments, which may result in increased latency and diminished service quality. By utilizing predictive analytics, organizations are able to anticipate these congestion periods and dynamically manage network resources, thereby preserving the quality of the user experience.

Predictive analytics also plays a crucial role in the management of fluctuating workloads. In the case of batch processing tasks with variable workloads, for instance, predictive analytics can accurately predict these variations, allowing for efficient task scheduling. This capability not only ensures optimal use of computing resources, but also reduces processing time, resulting in increased productivity.

Moreover, predictive analytics' significance extends to cost optimization. In a cloud environment, resources equal costs; therefore, misallocation can result in unneeded expenditures. Predictive analytics enables organizations to allocate resources prudently, avoiding overprovisioning or underutilization, by accurately predicting future needs. This strategizes accurate resource allocation thereby lowering the costs significantly and seamlessly creates a productive and economical cloud.

Summarizing, predictive analytics is potentially useful for optimization techniques by fostering business successfully with future ready resource provisioning system by identifying requirements of compute, network and workload variability. It enhances cloud service performance while lowering costs through the proactive and intelligent resource allocation. As the digital era develops further, the ability to precisely foresee future demands remains to be essential for effective and efficient cloud service delivery.

11.2.3.2 Real-Time Monitoring in Cloud Optimization

Real-time monitoring is crucial in cloud computing for controlling and enhancing the performance and functioning of cloud resources and services. It is a dynamic process that involves continuous monitoring of numerous variables related to resource use, network bandwidth, system performance, and various other variables. An extensive structure of rigorous and continual monitoring is required for detecting anomalies, pinpointing bottlenecks, and making performance improvements. This section investigates the significance and applicability of real-time monitoring in cloud optimization.

Cloud environments are incredibly dynamic and complicated, with numerous transactions and activities running concurrently. As a result, sustaining peak performance and spotting possible issues becomes quite the challenge. Real-time monitoring, which offers visibility into the functionality and status of cloud resources and services, helps to mitigate this. It facilitates the early detection of problems and allows for quick action to stop a little problem from growing into a bigger one.

Furthermore, monitoring makes it easier to spot abnormalities that could be signs of security risks or systemic problems. In the digital world, cybersecurity is an increasing problem, and stopping data theft and system incursions requires early detection of anomalies. To ensure the security and integrity of cloud systems, real-time monitoring is essential since it has the ability to identify unusual activity patterns.

A related idea is the identification of performance constraints. Cloud computing suffers an obstruction which consequently reduces its performance and diminishes the responsiveness. The ability to identify these bottlenecks quickly and maintain the highest level of service quality is made possible through real-time monitoring.

Planning for resource capacity and improving performance through optimized utilization needs real-time monitoring of services. It demands careful investigation into the resource demand and allocation patterns thereby imparting knowledge to the organizations fairly and convincingly. This allows efficient allocation possibilities with cost efficiency too, undermining the irrational conditions of over-provisioning or under-usage.

Real-time monitoring is an addendum to performance enhancements techniques with novel features of ML, DL, and statistical analysis. Algorithms for ML can learn from data generated by monitoring systems to anticipate future issues in beforehand. However, DL models can analyze intricate data patterns and offer precise tips for improving performance. Making conscious choices is simplified by statistical analysis, which makes it easier to spot trends and patterns.

Real-time monitoring is integrated into cloud optimization tactics, giving the opportunity to not only respond to incidents but also foresee and prevent them. Businesses may deliver high-performance cloud services by using real-time monitoring to continuously track response time, throughput, latency, bandwidth, makespan, energy usage, QoS, and cost. This active approach lowers costs, improves resource utilization, and enables organizations to maximally utilize cloud computing.

In conclusion, real-time monitoring is an essential tool for any company looking to increase the efficiency, security, and cost-effectiveness of its cloud infrastructure. By utilizing cutting-edge methods like ML, DL, and statistical analysis, real-time monitoring offers data-driven insights that support efficient and successful cloud operations. This promotes an environment of innovation, agility, and competition in the age of technology.

11.3 Role of Cloud Brokers in Cost Optimization

Cloud brokers become crucial integrators and optimizers of services provided by clouds on the part of cloud consumers. As an intermediary, they overcome the gap between cloud service providers and customers, facilitating the choice, provisioning, and management of cloud resources. With an emphasis on performance optimization and the measurements used for cost optimization, this section examines the crucial role cloud brokers play in cost optimization.

11.3.1 Performance Optimization: A Principal Responsibility of Cloud Brokers

Performance optimization emphasizes on increasing the efficacy and efficiency of cloud services. This is the fundamental functional paradigm of cloud computing. Cloud brokers greatly help to performance optimization with their specialized knowledge and capabilities. They must decide which cloud service providers to work with based on performance measurements, negotiate service level agreements (SLAs), and constantly monitor and improve performance to satisfy the demands of cloud users.

Brokers in the cloud are responsible for assessing the performance potential of various cloud service providers. To assess a provider's capabilities to satisfy performance requirements, it is necessary to analyze variables including processor power, network bandwidth, storage capacity, and scalability. These analyses of performance parameters help cloud brokers choose wisely when allocating resources and offering services.

Monitoring the effectiveness of cloud services is another duty of cloud brokers. Identifying possible performance-related barriers, such as inefficiencies and latency issues, is required. Cloud brokers use a variety of monitoring tools and methods to track key performance indicators (KPIs) such response time, throughput, latency, and resource use. Continuous monitoring provides insights that help cloud brokers pinpoint areas for performance improvement and put the required changes into place to improve the performance of cloud services.

Brokers in the cloud also play a significant role in optimizing performance via effective workload management and resource allocation strategies. With due analyses of the pattern of subjected workloads on Cloud and subsequent resource management, Cloud broker architecture enables fair resource allocation.

By analyzing the workload patterns and resource requirements of cloud consumers, cloud brokers are able to effectively allocate resources. They may maximize the utilization of cloud resources, ensuring optimal efficiency for consumers of cloud services while saving costs, by employing workload balancing techniques and clever resource allocation algorithms.

11.3.2 Key Cost Optimization Metrics

The capacity to extract maximum value from cloud services while minimizing expenditures is the core objective of cost optimization in cloud computing. To strike this equilibrium, a variety of techniques are used, and cloud brokers are essential in assisting cloud users on their journey through cloud computing. They use their complex knowledge of the cloud ecosystem as agents between cloud service providers and customers to address the issue of cost efficiency.

The function of the broker is based on the knowledge that cost optimization entails more than just cost reduction. Decisions must be made in a way to maximize resource usage, increase value, and improve efficiency. A cloud system that is cost-effective increases performance for every dollar invested, rather than being cheap. Brokers in the cloud use a number of techniques and assets to reduce expenses. Performance optimization is one of them, a method used to raise the general effectiveness and efficiency of cloud services. To do this, brokers choose the best cloud service providers based on performance measurements, negotiate SLAs, and persistently track and tweak performance to satisfy the demands of cloud customers.

Furthermore, the broker is in charge of assessing the operational capabilities of various cloud service providers, taking into consideration aspects like processor power, network bandwidth, storage capacity, and scalability. Brokers may make well-informed judgments about resource allocation and service delivery that correspond with consumers' performance needs and cost objectives by performing thorough assessments. Cloud brokers actively monitor cloud service performance in order to detect possible performance concerns. They use a range of monitoring tools to track KPIs such as response time, throughput, latency, and resource use. This constant monitoring allows cloud brokers to discover areas for improvement and take the required actions to optimize cloud service performance.

Workload management and resource allocation are two more key domains where brokers may help save costs. They analyze cloud customers' workload patterns and resource needs to ensure that resources are distributed efficiently to accomplish performance goals while conserving operating costs. Brokers that mediate the cloud provisioning operations, can maximize the utilization of cloud resources and provide maximum performance for cloud consumers. This is achieved by adopting workload balancing strategies and intelligent resource allocation algorithms. Cloud brokers act as intermediary for functional efficiency yet focus on cost-related measures in addition to performance optimization. They investigate workload patterns while services are offered and analyzes resource requirements in order to optimize scheduling and resource allocation. They employ complex algorithms to guarantee that resources are used efficiently and costs are kept to a minimum. Furthermore, to decrease storage costs, they employ storage optimization techniques such as data compression, deduplication, and intelligent data placement.

SLAs are critical for cost optimization. Cloud brokers negotiate SLAs on behalf of cloud users, guaranteeing that mutually agreed-up performance, availability, and reliability specifications fit with the client's cost expectations. Moreover, they continually monitor and control the expenses associated with cloud services, investigating cost related variables to discover cost-cutting options. Cloud brokers serve an important role in reducing cloud computing pricing. They greatly contribute to the efficient and cost-effective use of cloud resources through a comprehension of the cloud ecosystem, competency in performance optimization, and skillful use of cost optimization criteria. The brokers enable cloud customers to optimize their cloud expenditures while accomplishing their cost-cutting goals by selecting suitable service providers, monitoring performance indicators, and enacting price reduction strategies. Their contribution to cost reduction is critical to the acceptance and success of cloud computing.

11.3.2.1 Costs for Scheduling and Resource Provisioning

Cloud brokers play a vital role in analyzing workload patterns and resource demands in order to enhance the provisioning and scheduling of resources. Cloud brokers can cut expenses related to unused and overallocated resources by in advance scheduling workloads and allocating resources according to demand. To ensure minimized costs with structured use of resources we can make use of suitable algorithms and techniques to help cloud broker in optimized allocation of resources

In order for cloud brokers to optimize resource provisioning and scheduling, workload pattern analysis is essential. By thoroughly investigating the patterns of workloads, cloud brokers may acquire important information regarding the resource needs of cloud users. The research involved helps in deciding how to allocate resources effectively, ensuring that the essential resources are available when needed and preventing excessive overprovisioning. Cloud brokers can prevent resource waste and eventually cut costs by effectively coordinating resource allocation with workload patterns.

Cloud brokers prioritize resource provisioning to optimize costs by leveraging their expertise and advanced techniques. They consider factors such as workload expectations, specifications for performance, and cost constraints. Cloud brokers may deliver resources that closely match workload specifications by carefully evaluating these variables, which improves resource efficiency and lowers costs. Additionally, by taking a cautious approach to resource provisioning, they assist eliminate wasteful expenditures spurred on by overprovisioning and maximize price effectiveness.

Scheduling is an essential component of cloud brokers' cost-optimization methods in addition to resource supply. It necessitates skillfully dividing up and organizing work performance among the available resources. Cloud brokers increase scheduling by making use of an awareness of workload demands, resource accessibility, and performance objectives. They employ strategies including load distribution, job prioritization, and workload relocation in an effort to maximize resource utilization and save spending. By effectively scheduling workloads, cloud brokers may avoid instances when resources remain idle or neglected and save their customer's money.

Cloud brokers use advanced algorithms and approaches for optimization and addresses resource provisioning and planning challenges. These algorithms analyze a range of factors, including required workload, resource availability, performance metrics, and prices. Such algorithms enable cloud brokers to plan well for task scheduling and allocation of resources. They provide optimal use without overprovisioning by carefully distributing resources based on demand. This technique enables cloud customers to successfully control costs while maintaining a certain level of functionality and standard of service.

Cloud brokers play an important role in enhancing resource provisioning and scheduling by monitoring workload trends and resource demands. They carefully distribute resources based on workload demands to solve the issues of underutilization and overallocation. Cloud brokers make sure that resources are used as efficiently as possible and that performance goals are met by utilizing cutting-edge algorithms and methods. By carefully studying workload patterns, assessing resource availability, and putting intelligent scheduling techniques into practice, cloud brokers drive cost optimization efforts in the world of cloud computing. Their expertise enables users of the cloud to make efficient use of the resources at hand, resulting in significant cost savings and increased operational effectiveness. The vital function of cloud brokers in streamlining resource provisioning and scheduling emphasizes the significance of those people in reaching cost-optimization targets in the context of cloud computing.

11.3.2.2 Costs for Storage

Within the domain of cloud computing, storage costs constitute a substantial portion of overall expenses. Given this fact, cloud brokers, acting as proficient enablers of cloud services, assume a vital role in minimizing storage expenses through the implementation of diverse optimization techniques. By employing data compression, deduplication, and intelligent data positioning, cloud brokers successfully mitigate the storage costs borne by cloud customers.

Data compression is a significant strategy used by cloud brokers to reduce storage expenses. Data compression strategies aim to reduce the size of data files by removing unnecessary or repetitive information. Cloud brokers may drastically reduce the quantity of storage space required by using data compression, saving cloud clients money right away. Additionally, compressed data saves money when transferred among cloud services as well as between the cloud and client devices due to the fact it uses less bandwidth during transmission.

Deduplication of data is used by cloud brokers as an efficient approach for decreasing storage costs. Duplication is the process of locating and removing redundant copies of data, keeping only one instance, and referencing the remaining duplicates. Deduplication is a technique used by cloud brokers to lower the amount of storage space and associated expenses taken up by duplicated data. By doing rid with the need to keep several identical copies of a particular piece of data, this method maximizes storage usage and improves cost-efficiency.

By strategically placing data, cloud brokers are also essential for reducing storage costs. Based on criteria including the frequency of access, the value of the data, and the need for speed, they strategically distribute the data among several storage tiers. Cloud brokers make sure the most affordable storage options are used by doing this. While rarely utilized or archive material can be kept on less expensive storage solutions, often accessed or vital data can be kept on high-performance storage media. By matching their data storage requirements with the right storage resources, this tiered strategy helps cloud clients save unused expenses.

In order to cut expenses, cloud brokers constantly look for affordable storage choices. They look at the various storage choices offered by the cloud ecosystem and determine if they are appropriate for certain use cases. Cloud brokers help consumers of cloud computing choose the most cost-effective storage services by examining pricing models, storage capacity, performance attributes, and durability. This tactical strategy guarantees that cloud users utilize the best storage options while successfully controlling expenses.

To provide considerable cost reductions to cloud clients, cloud brokers use a number of storage optimization strategies. They decrease storage needs and cut back on unneeded expenditures by using data compression, deduplication, and intelligent data placement. With the help of these techniques, cloud users may more wisely use their savings and spend money on other crucial aspects of their cloud computing projects.

Storage optimization is a key area of attention for cloud brokers since storage costs make up a significant portion of cloud computing expenses. Cloud brokers effectively decrease storage costs for their clients by putting data compression, deduplication, intelligent data placement, and cost-effective storage solutions through practice. These optimization methods encourage effective storage use, get rid of redundant data, and strategically distribute data across various data storage tiers, which results in considerable cost savings. Cloud users may collaborate with cloud brokers to take advantage of their knowledge and insights, cutting storage costs without sacrificing data availability or speed. Cloud brokers will remain essential in managing storage efficiently as the cloud computing environment changes, helping businesses maximize their financial assets while utilizing the full potential of the cloud.

11.3.2.3 Cost Optimization and Service Level Agreements

SLAs, which outline the terms and conditions of cloud service providers' offerings, have a substantial influence on cost optimization. Cloud brokers actively negotiate SLAs on behalf of cloud users, ensuring alignment between the agreed-upon performance, availability, and reliability levels and the users' cost-optimization goals. By negotiating attractive SLAs, cloud brokers can reduce costs while maintaining the needed service standards.

By constantly tracking and controlling the expenses of cloud services, cloud brokers also aid in cost optimization. The discovery of prospective areas for cost reduction is made possible by monitoring cost-related variables including resource utilization, data transfer prices, and use patterns. Cloud brokers assist cloud customers to make educated decisions, hence optimizing their cost management strategies, by analyzing cost data and offering recommendations.

Cost optimization within the cloud computing environment is greatly helped by cloud brokers. They greatly contribute to the optimal and economical usage of cloud resources by utilizing their expertise in cost and performance optimization criteria. Cloud brokers help customers make the most of their cloud investments and reach their cost-optimization goals by choosing the best cloud service providers, monitoring performance data, and implementing cost-cutting techniques. For cloud computing to be adopted and succeed, cloud brokers' crucial role in cost optimization is crucial since it allows businesses to use the advantages of cloud services while minimizing expenses.

11.4 SLAs and Ethics

The cornerstones of the cloud computing ecosystem are SLAs, which operate as a framework for contracts between cloud service providers and their clients. These specifications include performance benchmarks, service availability, dependability, and other service-specific features that cloud service providers pledge to deliver [23, 24]. In the changing world of cloud computing, this contractual knowledge is crucial for establishing compliance, responsibility, and confidence.

11.4.1 Compliance and SLA Conformance

The delivery of cloud services depends critically on compliance and SLA conformity. Compliance is the ability of cloud service providers to continuously supply the promised services within the constraints of the SLA. Contrarily, conformity is adhering to the terms and circumstances that are clearly mentioned in the SLA.

SLA compliance necessitates constant monitoring and measurement of cloud service providers' service performance. To ensure compliance with the agreed-upon standards, providers must establish strong monitoring technologies, gather relevant performance data, and analyze their services on a regular basis. Providers may immediately discover deviations from SLA standards by proactively evaluating KPIs such as response time, throughput, latency, and availability.

Cloud providers typically use service level management (SLM) practices to facilitate SLA compliance and adherence. SLM covers the whole SLA lifecycle, from establishment and negotiation through monitoring, enforcement, and renewal, and provides a framework for cloud providers to manage SLAs. SLM frameworks design different processes, allocate roles, and provide escalation mechanisms to successfully manage SLA compliance. As a result, any difficulties with service performance may be discovered and remedied quickly, ensuring customers of the service's quality and performance.

Transparency is another critical part of SLA compliance and conformance. Cloud service providers must maintain broad avenues of communication with their clients, giving regular updates on service performance, outage notifications, and information on any deviations from SLA criteria. Such fast and accurate information fosters transparency, allowing consumers to make educated decisions based on real service performance. Customers can also assess the cloud provider's commitment to the SLA.

Ethical issues are prevalent in the debate of SLA compliance and conformance. Cloud computing companies must follow a set of ethical guidelines that prioritize user data fairness and accountability, as well as the preservation of consumer privacy and security. This encompasses data protection, data confidentiality and integrity, and adherence to applicable regulatory and legal regulations. To secure client information and prevent unauthorized access or modification, providers must apply strong security measures.

Cloud service providers are not completely liable for compliance and SLA compliance. When negotiating SLAs, customers must articulate their requirements, expectations, and performance targets. Customers may help cloud service providers establish SLAs that match their individual needs by giving precise information about their business objectives, desired service levels, and compliance requirements. Regular communication, performance monitoring, and feedback from both sides all contribute to the creation of a collaborative atmosphere that encourages compliance and conformity.

There will undoubtedly be SLA breaches and disagreements. To address such scenarios, strong governance and conflict resolution systems must be put in place. SLAs should include escalation channels and dispute resolution mechanisms for reporting and resolving performance issues. Such conflict resolution frameworks can aid in the effective settlement of conflicts, protecting the provider-client business relationship.

Finally, it can be quoted that safeguarding compliance and conformance with SLAs is a vital in the successful delivery of cloud services. The roles of providers and customers are equally significant. Providers must reliably evaluate their performance, hold to SLA metrics and terms of service, and guaranteeing transparency to the customer. Customers must present accurate requirements regarding their expected usage of services on cloud and actively participate in the process of monitoring and providing feedback. By advocating ethical doctrines, ensuring data privacy and security, and implementing active governance and dispute resolution mechanisms, it is possible to establish a trustworthy partnership. Compliance and conformance with SLAs play a crucial role in enhancing service quality, fostering trust, and ensuring the ecosystem's long-term success.

11.4.2 *Ethical Considerations in Cloud Computing*

Within the complex framework that is cloud computing, the ethical aspect is quickly gaining prominence and dominance. Regarding cloud computing, ethical considerations encompass a wide range of factors, including data protection, confidentiality, integrity, transparency, accountability, and adherence to legal and regulatory frameworks. They are essential to the discussion surrounding the design, implementation, and use of cloud computing services. Let's examine in greater depth this complex aspect of cloud computing.

In the ecosystem of cloud computing, ethics play a crucial role in establishing trust, ensuring accountability, and promoting justice. Due to the inherent nature of cloud computing, in which data is remotely stored and processed in virtualized environments, ethical considerations assume an even greater level of importance. When customers move their data and applications to the cloud, they must have confidence that their privacy and security will not be compromised in the process.

The protection of user data should be regarded as one of the most crucial ethical concerns in cloud computing. Providers of cloud services have an ethical duty to protect client data against unauthorized access, alteration, or disclosure. It is ethically required to protect the security and privacy of client information in addition to making sure that all applicable rules and regulations are followed. Data confidentiality entails limiting access to data to those who are authorized. Cloud service providers must have strict access control methods, encryption techniques, and security procedures to prevent unauthorized people or computer systems from accessing the stored data. Integrity of data, which relates to the concept that data being processed or stored in the cloud should not be altered or tampered with without the right permission, is yet another important ethical problem. To identify and stop unauthorized changes to client data, cloud service providers must include data integrity measures including checksums, hashing, and digital signatures.

One of the crucial ethical concerns surrounding cloud computing is transparency. Customers of cloud service providers have a right to be informed of all company operations, including those involving the management and processing of personal data. This entails giving precise details on data storage, such as where and how it is kept, who has access to it, what security precautions are taken, and how data breaches, if they happen, will be handled. Accountability and transparency go hand in hand. Customers expect a cloud service provider to be responsible for the security and privacy of the data they entrust to them and grant them permission to store in the cloud. This implies that the provider should accept accountability and take prompt action to address any issues that may arise in the case of a data breach or security incident. Furthermore, it is an aspect of the service to let consumers know when rules and practices regulating the administration of data change.

Cloud service providers are compelled by ethics to guarantee that their services adhere to all applicable legal and regulatory frameworks in addition to their legal commitment to do so. Specific standards for the security and privacy of personal information are provided by laws and regulations like the California Consumer Privacy Act (CCPA) and the General Data Protection Regulation (GDPR). In addition to avoiding any legal ramifications, following these rules is crucial for maintaining one's integrity and reputation with clients.

Customers are crucial to this process, but cloud service providers also have a big ethical duty to uphold. Customers of cloud service providers must be mindful of their ethical obligations while managing potentially sensitive information, such as personal data. They must use the cloud services ethically and in accordance with all applicable ethical guidelines and regulations.

In conclusion, ethics has a huge impact on how the cloud computing ecosystem functions as a whole. It provides the basis for building reciprocal confidence between cloud service providers and clients. Every facet of cloud computing is influenced by ethical issues, from the upkeep of accountability and openness to the safeguarding of data confidentiality and integrity. Together, customers and service providers must preserve these moral standards in order to make sure that the cloud computing environment is secure, fair, and considerate of the rights and interests of all parties. As long as it incorporates ethical practices into its core operations, cloud computing has the potential to continue to evolve and innovate. This will allow it to provide users with immense value while retaining their trust and confidence.

11.5 Conclusions

As we have seen, the expansive field of cloud computing offers numerous opportunities for business innovation and efficiency. However, it also involves considerable complexities in terms of cost optimization, performance, SLAs, and ethics. Organizations can maximize the potential benefits of cloud computing by understanding these complexities and applying effective strategies.

Cost optimization emerges as an essential aspect of cloud computing, necessitating a delicate balance between resource allocation, performance, and expenditures. In this context, cloud brokers play an indispensable role. With their knowledge of cloud services and market trends, these professionals assist cloud customers in making informed decisions regarding resource utilization, thereby driving cost-effective practises. Cost-effectiveness in cloud services is achieved through performance optimization, scheduling and provisioning of resources, and management of storage costs.

Compliance and SLA conformance play a crucial role in establishing a fair and transparent relationship between cloud service providers and their customers. SLAs specify the expected levels of performance, availability, and dependability, instilling confidence and encouraging accountability in the cloud computing ecosystem. Both parties must diligently measure and monitor their service performance to ensure SLA compliance. For the effective maintenance of these contractual agreements, robust monitoring mechanisms, transparency, and SLM practises are required.

In addition, ethics are a cornerstone of cloud computing, ensuring accountability, promoting fairness, and fostering trust. The ethical conduct of cloud services is founded on the principles of data protection, confidentiality, integrity, transparency, and compliance with legal and regulatory frameworks. The ethical obligation of cloud service providers to protect the privacy and security of customer data and operations goes beyond mere legal compliance. In contrast, cloud customers also have a substantial ethical responsibility. When using cloud services, they must be aware of the ethical implications, especially when dealing with sensitive data. Integrity of the cloud computing ecosystem is maintained by ensuring the responsible use of cloud services and compliance with applicable ethical guidelines and regulations.

The examination of these crucial facets collectively reveals the multifaceted nature of cloud computing. It is a dynamic field that thrives on constant monitoring, data-driven decisions, innovation, efficient resource management, strict compliance with SLAs, and strong ethical practises. Its transformative potential can only be maximized if these elements are comprehended and managed efficiently. Cloud computing continues to promote innovation, adaptability, and competitiveness in a digital era characterized by rapid change. The push for optimizing cloud operations and promoting ethical behaviour in cloud computing highlights the importance of this technology to contemporary businesses. This intricate combination of technological innovation and ethical behavior will shape the future of cloud computing and pave the way for the sustainable transformation of the digital sphere.

The challenges and opportunities presented by cloud computing will continue to evolve as time passes. It is imperative that organizations adapt to these changes by continuously evaluating their cloud strategies and investing in R&D. By doing so, they will be able to maximize the potential of cloud computing, drive business growth, and contribute to the overall development of this disruptive technology.

References

[1] J. Ahola *et al.*, "Best practices for cloud computing," Tieto- ja viestintäteollisuuden tutkimus TIVIT Oy, 2010. [Online]. Available: www.cloudsoftwareprogram.org/rs/2234/9ed65124-0873-400e-bc8a-9c85c1f1afa8/63b/filename/d1-1-2-techreport bestpracticesforcloudcomputing.pdf

[2] I. Foster, Y. Zhao, I. Raicu, and S. Lu, "Cloud computing and grid computing 360-degree compared," *2008 Grid Comput. Environ. Workshop*, pp. 1–10, Nov. 2008, doi: 10.1109/gce.2008.4738445.

[3] P. D. Filippi and S. Mccarthy, "Cloud computing: Centralization and data sovereignty," *Eur. J. Law Technol.*, vol. 3, pp. 1–18, 2012.

[4] L. Abraham, M. A. Murphy, M. Fenn, and S. Goasguen, "Self-provisioned hybrid clouds," in *Proceeding of the 7th international conference on Autonomic computing—ICAC '10*, New York, New York, USA: ACM Press, Jun. 2010, p. 161. [Online]. Available: http://portal.acm.org/citation.cfm?id=1809049.1809075

[5] M. T. Islam, S. Karunasekera, and R. Buyya, "Performance and cost-efficient spark job scheduling based on deep reinforcement learning in cloud computing environments," *IEEE Trans. Parallel Distrib. Syst.*, vol. 33, no. 7, pp. 1695–1710, 1–1, Jan. 2021, doi: 10.1109/tpds.2021.3124670.

[6] Muhammed Tawfiqul Islam, S. Karunasekera, and R. Buyya, "SLA-based spark job scheduling in cloud with deep reinforcement learning," vol. 1, pp. 1–21, 2020.

[7] W. Iqbal, M. N. Dailey, and D. Carrera, "SLA-Driven dynamic resource management for multi-tier web applications in a cloud," *2010 10th IEEEACM Int. Conf. Clust. Cloud Grid Comput.*, pp. 832–837, 2010, doi: 10.1109/CCGRID.2010.59.

[8] I. K. Kim, J. Hwang, W. Wang, and M. Humphrey, "Guaranteeing performance SLAs of cloud applications under resource storms," *IEEE Trans. Cloud Comput.*, vol. 10, pp. 1329–1343, Apr. 2020, doi: 10.1109/tcc.2020.2985372.

[9] Y. Zhao, R. N. Calheiros, G. Gange, J. Bailey, and R. O. Sinnott, "SLA-based profit optimization resource scheduling for big data analytics-as-a-service platforms in cloud computing environments," *IEEE Trans. Cloud Comput.*, vol. 9, no. 3, pp. 1236–1253, Dec. 2018, doi: 10.1109/tcc.2018.2889956.

[10] S. Khatua, A. Ghosh, and N. Mukherjee, "Optimizing the utilization of virtual resources in Cloud environment," in *Virtual environments human-computer interfaces and measurement systems (VECIMS), 2010 IEEE international conference on*, IEEE, 2010, pp. 82–87. [Online]. Available: http://ieeexplore.ieee.org/xpls/abs_all.jsp?arnumber=5609349

[11] M. Maurer, I. Brandic, and R. Sakellariou, "Enacting SLAs in clouds using rules," in *Euro-Par 2011 parallel processing: 17th International conference, Euro-Par 2011*, Bordeaux, France, pp. 455–466, Aug. 2011, doi: 10.1007/978-3-642-23400-2_42.

[12] S. Wee and H. Liu, "Client-side load balancer using cloud," in *Proceedings of the 2010 ACM symposium on applied computing—SAC '10*, New York, New York, USA: ACM Press, 2010, p. 399. doi: 10.1145/1774088.1774173.

[13] J. Cáceres, L. M. Vaquero, L. Rodero-Merino, Á. Polo, and J. J. Hierro, "Service scalability over the cloud," in *Handbook of Cloud Computing*, Springer, 2010, pp. 357–377, doi: 10.1007/978-1-4419-6524-0.

[14] B. Urgaonkar, P. Shenoy, A. Chandra, P. Goyal, and T. Wood, "Agile dynamic provisioning of multi-tier Internet applications," *ACM Trans. Auton. Adapt. Syst.*, vol. 3, no. 1, pp. 1–39, Mar. 2008, doi: 10.1145/1342171.1342172.

[15] C. Chapman, W. Emmerich, F. G. Márquez, S. Clayman, and A. Galis, "Software architecture definition for on-demand cloud provisioning," *Clust. Comput.*, vol. 1, pp. 61–72, Feb. 2011, doi: 10.1007/s10586-011-0152-0.

[16] R. Han, L. Guo, M. Ghanem, and Y. Guo, "Lightweight resource scaling for cloud applications," in *2012 12th IEEE/ACM international symposium on cluster, cloud and grid computing (ccgrid 2012)*, pp. 644–651, May 2012, doi: 10.1109/ccgrid.2012.52.

[17] S. Sankar *et al.*, "Cluster head selection for the internet of things using a sandpiper optimization algorithm (SOA)," *J. Sens.*, vol. 2023, p. 3507600, Apr. 2023, doi: 10.1155/2023/3507600.

[18] J. Kirschnick, "Toward an architecture for the automated provisioning of cloud services," *IEEE Commun. Mag.*, no. December, pp. 124–131, 2010.

[19] B. Furht and A. Escalante, Eds., *Handbook of Cloud Computing*. Springer, 2010. [Online]. Available: www.springer.com/computer/communication+networks/book/978-1-4419-6523-3

[20] L. Zeng, B. Benatallah, A. H. H. Ngu, M. Dumas, J. R. Kalagnanam, and H. Chang, "QoS-aware middleware for Web services composition," *IEEE Transactions on software engineering*, vol. 30, no. 5, pp. 311–327, 2004, doi: 10.1109/tse.2004.11.

[21] J. Yin *et al.*, "MUSE: A multi-tierd and SLA-driven deduplication framework for cloud storage systems," *IEEE Trans. Comput.*, vol. 70, no. 5, pp. 759–774, May 2021, doi: 10.1109/tc.2020.2996638.

[22] D. Saxena, A. K. Singh, and R. Buyya, "OP-MLB: An online VM prediction based multi-objective load balancing framework for resource management at cloud datacenter," *IEEE Trans. Cloud Comput.*, pp. 2804–2816, 2021, doi: 10.1109/tcc.2021.3059096.

[23] Anuska Sharma, "The ethics of cloud computing: A review," *Samvakti J. Res. Bus. Manag.*, vol. 2, no. Anon, pp. 57–64, Dec. 2021, doi: 10.46402/2021.02.17.

[24] Bernard Alaka and Bernard Shibwabo Kasamani, "The ethical switch: An automated policy and regulation framework for data dissemination in cloud environments," *2021 IST-Afr. Conf. IST-Afr.*, pp. 1–10, 2021.

Index

Printed in the United States
by Baker & Taylor Publisher Services